HEADS:

A Neurosurgeon's Memoir

For: Bernard R. Lerner, M.D.
(posthumously)
by doncha freeman

"…the Greeks didn't write obituaries, they only asked one question after a man died, 'Did he have passion?'"

**In loving memory of Bernard R. Lerner, M.D.
the most extraordinarily passionate and the kindest man**

*Holding my hand, before you left me, you shed one perfect
tear and opened your eyes, closed for so long.
I said good morning, darling, hoping you would still be mine,
believing it might be true.*

Praise for *Heads: A Neurosurgeon's Memoir and A Gentleman's Guide to the Joint*

From *Daniel A. Thomas* attorney and **co-owner of Goldsmith-Thomas Studios** *(Perfect Stranger and Kit Kittredge: An American Girl)* This memoir has captured a host of intriguing characters. The potential for this book and future exploitation of *HEADS* in film and/or television is great. The popularity of medical and legal dramas makes the time right for a hybrid project such as *HEADS*. This memoir is both unique and unusual, but completely engaging. Transforming one's life pain into a passion that can also sustain is both difficult and impressive, but you manage to do it quite well.

The mind-blowing part of this story is that it is based on the author's actual experiences. There are descriptions of events that could only have been written by someone who was there, who has intimate knowledge of the nitty-gritty of the drug culture, the prison culture, the medical culture, and the weird and amazing fusion of all three. Think 'Fear and loathing in Las Vegas' with a neurosurgeon in the driver's seat.

Thomas Cathcart Co-author of the New York Times best seller "Plato and a platypus walk into a bar: understanding philosophy through jokes".

I heard many of the events in this book directly from the author's mouth, and it's a real pleasure to read about them as they happened. More pleasurable is the knowledge that my former student, my fellow physician and my boon dinner companion for many years since he left 'camp', can speak of his life with such candor. The humanistic characteristics and medical skills displayed by Dr. Lerner, along with his rough and ready personality and his ultimate conversion to peace on earth are portrayed with ribald humor, much sensitivity and great insights by doncha. Events are told with touching pathos, creating a pleasurable read. Laughing out loud, as the pages raced to the finish line, I experienced an

amazing range of emotions that took me along on a perilous, but victorious journey.
Louis G. Keith, M.D., PhD, ScD (Hon) Emeritus Professor of Obstetrics & Gynecology

I find the book extremely enticing. The best news is that there is no story here without "real" life and there is no real life without a story…this one is quite remarkable. I am intrigued by it, not as a professional, but as an ordinary person who vicariously seeks adventure, growth and insight. I just know that I will see this story on the red carpet some day soon!
Brenda Russell Williams, president Russell Williams Group, Inc.

HEADS IS COMPELLING AND VIVID. THIS IS AN ARRESTING MEMOIR THAT IS RICH WITH INSIGHT. DR. LERNER AND MS. FREEMAN HAVE DECIDED TO TELL ALL AND THE RESULT IS RIVETING. READERS WILL MARVEL AT THEIR INTELLIGENCE AND RESILIENCE. SIMPLY PUT, IT'S A GREAT READ.
JOAN EDELMAN, LAKE FOREST, ILLINOIS.

Holistic and clean, doncha has woven many layers into this tapestry about Bernard and her life with him. Each time I read this multi-faceted story I discover new meaning in it. These extraordinary people faced trauma and yet created – what some lives become - a work of art. A pithy and powerful read! Martha Channer – MC^2 The science of Design

HEADS is a poignant and riveting look into the inner workings of one of our most important professions, as well as the compelling tale of the relationship of two very remarkable people.
Leonard Riforgiato, Heywood-Wakefield Furniture Company

Muscular!
Mel Zellman, former head announcer of WFMT Chicago

Acknowledgements

From the inception, Bernard's memoir benefited from moral support and guidance. For that, I wish to express gratitude to my mother, Deedee Freeman, always a good sport, an avid reader, a woman with the patience of a saint and a heart of gold.   Jennifer Amo, my dear friend, midwife, and astrologer, lightening this labor of love taught me how to use a computer - I couldn't have gone an inch without her support and friendship. Martha Channer helped with editing suggestions and crucial tips on structural analysis. An incredible talent, an artist and director of the fabulous MC^2 The Science of Design, Martha has been an inspiration to me since our days at Barat College. Joan Edelman, dog trainer extraordinaire, my lifelong friend truly enriched my life; she read for devotion and carefully with perfection as she does everything. Danny Thomas, attorney and co-owner of Goldsmith-Thomas Studios, your interest meant so much to Bernard and me. David Pearline, I thank you for reading and rereading; your suggestions were invaluable, but most of all I am grateful for your kindness. You helped me until I was sure on my feet. Julie Clark Lampert, who understands me so well…like Katie, my Grandmother, inside me always, I am more grateful for your support than I can say. And, Ellen Cornell, a woman who has known suffering, empathizes as deeply as she reads.

I hope *Heads* birth makes all of you proud because I'm proud to put it out there on Bernard's behalf. Sarah and Philip Lerner, Bernard's loving parents, guided Bernard skillfully to become the talented healer they knew he could be. Most of all, the guys from FPC Duluth, without them Bernard's trials and tribulations wouldn't make any sense. Finally, a word to the incompetents: This book would never have been written if it weren't for you messing up so badly. Take care with other people's lives. Thanks for the journey; it was quite the trip.

My hope for the future is having time enough to work knowledge and experience into wisdom.

doncha freeman
Miami Beach, 2010

Dear Reader; The events in this book are real. Considering the length of the time period in between living them and writing about them, conversations and events are not exact; they are, nevertheless, authentic and every bit as meaningful.

Timelines have been altered on occasion, as well as names that begged modification. However satirical, they are well deserved.

A Brief History

I knew in my bones from the time I was a kid that I was born to be a surgeon. I hung out in my father's medical office and I trailed after him on hospital rounds. Listening to his flare-ups against incompetence was only part of my early medical education. Further coaching came from my neurosurgical nurse mother, an assistant to Max Minor Peet, one of the founding fathers of neurosurgery.

Sarah Lerner, a far-seeing woman, was adamant in her belief that medicine needed improvement - vast improvement. My mother was confident in her conviction that I was going to rise to the occasion. It's true that Jewish mothers can be fanatical about their sons. And, as it happens, these sacred beliefs sometimes catch on.

Committed by a code of honor, a bond shared with my parents, I vowed to engage in the process of transforming medicine. I never thought about what rocking the boat might entail. Capsizing was never part of my vision. I held the firm belief that my devotion would keep me afloat. But then, I was not an all-seeing God. I was only a kick-ass neurosurgeon who saved lives on his own turf.

My thunderbolt direction struck me during my residency at The Mayo Clinic. Operating a Zeiss counter-balance-beam microscope did it for me. Manipulating a free-floating bit in my mouth enabled me, for the first time, to operate at thirty times the magnification over the naked eye *throughout* the procedure... *and* every move I made was omnipresent on camera, in the four corners of the room. Out of thousands of surgeons, *maybe* fifty were ingenious or coordinated enough to get around the dexterity requirements. The rest functioned *the good old-fashioned way,* with the naked eye and the assistance of loops. Small magnifiers with a light source may be useful for coal miners, but it was no longer an adequate way for surgeons to perform. Great surgeons stay on top of technological advances. Having a Zeiss counter-balance-beam microscope wheeled into the OR *only* to charge for the use it, which some surgeons actually did, I felt morally obligated to point out to the geniuses that accordingly their results would be disappointing.

Because microneurosurgery was revolutionary in the 1970s, and most doctors at the time weren't jocks or pinball wizards (another sport reliant on hand-eye coordination), their shortcomings - right off the bat - were two-fold. Being of a revolutionary bent and seeing that I could ski on glaciers and run a mile just under world-record time, I enlisted in a fellowship with the luminous and illuminating Professor Yasargil, a Houdini with this terrific scope. If I weren't headed for Zurich on a mission to master the instrument soon to become instrumental in my meteoric rise to fame, I'd hang up my jock-strap.

It didn't take long for me to learn that Professor Yasargil could maneuver his way out of anything. Any difficulty he encountered he dramatically diffused. I developed that faculty easily in surgery, and I was a hell of a quarterback in college; unfortunately, I never got the hang of it in the so-called real world. Professor Yasargil, if the truth be known, is idiosyncratic, too. For instance, he wouldn't operate if the Mediterranean tides weren't to his liking. Let him try that one at Northwestern University Hospitals; Northwestern's inquisitors would exorcise his rank individualism right out the door, but not without him telling them a thing or two first.

Under Professor Yasargil's amazing tutelage, and because of his extraordinary talent, I became a proficient with a Zeiss, one hell of a microscope. To start, I operated on over a thousand rats - one rat at a time. Prickly, until I conquered the hand-eye coordination, the trickiest part. Any surgeon worthy of the oath masters technique. No two ways about it. A surgeon isn't much if he isn't an ace.

Related to super-heroes, it's all about the quality to bail out those in jeopardy. It's magnificent when physical agility, a keen mind, and super-empowered vision employed fixedly to save lives can do exactly that. Six months of accelerated training and I was raring to circumnavigate in the operating theater solo. My microscope was *my* super-hero x-ray vision. Biting on a surgical bit, I operated upside down, sideways, inside out; whatever it took I did it magnified, because I was able, and I got a kick out it. In my book, nothing is more heroic than saving lives.

Coming on board at Northwestern University Hospitals in 1976, after Anthony J. Raimondi seized power, was another landmark big break in my uncertain history. The frosting on Northwestern's cake was no longer WASP-white only. Northwestern's WASPy board of directors was particularly fond of the color green. Besides, ethnic was in. The liberal and wealthy Doctor Raimondi took on the Department of Neurosurgery at Northwestern University Hospitals, I heard, for one dollar a year. An additional bonus came in the way of endowments he would bring in. His position as Chairman of Neurosurgery at Cook County Hospital was proof of his aptitude, doing exactly that. That's where I met him. I have to say I was impressed.

Fresh with the imprint of Mayo Clinic and newly returned from Zurich, by all accounts I was wired to cut. Professor Raimondi prized my programming for his voracious program at Northwestern. The pre-revolutionary regime's unenlightened attitude of *let them eat cake* left the department anemic. Tony and I were the first transfusions.

Before Tony roped me in, my action came from County Hospital. On the west side of Chicago, it was *the meanest place in the whole damn town.* On top on that, helicopter landing-pads brought in more trauma. Hard to beat that combination outside of a MASH unit. For giving Death a run for the booty, we didn't have to go to Saigon. Although, I have to say I took my surgical hat off to surgeons back from Vietnam. They were tough. They *handled* everything, even the burn units.

Working with them and the *demanding* Professor Raimondi was, without question, empowering and intensely invigorating. These surgeons knew how to call the shots. For that, and, loving Tony, knowing he could be counted on for anything, I took him on as a role model. Our similarities didn't end with devotion. Tony and I looked so much alike (silver grey hair and all, from the time I was in my thirties) that the Japanese residents called me Son of Raimondi. I got a kick out of it every time the valets from the garage brought me his Porsche or yellow Maserati Bora that he took up to 235mph. I *had* to take it out to see what I could do. Then, I had to have one.

In perpetual motion, headed toward new ages of expanded horizons, I was on my way driving fast cars and riding smooth bikes. Traveling the tri-state area in record time, I spread the news about what I was doing at Northwestern. A constant influx of spinal reconstruction patients followed. In no time, the procedure became a micro-neurosurgical exercise, a warm-up for critical cases. Never turning anyone away, the overflow of beds spilled into the hallways. The administrators, not approving of the cluttered hallways, weren't complaining too much because, after all was said and done, Northwestern was no longer in jeopardy of losing its Veteran's Hospital.

Indeed, this coup was personally gratifying, allowing me to operate to my heart's content. Three major intra-cranial procedures a week was my idea of something to rave about. I was crazy about doing heads. Lesser attending physicians could suck up martinis and fame, discussing hospital politics, teeing off, instead of cutting. I was glad when they played elsewhere. Picking up their slack, is it any wonder that I never knew what was happening outside the hospital? With all I had going on, I didn't even know what popular music was playing or what movies where at the theaters. Luckily, breathing requires no special effort.

Managing my temper is what caused me to sweat every time two of the worst attending men hung around the OR. Tying fly-fishing knots and spouting gibberish, easily ignored, until these loose cannons scrubbed. Replacing one of the culprit's pedestrian bow ties with a rogue's noose would have been too good for him the day he dropped a drill, so sharp it could cut a diamond, on the patient's brain. When the other idiot claimed sacrificing his patient's vision was unavoidable because the case was tough, I notified Tony that there was no reason for anyone to cover me.

Tony and I were having one of *those* conversations in the Gothic foyer of Northwestern's Wesley Pavilion (where a huge portrait of Loyal Davis, the last chairperson, hung until Tony had it removed). Dan Ruge, a decent spine man in his day from Loyal's regime, would walk past us waving, saying, "Ta-ta, good evening." No matter what was happening in the hospital, at five o'clock sharp, Doctor Ruge crossed Lake Shore Drive to stroll the shores of Lake Michigan, weather permitting, *always* with cocktail in hand. The alternative was a highfalutin neighborhood cocktail lounge.

Considering blood made Doctor Ruge excessively nervous, I thought it peculiar that he came so far. Despite Uncle Dan's quirks, (he also wore seersucker suits) he was straight up. Unlike many of the socially arrogant in his pack, he knew his limitations. My privilege was covering the cases that were out of his league.

I was sorry when Uncle Dan left us to attend President Reagan, but Nancy wanted him; probably because her daddy, Loyal Davis, thought so well of him. Tony had been delighted when Loyal said his goodbyes, and he wasn't sorry to see Uncle Dan go, either. After all, Uncle Dan wasn't really a relative, and pedigrees were just lap dogs to Tony; he didn't like cleaning up the mess they left behind. Before departing for the White House, Uncle Dan bequeathed me his operating shoes. I told him *they're too small for me*; he shook my hand and said *I know*. Actually, they were remarkably comfortable. I wore them like a second skin, until the soles were worn through, mimicking my life.

I stepped into those shoes the day I operated on a twenty-seven year old house painter with an aneurysm. No anti-Semite he, this patient marched into Raimondi's office demanding *a Jew doctor*... and he wasn't messing around. There are patients who believe a huge benefit is bestowed upon them if their doctor is Jewish. You can bet if anything went wrong, they'd scream *I want a Jew lawyer.*

Heads from the morgue in hand, I set out to define the complex anatomy of the patient's cavernous sinus and to map a route to the pathology. My other goal was to find a means of protection, in case there were unforeseen difficulties.

This sixteen-hour neurosurgical procedure was the first external-to-internal double-barrel by-pass and internal carotid artery trap ever performed. It would save countless lives. You would think I committed a crime from the reactions of surgeons who were not fans of mine. When their patients questioned them, asking the definitive *Why is the person in the room next to mine, who had the same diagnosis as me, leaving the hospital while I'm still in bed,* there's going to be trouble. So sure of who I was and what I was doing, I became all the more vulnerable.

In my compulsive reflections, I've often considered how my unbridled self-satisfaction created a venomous dislike for me in several colleagues, reminding me of alpha bengala snakes. Next in line were the human upwardly-mobiles, stumbling onto my path with their big clubs to impede my way. Apparently, my fatal flaw, the thing that did me in - in addition to my exceptional skill as a diagnostician and my talent as a top gun neurosurgeon - was insufficient savvy about the treacherous real-life games pathological people play.

Tragically, it is an historical fact that those who lead the way off the beaten path can, and often do, wind up in prison, psych wards, homeless, or worse, hopeless. The dark night of the soul crept over me like a lunar eclipse. It was impossible for me to devote nearly twenty years of my life and have it demolished, with all the implications, without misery and a fatalistic dose of acting out. I do not go gently into that good night.

PROLOGUE

A carefully constructed world on the verge of a crushing breakdown was mine. An historic collapse would change my life forever, to include future possibilities in neurosurgery. Buried in my work, I didn't see it coming. Actually, it shocked the hell out of me. I was completely confident that the safe harbor I created for patients, and anyone in need of my pioneering know-how, would define my entire life. Because I played a leading role in the rapid growth of microneurosurgery and in life-and-death dramas, giving it my best shot twenty-four seven, I believed I was the master of my own universe.

The successful demonization of Bernard R. Lerner, M.D., also known as a fall or getting knocked on my ass (depending on the language you speak) became *painfully* obvious during the Eighties, the decade of decadence. Unfortunate reversals of fortune are by-products of extremes.

Asked, given the opportunity, would I change the events that led to my fall from grace? I answer, "Absolutely! *If* it were possible to arrange the procedure and spend my life in the service of others." The catch is, I wouldn't have the vaguest idea of where to begin. Subsequent dealings were convoluted and sordid - not immaculate like the brain. And, as it turns out,   beyond my scope of understanding.

Where do we find meaningful instruction, finely tuned, all mapped out in this experiential and sometimes cruel world? What happens after our plans go awry and the dark night of the soul creeps over us like a lunar eclipse?

An indispensible attribute for doing well, when the shit hits the fan, is to *not* travel like a tourist, but to be fully plugged-in. I'm not entirely wired that way. My vote has always been for spotless sunshine of everlasting joy. Not an option when survival of the shittiest seizes the day. Let's face it, there's an awful lot of absurdity in life.

When detours are nightmarish roller coaster rides, and darkness prevails over light, hang on to your gonads and other precious heart parts. It's the logical thing to do when mighty but unenlightened forces come after you with a vengeance and a machete. Nefarious types think absolutely nothing of separating a uniquely talented neurosurgeon, or other persons, from all that they sweated for in building a worthy life. They do not judge their actions to be wrongfully executed ambition, because they do not care.

Chapter One
County Hospital
1989

A worthy life is a subject deserving exploration. For me, it all begins with my intention to make my services available in the emergency room at Cook County Hospital - a dingy district where ambulance and cop sirens shriek all day and night. The trick with incoming wounded in this trigger-happy war zone is to be slick with a surgical blade. Neurosurgically lowering the numbers of the corpse population keeps me razor-sharp and meditatively peaceful, unlike anything else, with the exception of love.

The unmistakable growl of my Harley-Davidson pulling up curbside attracts a fair share of attention on these mean streets, despite everything else that's going down. That's all right with me, I like being noticed. Sliding from the leather seat, feeling the way humid does when it sticks to hot, I lean against my bike, light a cigarette, and begin to wonder if the devil does care.

Only some things are for sure, like the fact that a bottomless drag satisfies my lungs with a potent nicotine rush. Pleasureful poison innocently disguised in white. Ahhh, I take another drag on death. Blowing shades of smoke rings into the moonlit night, I watch the neighborhood drug dealer prowl.

He thinks he's smooth but everyone knows what he's after with those fast paws. Ready steady cash money is no problem for him. He provides the stuff that goes up the nose, curls the toes, makes 'em say *Hallelujah!* and *Amen!* Crashing down from the heavens, users habitually wish they were dead. Can't help it once you're *that* high. They've got you comin' and goin'.

"I'm lucky no one notices me comin' or goin' any time of the day or night," Fast Paws tell an anxious med student copping dope. "So be cool, man."

1

No shit Sherlock or you'd be in jail by now.

More on the mellow side, Johnny Lee Sunshine, a street philosopher, distracts me as he lumbers over. His hair pick strategically located in his untamed afro bobs up and down, and his boom box is always in tow. Regulars gather around as we exchange a street *peace and soul* handshake. Flashing those pearly whites, "Righteous" is all he has to say before we begin our routine, street performance for the locals. I know many people who can talk all day long; I like a person that can sing and dance, too.

We're into it, until a squad car pulls up. The cop separating the donut from his face yells out the window, "Turn that fuckin' boom box down before you wake the dead in cold storage. The morgue is only a block away." I step forward and he slows down, about to get out of the car with his big stick. "Sorry, Doc, I didn't know it was *you*. You're not wearin' one of them fancy Armani jobs." Having said that he leaves us alone.

Turning up the volume puts us back in the mood. Gruff, but warm, our deep tones harmonize with the soulful Josh White singing "St. James Infirmary".

> *I went down to that St. James Infirmary, and I saw some plasma there, I ups and asks the doctor man, "Now was the owner dark or fair? The doctor laughed a great big laugh, and he puffed it right in my face, He said, "A molecule is a molecule, son, and the damn thing has no race."*

Worthwhile entertainment: eighteen minutes skin-to-skin, time enough for a few tracks from *Free and Equal Blues*. Our approving audience nod their heads as we come to the end. Johnny Lee cuffs my arm and laughs. "I saw you boxin' at Tony's Gym. You're good Daddy-O." Imitating my boxing style, bobbing and weaving, he chants, "Fly like a butterfly and sting like a bee, Mohammed Ali got nothin' on me, 'cause I'm the Doc, I'm the greatest."

2

"I look that good?" I suck up the approval.

"Word is, you was a drag-racin' tougher-than-shit kid livin' right here in the hood. Is that right, Doc?"

"Yep."

"Can't take the dude outta yo' bad ass." He feints a punch.

"Thanks for the vote of confidence, Mr. Sunshine."

Happy-go-lucky, snapping my fingers and shuffling my feet, I dance to many beats. Inside the halls of academia, I'm Bernard R. Lerner, M.D., the youngest associate professor in the Department of Neurosurgery at Northwestern University Hospitals and a frequent volunteer at Cook County Hospital. On the street, I'm the Doc. Obviously, I'm not your garden-variety country club type of doctor, but don't go to extremes and label me typical alpha male type, either. I'm a man on a mission. With steely confidence, I've made it my business to take neurosurgery so far into the future I revolutionize the science.

Still, the best part of me has never left County Hospital's quarter. Drawn to the socially wounded, my first set of rounds is complete before I enter the hospital. I never forget to tend the homeless. I hope no one forgets to care for me if the shoe is ever on the other foot. Life is so precarious. I'd never turn my back on anyone who needs me, and I never will.

Singing the blues or Frank Sinatra, I mingle among the street's downtrodden inhabitants. On the mark with a quick eye for disease, I don't make an issue of it. They don't go for that. Instead, I hand out money with a here you go, Pal or Dear, treat yourselves to supper after the show. My smile seems infectious; I'm glad to hearten the disheartened whenever I am able.

All the top surgeons invited to operate at Cook County are encouraged to teach neurosurgical residents rotating through the service. Those who show up to hone their skills can be counted on one hand when operating is an unpaid labor of love. Some of my colleagues, from the Lake Shore Drive side of town, don't understand why anyone would spend time cutting anywhere other than the pristine and prestigious halls of private hospitals. Presented the world on a silver platter, they are numb to the medically disenfranchised. Most of them - and they are a restricted type - discount the advantages of working at County. *In the gutter*, as they so generously put it.

In the tradition of any other irreverent iconoclast, when conversations beg variety, I improvise. "How can I pass up a seventeen-hundred bed hospital when it's the place to be for any surgeon hot to cut? County's abundance of trauma quenches my vampiric thirst. Pathology cross-matches and types three units of blood - two for the patient and one for me - I'm not greedy." I do that Bella Lugosi, let-me-suck-your-blood thing, and the mocking becomes judgmental. "Grow up, Lerner," doesn't inhibit me.

Ignoring my detractors, supporters declare, "*You* vampires are something else." Encouraged, I uphold the truth. "Death hangs out everywhere, and I've never known the Marauder to give *anyone* a second chance," I tell the residents and interns, and anyone else that cares to listen. "Walking in the shadow of death, with reverence for life, is the everyday world of great surgeons." I like the applause and "You're a splendid teacher, a great surgeon and a real human being," pronounced by Mario Ammirati, a top-notch resident, goes the distance to make my day brighter.

Another insight into the clandestine surgical society of carefully guarded secrets is the fact that medical professionals ingest a fair share of drugs. Addiction is an occupational hazard, a result of super-human grueling demands and impossibly long hours. I was on call every other night, all night long, for eight years, facing horrors most people never encounter in a lifetime. Couple this with the certainty that humans are habitual creatures and you have a sure-fire prescription for dependency. Fifty percent of occupied beds in hospitals are for patients with diseases related to alcohol - the state-approved lethal substance. This is not an excuse; it's the actuality, so put away the cross and don't shoot the messenger.

Whatever the drug of choice, a surgeon unable to sustain the rigors of thirty-six hour days will turn to mother's little helpers. When long hours rule and are not the exception, staying awake without drugs, *plentiful in the environment*, often becomes impossible. Necessity, like any other dictator, will exact a harsh penalty when circumstance doesn't count for much. It's a Catch-22; an unfortunate way of life for too many of us suffering sleep deprivation and other maladies. I medicate chronic pain from old football injuries. I'm not judging anyone and I don't want to be judged. As long as colleagues do well with patients, I'm satisfied when personal issues are addressed privately.

It's the seemingly straight-arrow types, pretending to be so bloody superior, that end up with nicotine stains in their underwear. Reeking from alcohol, they crap in their pants, taking on cases for which they have no talent. To cover extravagant end-of-the-month expenses they engage in dangerous sport, with no athletic ability whatsoever.

Timmy, a kid I'm especially fond of, had the misfortune to be a casualty of this inferior breed. Personally, I have witnessed too many botched surgeries, and every time it happens it blows my mind. My subspecialty seems to be cleaning-up the catastrophes of surgeons who go in over their heads. When I called the surgeon who failed this child and insisted Why *didn't you send Timmy to me in the first place? You could have kept the money*. Hanging up on me ends Timmy's tribulations for him. I wonder how he sleeps at night.

My first step into Timmy's room, Timmy's worried-sick broken-hearted mother cries, "Help me, Doctor! Timmy is always looking at teenage girls in fashion magazines. He doesn't act like my child anymore." Timmy's father turns away from us to stare at shades of watery blue on the TV. I'm a father; I understand his pain. Timmy's blemished scalp that looks like transcontinental railroad tracks will heal. Gratified as I am to have saved Timmy's life, I'm sorry to say it will take a long time for him to recover somewhat functionally with a persistent neurological deficit. If it weren't for me, and Timmy's desire to live, he wouldn't be getting ready for an imaginary night out on the town. Finished examining my handiwork, I check out his. He's busy cutting out perfume bottles from a magazine.

"I give my dates nice presents, don't I?" He giggles. I show him how to scotch tape the paper perfume bottles to the models in the magazine. "I want to take them to see a scary movie. Then we'll eat ice cream." Timmy beams with pride, holding up the magazine for his disturbingly quiet parents to see. Because their silence is painful, I interject "That's great, Pal."

Embracing me with his wide clear child blue eyes, he points to my boots. "I like your cowboy boots, Cowboy Doctor. doncha brought me a book about cowboys. I *really* like doncha." He giggles and giggles some more.

I tousle his hairless head. "Me too, Cowboy, I'm crazy about doncha. She's the love of my life. I have to head over to the emergency room now. I'll see you tomorrow."

He doesn't notice when I leave. He's already alone with his dates, no different from any other guy hoping to get lucky.

The emergency room is a titanic sea of misery that jump-starts my adrenals. The first thing I get on is a local barroom brawler, vibrating as though he's connected to an unseen electrical socket. Doing combat with Chicago's finest is dangerous to one's health. "I need an operating room," I call out to Nurse Kelly. And don't stop moving the way you do."

"I enjoy watching your ass, too, Doctor. I hate to disappoint you, but all operating rooms are engaged."

I grab a drill from a minor craniotomy kit and bore a hole in Mr. Strange's cranium. Observers look a little stunned witnessing their first unsterile procedure. I calm them explaining, "Anesthetizing isn't necessary; there aren't any pain fibers in the brain. Improvising at Cook County Hospital becomes second nature. I don't know how many times I've delivered C-section babies in the elevators." A blood clot, the color of crankcase motor oil, squirts out of Mr. Strange's brain. "At Northwestern, called to task over insurance issues for performing this same procedure, I raised the question *What about the life I saved*? Never mind that. I was warned *stick to the rules*. The almighty rules. The good news is Mr. Strange will be fine. I'm out of here. My woman is waiting for me to take her to dinner this fine evening. I'll check in on this madman later."

Returning to the hospital after midnight, I find my much-recovered patient tipping back a bottle concealed inside a brown paper bag. Mr. Strange takes a healthy slug and gurgles, "You're my savior, Doc." Tears fill his eyes as booze runs down the sides of his mouth onto the dirty bed sheets, stained with food and vomit. When I do the unpardonable and take away a fifth of whiskey, I unleash tidal waves of curses beginning with "You satanic bastard, how dare you deprive me of refreshment! And another thing, you control freak, snakes are crawling through every fucking orifice of my body and elephants are jumping through goddamn purple people eatin' hoops..."

"At least you have some entertainment while you're here. Some of our guests miss out on the weird Technicolor visuals." Howling, "Eat shit and die," the way he does, reminds me of how easy it is to go from savior to anti-Christ. Tears of gratitude are the fastest evaporating substance known to man.

Answering a page, anticipating it might be doncha, hoping she's not pissed off that I didn't go out dancing with her, I'm disappointed. It's not doncha. It's the triage nurse at Northwestern. Knowing flattery appeals to my vanity she lays it on thick. "Doctor Lerner, I know you're not on call tonight, but you are the best." Nurse Duffy's Irish brogue is lilting and pleasant to my ear. "You are, however, one of the last doctors on earth devoted enough to make house calls. Unfortunately the darlin' on call isn't respondin'. Please bring that adorable bum of yours over to Northwestern's ER. Help us out. We have a situation."

"I'm on my way, but *you* have to call doncha and tell her I'm detained."

Chapter Two
Northwestern University Hospital

Newborn ducklings couldn't follow each other, one after the other, with more abandon than Neurosurgical residents wandering around the Emergency Room. "Collect yourselves at the viewing screen," I order in a well-modulated tone to hide my displeasure, flipping Mrs. Seymour's angiogram in place. One of the members of the flock, a cocky third year resident, folds his arms over his chest and squawks, "Rotten luck; looks like it's over for her" hits the back of my head and a glacial air comes over me. With the conviction of General Patton before the invasion of Sicily, I address the residents. "Our mission is to evacuate the hematoma, clip the aneurysms and peel off the arteriovenous malformation. Any abnormal pathology in our way goes too. Now then, you eight-year wonders, you've supposedly passed your National Boards..."

"You know I've passed my boards."

"That's right, Fussins, you've been granted a license to practice on the unsuspecting public. Tell me, how is it that you ignored the symptoms and assumed a diagnosis so final that it should be spoken solemnly as a prayer." Face to face with this impertinent resident, who never knows when to remain silent, I pull no punches. "You're a pathetic excuse for a neurosurgeon. No bastard who didn't care in the first place ever saved a life."

"I was stating..."

"Drop to the floor, now, and give me twenty!"

Fussins makes a big show of it as onlookers gather around. Between gulps of air, he wheezes. "I could... do.... fifty pushups... with one hand.... tied.... behind... my... back."

I shake my head in disbelief, amazed at the puny effort.

"For those of you that crave the opportunity to stand victorious against overwhelming odds, the operating theater is the arena of this battle. Let me enlighten you; all the power and magic in this crazy world happens inside the brain. Proceed with reverence to assure your performance is worthy of the task. If you're hungry, eat. If you need to take a crap, do it now. This isn't going to be a chip-shot."

The pre-op holding area is bare bones impersonal, except for the crucifix on the wall and the families waiting. To be on the safe side a priest gives last rites to the patient going under the knife. He considers there may not be an earthly tomorrow for surgical patients. That's *not* the case when the knife is mine.

Alone with Mrs. Seymour, her hand in mine, I whisper, "I won't let anything happen to you, sweetheart. I promise you, you'll do well." Confident that our souls have connected, all matters of magnitude being equal, I'm ready.

"First, I'll clip the aneurysms, and since the arteriovenous malformation is right in front of us let's take it, too. You do see it, don't you, Doctors?" I glance up from my microscope for a sign of comprehension. "I'm going to peel these monsters right off the surface of the brain."

Gluck grandstands right on cue. "You should, *of course*, perform individual operations for the aneurysms and a later one for the arteriovenous malformation, but you won't, not you."

"You know perfectly well, Gluck, I wouldn't open someone twice when I can handle it in one go."

"Grown-up surgeons operate with caution, Doctor Lerner. They don't need to show off with excessively expensive microscopes, like it's a toy."

"The greedy bastards wouldn't take the time away from their money-producing hand-holding practices to learn how to operate this beautiful instrument. Do us all a favor and make yourself useful. Arm three veri-angle clips on three veri-angle clip appliers. Then, have several Sundt-Kees clip grafts ready in case we run into trouble. Gluck, *do not* come back into *my* OR without surgical trousers. Microorganisms common to the vagina contaminate the operating field. You *should* know that by now."

She storms out, taking her unshaved patchouli scent with her.

"Your confrontational streak isn't winning any popularity contests." Mario Ammirati, the best resident in the group, shakes his finger at me. "Talent is no excuse."

"It's not purely a blessing either. Unconventional behavior is a predominant trait of our breed. After all, we're artists. When the surgeon is the surgery, the art and the artist are not of separate value. Only a Michelangelo should open up a spine or play peek-a-boo with the brain. Do you think it matters to me if Herr Chairman Nahrwald disapproves of me? You don't have to approve of an artist to buy their paintings, listen to their music, or read an author's fiction or nonfiction. The same courtesy should be extended to me. What's more relevant is my patients *love* me."

"And so they should. I still think it's unfortunate that Nahrwald only thinks of you as the pain in the ass nonconformist inherited from Raimondi's regime."

"My friend, the glory days of medicine are over. And we, the rock-star neurosurgeons inherited by the new clout, just keep on cuttin'. Nahrwald didn't do medicine any favor ushering in corporate medicine and neo-conservatism. I'm against a machine that competes historically with the Catholic Church as the bane of modern medicine. I could never approve of the Machiavellian ways behind the scenes. I wouldn't want to end up a patient in a hospital run like a machine by businessmen. Take the heart out of medicine and it has no authenticity. Doctors no longer diagnosis; they rule out by running every test under the sun. The attention given to patients is miniscule…but the cost is astronomical. Healing is not only ineffectual, it's feeble. Diseases don't read textbooks. My strategies make miracles possible - not on a spreadsheet or Wall

Street - but in the operating theater. The best results are achieved by carefully listening to patients *before* you even examine them. In that way, Mario, I'm no different than you!"

"Aren't you worried about getting your tit caught in the ringer?"

"Even when the dust was flying so thick around here that daylight was blocked out, all I cared about was saving lives. There's nothing between life and death but the skilled intention of the surgeon. I have no time for hospital politics. There's no place for ego when you open a head. Lately, all I hear from some of the residents is how cool they are because it's easy to get laid when they mention they're neurosurgeons. You laugh."

"What do you say to them, Bernie?"

"Only, if you're trying to impress me, function, at least while in the OR, as a highly specialized neurosurgical instrument with the objective to get the patient out of the operating theater neurologically intact, speaking coherently, and moving all four extremities. Save the drivel for cocktail parties."

Lately, Nahrwald begins his days sending terse little notes to me in the operating room. Today, it's: *Dr. Lerner, join me in the surgeon's lounge.*

"Tell his highness to scrub and join me in the OR if he wants to talk to me" is my sent reply.

To my surprise, Nahrwald puts in a personal appearance. With all the finesse the man can muster, he simpers, "Doctor Lerner, would you mind if I bring a sensitive matter to your attention in front of others?"

"Shoot."

Showing no interest in the surgery, Mrs. Seymour, or the raring to go, eagerly listening entourage of nurses and physicians, Nahrwald clears his bony throat. "Doctor Gluck has been by to see me, Doctor Lerner."

"Charming."

"She told me about how you inferred that her perineal fallout contaminates exposed brain…"

"What's your point?"

"That is *not* an appropriate way to talk to a lady."

"I thought she was a surgeon at the time I said it or was she posing?" I imitate the posture he assumes for camera shots he has taken on a regular basis. Marginally under my breath, I exhale, "You're such a shmuck."

"What was that you said?"

"I said good luck standing in as Gluck's champion."

"I never…"

"Don't deny it. You constantly defend her bad technique. As if that isn't enough of a distraction, I have to put up with the additional insult of her stinking body odor."

"*Really*, Doctor Lerner."

"No kidding. What's worse is, she operates with six fingers on each hand. I eat a box of antacids whenever she scrubs. *You,* of all people, should know what I mean." I give the whip time to absorb the insult. "Would you like me to discuss technique with you, or may I focus exclusively on my patient?"

He bails out.

Millimeter by millimeter, by the tenth hour of surgery, the arteriovenous malformation has been peeled from the cortex of the brain; six inches of wormlike vessel have been resected. With a substantial amount of work ahead, after an intense silence, I hum *Ode to Joy.*

The circulating nurse mops the sweat from my brow. I reject another offer to take over. *I'm* Mrs. Seymour's best shot. Just when I thought I got rid of all the gatecrashers, the head nurse attempts to head off a rather imposing figure. "Doctor Hook is a visiting cerebral vascular neurosurgeon from Heidelberg. He *insists* on observing." Glancing up from the scope, into the one good eye of Keith,

I recognize the imposter behind the mask. Keith is not a surgeon, despite the remarkable coincidence that he is scrubbed, gowned and gloved and everyone addresses him as Doctor Hook. Keith is doncha's officially undiagnosed bi-polar personality disordered brother.

"Doctor Hook, are you here to assist or observe?" I play his game.

Positioning himself at the viewing scope, the character milks his part for all it's worth, articulating well thought-out observations in a phony German accent. I suppose he's coming close to the point of his visit when he gets real. "Sorry to interrupt, Bro,' I'd like to stay but I have to go. This is so fucking amazing. You blow my mind. Take a break with me....it's important."

Alone with him in the locker room, I have to laugh. "I don't know how you convinced them to let you in the OR and I don't think I want to know."

"I'm fully aware that I'm a pain in the ass, man. It's not that I don't love ya. I do. Now, do me a favor and call the garage." He hands me the phone. "I need your Ferrari. Next time, I want to participate. Nothing fancy. Just a little knick-knack kind of brain thing. Initiating me into the service would be *very* cool. You've got balls, I'll give you that." He stuffs an Italian beef sandwich in my pocket. "I'm proud of you. Be sure to eat the sandwich I brought for you, dolly."

Alone in the locker room, with a few minutes to myself, I take 2-mg of dilaudid for my aching hips, down a cup of black coffee loaded with sweetener, inhale the killer beef sandwich from Taylor street and head back.

After twenty-two hours, Mrs. Seymour's brain, decidedly decompressed, pulsates with excellent color. Satisfied with the results, I pop off my bloody surgical gloves and shoot them into the surgical wastebasket. I've successfully completed a surgery that witnessed the rotation of four residents, three sets of scrub nurses, two neurosurgical anesthesiologists, and Keith. Exhausted and exhilarated, my day made, I can put another notch in my scalpel.

In the waiting room, Mrs. Seymour's grateful and much relieved family receive the good news. I must be invisible. They thank the Almighty for saving their mother's life. Not unaccustomed to this practice, I avow, "In case you didn't know, I was also in that operating room for twenty-two hours. Good evening." *I don't like being excluded from the credit I deserve and crave.*

Outside the door of my last patient on my last rounds, Gluck paces, anticipating her prey. She-devil pounces. "You think you're some kind of god, don't you? You're nothing but a showoff."

She stops me in my tracks. "Get this through your head, Gluck, I'm not trying to win a popularity contest. And gods *are* showoffs; I thought mythology was your specialty."

"You think that's funny. I heard something funnier like *you're* under indictment. Since you find everything so amusing have fun defending yourself in this, you chauvinistic prick."

"It's not chauvinism; it's your irresponsibility that turns me against you. Good thing I checked on Mrs. Seymour, again. I had to change some of the orders you wrote. Obviously, you were preoccupied with matters of far greater importance to you."

"I was going back in, after I consulted with Dr. Fussins."

"Fussins abilities happen to be another one of your illusions. Look around you; you're in a Wasp's nest. Not a good place to be when ethnic is on its way out. All the surgeons that were as talented as gods left, and I should have gone with them."

"Fuck you and your buddies." Turning her back on me, Gluck flips me off over her head with both hands. She must think the gesture symbolizes a victory of sorts. She reminds me of Tricky Dick Nixon.

Walking the long bridge corridor alone - no entourage of residents or interns – nothing but the echoing of my footsteps are behind me, resounding in my brain, haunting as a refrain from Chopin's *Nocturnes*. This defining moment, at the crossroads of the improbable and the incredible, I am aware that I'm going to pay a heavy toll for my soul's complications. All the magic and all the knowledge I possess will not change my destiny. The door behind me is closed. I have no illusions about an ongoing career at Northwestern University Hospitals. Even so, there is no lock strong enough to keep me from attending the patients on my service until I release them into competent hands. I stare down at mine and breathe in the renewing spring evening air, refreshing as birth. My life is about to take the strangest turn; not a simple twist of fate, I'm hardly prepared for the outcome. In spite of that, there's still the pleasure I experienced, and feel, from the masterful repair work called healing.

Chapter Three
The News

I know that pure love is the magic elixir for all souls lost and weary, or for those who simply need a good stiff drink after an excruciatingly long day. Mental and physical exhaustion is merely part of the equation. There's also a nagging forewarning about my imminent debut on the evening news.

Still, I'm lucky to open the door and find what I truly need: doncha waiting. doncha in candlelight and Frank Sinatra singing, *I've got a crush on you, sweetie pie, all day and night, sweetie pie, pardon my mush but I've got a crush, my honey, on you...* Singing along with Frank, doncha gently presses a perfectly built martini to my lips. An embracing shelter of knowing, that's what love is. Drifting, drinking my martini, floating on a wave of memory, I return to the place in time when we first met.

October 4, 1980. Present in all her glory, she was more sensuous than the inside of a ripe fig; not to mention academic, coy, ironic, and hauntingly beautiful. Finally, a woman I craved with every fiber of my being. Admittedly, I was instantaneously in love, or, at the very least, seriously consumed with lust. However quick I was to disguise the internal pant going on that could blow off the top of my head, my Cheshire cat grin didn't do much to deflect her attention from my desire to explore her meticulously in thoroughly nonmedical ways.

"Take off your clothes ms. freeman and stand with your face to the wall, back side towards me. I want to examine you." I spoke in my most professional tone; she was not going to sniff out my heat.

Showing no emotion, Eden's veteran temptation slipped out of her diaphanous dress, moving the way liquid is fluid. The cadence of time changed when that amazing hair, all wild reddish tangles in waves, came undone, tumbling down to the curve of her waist. The longest strands tickled the dimples at rest on the top of her butt cheeks...*they* begged attention.

Visualizing a long line of wounded bodies in her path, I thought someone somewhere might have gone into business selling revolvers with one bullet in them to her ex-lovers.

Suffering, as she was, the effects of a cervical spine injury and a radiculopathy (nerve pain radiating from the source) was reason enough to make house calls. I will have her I told myself. With the slightest edge of coolness in my voice, I asked if she was a dancer, knowing perfectly well that only dancers move that way.

Her meditative reply revealed she read my secreted thoughts. "Hmmm, yes...well, healing is a lost art.... medicine a torturing science....you have a disarming voice, Doctor Lerner. You give the impression of intimacy."

"Are you saying I want to screw you, ms. freeman?"

"I'm sure you'd never screw anyone... not if you want to affect the heart of the matter."

Immediately after our rendezvous, (I mean the examination) I overhear a fragment of her breathy telephone conversation. She told her friend that her doctor is a magnetically powerful man with a rugged face and earthy good looks. She said I moved her. She called me a beautiful genius because I made a diagnosis after five clueless idiots tortured her needlessly. I loved when she said I have a Ben Casey-Doctor Kildare thing going on, with a twist. I'm in love is how she ended the conversation.

I penetrated her deeply. Oh yes, I knocked her silky little socks right off. The scandalous thing is we didn't even kiss, not for months. Not until her birthday on December 11th. That was our first kiss. I laugh aloud. My mind returns to the present when doncha asks me "What's funny? I thought you were asleep."

"Just thinking."

"Funny thoughts?"

"As a matter of fact, yes.... and beautiful."

She massages my tired muscles. She spoils my aching feet. Further pleasures are toothsome treats. doncha is the mistress of indulgence. She is the high priestess of tolerance for pure faults. I take her in my arms. "I want to swallow you whole. I want to inhale a bottomless breath with you in it."

Please, I plead, intense with a crazed passion, *if there is a higher power in this universe hear me now and don't take this beautiful woman that I adore away from me.* With the impact of the possibility of losing her, I tremble. *What am I going on about? What exactly do I think I'm facing? I have no idea. Snap out of it.*

Switching to another venue, I relay with unveiled humor Keith's visit to the OR. No sooner do I end that Keith story than another finagles its way in. There are so many; however, this one nearly ended my life. "Tonight, I saw a kid that reminded me of the time Keith took me into the underworld of the Cabrini Green housing projects; scary place to be driving at hundred miles an hour. I swear I can't tell where your crazy brother's personality ends and his mania begins. Nevertheless, I can tell you this, he drives as well with one eye as any racecar driver does with normal vision. His peripheral vision is incredible."

"I wouldn't go in a car with him if it was raining cyanide. He's been driving that way since he was twelve."

"Are you kidding? He's been driving since he was a child?"

"We weren't socialized properly. My parents were legendary freewheeling kids when they had us. My mother, dreamy like Luise Rainer, and my father was a Kirk Douglas look alike and macho ... and in the car business."

"What about me?"

"You're more the James Dean type, sweetheart."

"And you're like your leggy Auntie Jacky. *That woman* has Rita Hayworth appeal. To be honest, I've never fully recovered from *your Gilda* days."

"You had it coming, so leave it alone. Besides, you were equally as wild when you were a lad so don't look so disapproving, Sarah's monster."

Taking another pull off a joint, my forever flower-child plunks into a one-sided argument on the trade-offs between freedom and structure, as if the twain shall never meet. I listen to her speak and I think of how much she reminds me, in her quirkiness and braininess, of Sarah.

"My mother was indomitable in her conviction that I was destined to be an even greater neurosurgeon than Max Peet. Max Peet inspired Sarah even before she became his neurosurgical scrub nurse. He saved her life."

"So Freudian."

"Sarah Lerner was a perfectionist, outshining the call of duty. She put me on track after picking me up on a beach in Mexico, when I should have been in school. Determined to direct my future achievements, my mother enlisted department heads to tutor me. She even sat in on my classes; she wasn't taking any chances with me. My mother worshiped excellence the way the truly religious worship God." *I'm glad Sarah will never know about what's happening in my life now.* "Anyways, let me finish telling you my story about Keith transporting me through hell, complete with salvation."

"In the situation, salvation boggles the mind."

"Being around Keith is a trip, but I don't like losing my bearings. Wild man takes me to a crack house neighborhood; *supposedly,* I was taking a ride with him to make a brief stop, not one that would have lasted through eternity. All he had to say for himself, while I was ducking down in the seat trying not to get killed, was *these guys don't seem to see eye to eye with me.*"

"Crazy."

"Then, he insists I take a gun from the glove compartment and shoot back at them."

"You didn't..."

"Of course not; I hate guns. It gets worse. Cornered in an alley, dragged out of the car surrounded by crazed underworld types, I thought this is the end."

"That's terrifying! Did your life pass before your eyes?"

"Fortunately, no. Marmalade, a member of this gang about to murder us, recognized me. I decompressed a gunshot wound to the head on his buddy. A simple neurosurgical exercise on Jimmy Brown saved our asses."

doncha's face blanches against the blue light of the TV screen; her hand trembles turning up the volume. *Doctor Bernard Lerner, an eminent neurosurgeon from Northwestern University Hospitals, has been indicted by a federal grand jury for filling prescriptions for dilaudid and opiates for fictitious people, dead people, and compliant people.*

"Have you saved anyone in the DEA lately?"

My first reflex is "I need a dilaudid and a few valium to chase it. Pass the joint over."Taking a deep pull, I chase it with a stiff martini.

"When did this begin?" she asks softly, sitting next to me.

"While medicating myself for chronic pain from old football injuries....I tried to withdraw but it interfered with my performance."

She smiles like an angel. "You're performance is sublime. I meant..." I press my lips to a solitary tear on her warm cheek. "I do the best I can with what I've got."

"I meant them harassing you." She fires at the TV, "Trying to turn a neurosurgeon into a criminal, how many points is that! Go after real culprits, morons." She comforts me with the strength she's determined not to waste on anger.

The Fed's want a prison sentence; drug rehab is too good for smart-ass wonder boys. *That's the news folks! Everybody loves a hanging.* Reflecting an awful darkness, fear erupts inside me. I feel doncha's gashed silence bleed. *What will I do if she leaves me?* I unexpectedly become conscious of another addiction. I am seriously addicted to doncha.

In the morning, I call a well-known criminal attorney, who indicates to me via his cherished client Keith that if I don't *beat the rap* I will lose my license to practice medicine. Julius Echeles, a short-tempered bellowing barrister, does not use sugarcoated language. Too many years defending unbreakable criminals and a motley assortment of sociopaths and he no longer hears the truth spoken in modulated tones. Looking back, I have the perspective that retaining a criminal attorney wasn't the best idea. Some things become clearer through the retrospectascope.

Facing the day no longer holds the same charm when stepping out the door means reporters shoving microphones in my face besiege me. Typically, it's, "With all the self-medicating you've done, Doctor, what's the worst thing that ever happened to you in the operating room?" Standing firm like granite to keep the crowd from trampling me, I answer, "Watching someone else operate." They expect more but the truth is simple. "There's nothing more to be said."

Tuning them out, I tune into doncha's voice inside my head. *Forces of the universe touch us and change everything, forever.* Now I know what it's like to be haunted and hunted in a world of bullies where the rabbit does not have the gun. Of course, all bullies know the rabbit never has the gun. The rabbit wouldn't know what to do with a gun. A surgical blade is of a different metal altogether…and so is character.

Chapter Four
India

When a federal grand jury hits me with a formal accusation, I'm dealt a hand from hell, portending a serious nightmare. Played out, an indictment is for those deemed felonious or blameworthy in the *all-seeing eyes* of the *all-knowing* law. What could be worse? Only a proctoscope shoved up one's ass for the duration of this fantastic fiasco.

Dancing on fiery red carpets burns gaping holes through the soles of my shoes. Roasted, chewed up and spat out by publicity makers, my resources diminished, I'm left in the shallow end of my bank account. Positive my life couldn't get any more one-dimensional, morgue members of the Illinois State Medical Society clue me in that my malpractice insurance will not be renewed, and not because of malpractice. A faction of deadheads, posing as worthwhile physicians, made a unilateral decision. Knowing perfectly well that I cannot practice neurosurgery without carrying two million dollars on top and one million behind in malpractice coverage, the dirty double-dealers were determined to have me out of the game by hook or by crook. *Someone* would tap-dance on the grave of my virtuosic career.

None of their underhanded transactions prevents doncha from flying into hallowed chambers on her proverbial broomstick. My champion, labeled witch (with a capital B) from one end of town to the other, doesn't care what they say about her. She knows their game.

While she flies around vindicating me, I'm amorphously detached and free-falling. Hell bound, depression imbues the blue barrenness of my fractured existence. Out of this melancholia, to prove justice has at least one good eye, the universe grants me a portion of clemency. Was I begging? You bet.

I receive a concise correspondence from Lord Andrew Wakefield III. *Dr. Lerner, please come to India and to my rescue immediately, as I am, again, in critical need of your neurosurgical talent. If you do not come, I'm sure I do not know what I will do. I do not trust anyone as I trust you.*

No brain racking decision there; in a nanosecond we're packed up and ready to go; everything else has been made ready.

In India, chasing away beggars, the driver desperately pleads, "Please do not give them money, Sir and Madam, or it will be a never-ending journey. They will never stop coming."

The man doesn't sound cold; he actually has a gentle voice. Still, I have to tell him "That's cold." I can't face *that's reality*. An admission of that order would be as unearthly as witnessing skeletal maimed masses swarm from stacked shelters of cardboard boxes they call home. We give these people - humanity served up raw - the cash we have on us. It's a drop in the ocean.

If only the necessities were available to them. Food, disinfectant soap, clean water, toilet paper, and medicine would go such a long way to improve their lives.

Hating my inability to do anything in the service of deplorable conditions, I close my eyes. The vision doesn't erase; it's indelibly imprinted on my soul. "Why does any of this happen?" doncha squeezes my hand tight. "As long as the question remains a question, appalling realities will exist. There is no reasonable answer because there is no justification for any of it."

In view of the sweeping changes in my surroundings, I reorganize my thoughts to avoid stressing my patient. Content in my presence, Lord Wakefield smiles and greets me. "Doctor Lerner, this is indeed an honor. You traveled a far distance to come to my rescue. I am a fortunate man." Lord Wakefield speaks in a refined and somewhat wracked whisper, without much movement of his facial muscles, producing that stiff upper lip effect. "Am I going to die? Be honest with me; I want to know the truth."

I understand his starchy dramas and the drastic change in scenery calls for niceties, even if the extremes are perverse. "I could do this one in the closet with a jackknife." I draw a picture for him to illustrate the simplicity of my intended course of action. "I'm going to connect healthy vessels to the occluded vessels of the brain for a fresh blood supply. Right now, the blood vessels to your brain are not receiving an adequate blood supply. It's a simple matter of bringing vessels in from another source, which is very straight forward. Relax. I'm the best, remember, that's why you sent for me." I sign the completed sketch and hand it to him. "A souvenir. See you first thing in the morning. Get some rest."

Stepping into the heavy evening air, the potential of a monsoon brings to mind how unsettling large-scale systems can be when shifting direction. Personally, I'm like a tempest brewing, but that will not affect the result of my last surgery, as it may turn out to be. I'd stake my freedom that my patient has nothing to fear, concerning my performance. I can vouch for that.

Several days are all it takes for Lord Wakefield to recover. The hospital staff and I escort him to his chauffeur driven Mercedes. Presented a solid gold Dunhill lighter and a much-appreciated check, "A small token of my appreciation, Doctor, and it would please me immensely if you and doncha would be my guests in Goa, on the Arabian Sea."

"That would be right up doncha's alley. The little cat loves the sea."

Well, the little cat, dressed in a sari looking like a goddess, has plans of her own. "I'm ready to see the Taj Mahal, Bobby." (That's what she calls me. Bobby. Has nothing to do with my middle name. She claims it's a past life thing, which is a strange coincidence, taking into account I gave myself the middle name Robert, sensing a connection to the name when I was a child.)

"Lord Wakefield has arranged a holiday for us, in Goa." I give her that I can't help it look, not that the news is so awful.

"Let's go to Agra first. Okay, Goa first....but, I'm definitely not leaving India without seeing the Taj. I'm sure Goa will be lovely."

No one does a U-turn faster than donch.

Chapter Five
Goa

The warm cerulean blue waves of the Arabian Sea wash away woes so thoroughly you almost forget how hard life can be. With golden beaches, salty breezes, laid back natives, and mass quantities of mangoes, the lifestyle in Goa is what I would call uncomplicated. Serenely swaying in a hammock, under palm trees as graceful as flamingos, we whisper warm words while the tangerine sun sets. It's no wonder the Portuguese stayed on. The bells ringing-out from whitewashed Catholic churches remind us the Portuguese settled here. Peace on earth. East meets West. doncha loves that, it's her ideal.

Lingering on never-ending garden paths, the fragrant air intoxicates; like all beauties, Goa makes us heady. doncha, too, wants to colonize. "Let's stay here forever, Bobby," she begs wrapping herself around me. She does not want to let go of me, or this idyllic island. Her pleading saddens me when I cannot answer it.

Eating Indian food without silverware pleases her; tactile, doncha does it all time; here it's acceptable. It's rather erotic watching her savor the cuisine's warm exotic scents and flavors. Relaxing is a welcome change of pace....it's the shark-infested waters that trouble me. Because I love to swim, I want to be in the sea. Sad to say, even the most seemingly carefree worlds have hidden dangers. I'm not going to let that bother me, not now. doncha says the moon is balsamic, the time before the new moon, a time to make a wish.

Waking early, we traipse down the hilly path. The morning sand and sea sparkle, variegated like diamonds. Joined by several children, traveling with a cow crowned with wreaths of riotous colored flowers around its holy head, I turn up the volume on my Walkman. "Check this out." Needing little encouragement, we all dance down the hill, looking like Gopis, the cow herders who followed Lord Krishna. Everyone loves a blue prophet. Everyone loves Stevie Wonder.

On the beach, sun-bleached tents in soft shades of honeydew and cantaloupe capture our eyes and our imagination. The dancing pop-beat Gopis giggle and gesture entry is forbidden them. While the holy cow suns, the children swim in divine waters. We, on the other hand, are determined to discover what contraband lies ahead.

"Sex? Drugs? Toilet paper?" doncha, wants to know what these teepee-like structures hold. Directly on my heels, she greets the bone-thin nearly naked crinkled Indian with dreadlocks to his waist. In the filtered light, he welcomes us to his place of business with many namastes. My eyes wander. Unset stones and polished jewels priced dirt-cheap aren't what we're looking for. After some halting and rather amusing negotiations, the native directs us to another tent.

This one has a distinctly musky odor, vaguely familiar. "Opium." The native invites me with a pipe. I accept his hospitality with a few savory puffs. "Nice." I cough.

"It's time to go, my love." doncha guides me out the door to return to the villa, where we can indulge ourselves in surroundings that are more predictable.

Trying to figure out how to best work this out, we place the lit substance under a glass and inhale the opium fumes through a straw, our rendition of a hookah. Several days are lost to the reveries of this mysterious drug. We find ourselves laughing like idiots and making love like the monkeys on the temples. Wild and untroubled for these few days, doncha and I do not want to awaken from the freedom of this dream world.

Back on planet earth, having fresh baked nan and chai tea for breakfast, I'm lazy and complacent. Under the canopy in the frappi and lavender scented garden, gazing out over the handsome rolling lawns, I sigh with a tinge of regret, knowing I can't remain in this state. Addressing doncha's imploring, I can't help ending my thoughts with "Your ideals are not the way it is anywhere on this planet or in the known universe."

"Bobby, I'm begging you; let's stay here. You just think you have to live in a prescribed manner. That's socialization. It's not authentic."

"We have to go back, sweetheart."

"You're such a....such a doctor."

"I know."

Lord Wakefield pays us a surprise visit with a man called Manza. They find doncha, fed up with my stubbornness, reading in the arms of a Buddha statue as if it were a hammock. Lord Wakefield doesn't mind her antics. In his opinion, she's irrepressibly adorable. *She is*. Manzah, an influential operant in India and the United Arab Emirates, not sure what to make of doncha, forges ahead with his intended proposal, not finding any immediate objection to me.

Telling me he has considerable financial holdings in the oil producing Arab world and that it is in his interest to build a state-of-the-art hospital in Dubai, he concludes, "Would you be willing, Doctor Lerner, to oversee the development of the neurosurgical wing?"

Served pink gin and tonics, I think it's expedient to pass on the booze. The urgency of this opportunity becomes clear taking a first class ticket in hand. "Now? Is this today's date on the ticket?" I've lost track of time.

"If you please," Manzah answers succinctly.

Lord Wakefield, trying to manage doncha, has engaged her in conversation. "Women like you, charming and free spirited, are generally not well received in the United Arab Emirates."

I do my best to assuage her indignation. Unsuccessful at sweet-talking her, I end the amiable schmoose and take a no nonsense stand. "I'll meet you *after* I complete the project. I'll make it up to you. I promise. You bring me luck and I adore you." I pack up, kiss my love goodbye, and walk out the door singing, *"Luck be a lady tonight, luck be a lady…"* Before she can tuck her panties into my pocket, I'm gone.

Even without being there, I can hear her say, "The first place I'm going, Andrew, is Agra. I'm going to witness the Taj Mahal, the greatest expression of love in architecture, without Bernard. It doesn't seem right, but then what has *right* to do with anything."

Andrew raises an eyebrow. "That, my dear girl, is no mystery."

Scrutinizing him, she questions, "Will men forever maintain the status quo, no matter how unhappy it makes everyone, including them?" Lingering in the garden, the conversation wanders without prescribed answers. doncha's discontent, glossed over with an enchanting but woeful smile, doesn't change a thing, to include how much we want to be together.

Chapter Six
Abu Dhabi

At Abu Dubai International Airport, all international flights deplane on the runway. It infuriates me that we are kept waiting on the tarmac in over a hundred degrees of repulsively humid desert heat. Sweltering and crimson, not sure if I'm roasting or boiled, my melting eyeballs, by sheer force of will, are fixated on the immigration officers, holding the works up, shooting the only breeze going.

A bull in a red pen couldn't be madder. Doing my damnedest to control myself and figure out what in the hell is going on, Ali, the man who sat next to me on the flight talking about women's lingerie, is at it again. I snap at him, "Tell me something useful - like how I can get those idiots doing their paperwork in this appalling heat to move faster. Don't they have air-conditioning in this God forsaken country? It's supposed to be one of the richest countries in the world? I'm melting like a fucking Popsicle. Smell my pits."

I freeze when I hear the immigration officer asking about religious preference.

Never having considered the ramifications of being a Jew on Arab soil when I took on this assignment, I'm freaked.

Deliberating on what I should say becomes a mute point when at least twenty greased lightning Israeli jet interceptors rocketing off the steaming Persian Gulf, flying in *low,* head in the direction of the only upright person left on the runway. Everyone else had the good sense to take cover.

Consumed in a cyclone of pearly white sand sinking razor-sharp teeth into my blistering body, choking on dust, I whip my Star of David from my neck. Waving it in the air, shouting for all I'm worth, "Hey! Fuck! Stop! I'm one of you, you Kamikaze Sheenies."

My efforts are answered with a downpour of flowers intermingled with postcards that have Israel written across a map of the Middle East. Unable to see or think straight, I'm convinced my rational mind has figured it all out. Bursting with rage, I cry into the heavens above, "I'm not Job….got that, God. I'm Bernard Lerner and I've had enough! Do you hear me! I'm begging you to leave me alone!"

"You shouldn't speak to your Lord God that way."

Expecting I'll be scourged into the everlasting, a flight attendant breaks up a tortuous repartee between the Almighty and me. I'm informed with certitude that this ritual showering is timed to coincide with the five times daily Muslims and other Arabs are at their prayers. Shaking flowers from my head, I spit out more sand. "Why wasn't this mentioned *before* we deplaned? What is it with people?"

Left alone, a bitter after taste reinforces my apprehension. I'm a pariah on unfriendly soil. There's nothing novel about that… just another lovely day in my sensational life, soon to be a double-feature. Fearing hidden authorities may know my secret, I get the picture why Manzah didn't travel with me. He wouldn't be caught dead with a Jew on Arab soil.

Three half-tracks stand armed to the teeth with fifty caliber submachine guns in front of the U.S. Consulate. The greeting officer has his orders. "A person must declare themselves before they're admitted, or else." The *or else* makes me queasy when "Welcome to paradise on earth, Doctor Lerner," sounds treacherous. I don't care if Dr. Strangelove is representing Uncle Sam. Sporting ostentatiously tall black boots, clicking his heels, I call him Herr Wrightenhauer. Using the German Herr for Mister seems appropriate.

Herr Wrightenhauer expresses himself succinctly with his I eat nails for breakfast deportment. I immediately intuit his urgent dislike for me. Otherwise, I'm possessed with an rather impressive onslaught of paranoia. I feel it in my bones; Herr Wrightenhauer is a Neo-Nazi SOB.

Unconsciously touching the Star of David in my pocket, I pray this hard-core serious as a Gestapo baboon doesn't know my history. He'd arrest my ass and torture me for kicks. To flee the stone cold delusional heavy, insisting it's just Wrightenhauer, and his proclaimed vision of absolute paradise on earth post haste is the plan.

Shivering in the desert heat with thoughts that leave me panic cold, I can't distinguish what's in my head from what I put out there. On top of that, I'm drier than antique bone from the mass quantities of sand I've inhaled. I also have a sneaking suspicion that the Consul General's mad dogs, who charged out from behind the scenes after me, are not going to let me out of their sight. In this golden-domed mosque city, the boys with the elevated black boots will tail this sandal-footed nomad for the duration. I'd bet anything they are determined to know where this Jew is at all times.

Presently, shaking and sweating, consuming a quantity of alcohol to steady my nerves and appease my cross drug addicted needs, I disclose to the bartender pouring me another that all addictions need to be satisfied in one way or another.

Despite my drawbacks, in a matter of weeks, I design a highly sophisticated state-of-the-art operating theater, the exclusive province of the rich. I hand over the plans to a shrouded man wearing traditional Arab clothes. He has nothing to say to me, despite my attempts to engage him in conversation.

After a fearsome loneliness, I meet up with six full-sized hard-drinking Welsh offshore oil riggers, sitting in a cloud of smoke with pints in their hands and booze on their breath. My morale escalated, I tell them not for the first time, "I'm so glad to know you guys." They bellow their motto, "Have another one on us, mate." I reciprocate and so goes the camaraderie; until the day of my departure we have a blast.

Because Middle East disturbances add to the unpredictably or predictably of life, depending on your point of view, airlines ready to close their doors. With partial payment from the sheiks, two days before my planned departure, cutthroats deliver a personalized message - the America translation is — *don't count on any more green backs. Get the hell out of town, Jew boy, your invitation has expired.* Nothing subtle about desert thieves; I see the knives in their teeth.

The oil riggers, six good men tried and true, sponsor a night out on the town in my honor. Mighty, fully tattooed and intoxicated (pissed, as they say) fellows display themselves admirably in T-shirts and jeans, impressive over articulated muscles. I have a fuzzy recollection of standing on a table at a Bedouin wedding party, wearing my buckskin jacket, singing *Rawhide.* I also have a vague memory of militia beating me to a bloody pulp. The numbers were so unfair. We cowboys, taken back to the compound under guard, didn't go without resistance, or we wouldn't be cowboys.

Morning hits us hard. The misbegotten escort us to the airport and put us on our respective flights. Heroically, I limp to the gate with my friends cheering me on. A busted nose, a fractured rib, and a beauty of a black eye are a pretty picture, up to the point when no one is looking. *Act out much?* I quip to my reflection in the mirror before I throw up. The thunderous roar, from flushing the commode in the air, makes my head explode and threatens to suck me into oblivion.

doncha, waiting for this desperado at Heathrow, frowns with concern. "I am reluctantly here to collect you, Bobby. What I want to do is abduct you and not return to the States." Her serious hesitation about going back to the land of the free and the home of the brave has become more complicated. "Where would you be safe?" She asks strategically placing kisses on my bruised face. She handles me gently. *"Damn,* Bobby, you're an unholy mess."

"You should see the other guys," I counter with renewed enthusiasm. Telling my side of the story, I vent some serious complaints against the U.A.E. You know I'm not going to be messed with; when physically threatened I will respond aggressively. My street smarts are still intact. You think I belong in the gutter, don't' you?"

"I do not judge you. I simply love you the only way I know how. Are we still taking the flight back to the States? With my heart and soul, I beg you not to do it. It would be suicidal. Straighten things out from this side of the Atlantic."

She's speaking to herself. I'm not listening. "The most exciting thing besides my buddies was playing James Bond while the Consulate's people tailed me. And the camel races at the Abu Dhabi Downs were sensational…."

No sooner am I on U.S. soil than I wish I wasn't. The villainous DEA agent Hockstrap is waiting for me at U.S. immigration. Playing macho, conspiring with another scrawny scoundrel wearing dark motorcycle cop glasses, they exude second-rate porn. WHOOM! WHOOP! Hockstrap slaps those cuffs on me. "Broke your probation; I knew you would," he chortles. Satisfied, having witnessed Hockstrap initiate his dirty deed, his sidekick abandons himself to the shadows.

"What are you talking about? I'm not on probation."

"I caught you fleeing the country red handed, asshole. Go on deny it. We're standing right here in immigration."

"You didn't catch me *leaving* the Country."

Stunned with the absurdity of the situation, doncha steps in to mediate. "Bernard wouldn't have *returned* if he *fled* the country, that's illogical. Do you understand that he's returning from a business trip and…"

doncha is left alone, once again, while I squander another night in a *made to make you miserable* prison cell, conceding I wind up in rather shitty places for a man of my refined sensibilities.

In the morning, I am relieved to find my attorney, Mr. Echeles, present in court. "You look awful, Doctor Lerner" is how the charmer greets me. Pleading from parched lips, "My passport is valid. It wasn't taken from me," Echeles reads me the riot act, while King Kong Hockstrap beats his breastbone. "I apprehended this treacherous criminal. Incarcerate him until the trial, Your Honor, or he'll take off again."

"Look at Hockstrap. To give me the evil eye, he has to turn his entire body side to side to find me. He's so unnaturally rigid, he looks more like an action figure than a person, which would be comical if he weren't so dangerously calcified and stupid. The law gives the oddest types stature and a voice and puts me in debt and in jail."

My lawyer professes, "I'm not interested in that; I want to know why you left the country."

"Simple. I can't pay attorney fees if I'm unable to work." I light a cigarette that I am powerless to smoke; my lips are too painfully swollen.

"Point well taken. An additional twenty thousand dollars for this hearing and a fifty thousand dollar bond…"

All this bullyboy self-satisfaction gives me the creeps. Preferring not to speak to thugs, I keep the rest of my wayward thoughts to myself while he rambles. *I must be in the Twilight Zone. This does not happen in real life…oh yeah, what about Berlin in the 1930s…..or McCarthyism….shit!*

What hallucinogen is Hockstrap on, complaining, "What are you doing, Your Honor? You can't release Lerner on bond. He'll procure opiates and cause physical harm to others."

Assbern warns, "Another word and I will find *you* in contempt. You could spend the night in jail, Agent Hockstrap."

Pitching his body toward me, the instrument of torture crushes the words "I'm going to see you hang."

You would think I was the one threatening him with a night in prison. *What's up with that jerk anyways?* I rub my bruised ribs and look out of my almost good eye. It's all a blur.

Chapter Seven
Counsel's Advice

At another one of our many get-togethers, Echeles chokes me with a surfeit of minutia. Persisting with strong-arm advice, he insists I signup for a stay in a rehabilitation center, pushing the papers towards me. I lean back in the chair. "I've heard nothing creditable about those places, except that they lack a certain gritty reality for the serious abuser. Going into rehab is redundant. I've already stopped taking medication the good old-fashioned way - cold turkey. Let me tell you something, Mr. Echeles, a jones approximates a medieval exorcism. Telescopic vomiting is comic relief when a seizure can kill you. I've paid my dues."

In a rare moment of compassion, Echeles displays a tender underbelly. Quick to flip to his tough side, he points a gnarly finger at me. "Sign the papers. You're going into rehab. End of story."

It's true the demon drug wracked every fiber of my being before its expulsion…but listening to Echeles is insufferable. All he cares about is his habit. He'll rack-up a big fat bankroll, hightail his gargantuan walrus butt out of here and get on the first junket to Vegas to mindlessly blow the wad. And where will I be? Blowing more money on rehab?

Strung out by the outlandish nightmare I'm living; trapped in the grip of the evil twins withdrawal and craving, constantly snapping at my heels, my entire being longs for the relief of pulverized dilaudid lit with cocaine. Regrettably, this mixture over time forms a salt that precipitates into the muscles and tendons, dramatically altering body chemistry. A few of the nasty end products noticeable right off the bat are sleeplessness, shaking, bone and joint pain and just plain bad juju. Might as well suffer rehab's rack as any other. A cold chord of fear clangs in my brain.

Alarm bells go off. Having witnessed gross incompetence and more than a little deviousness in this world, I am not at all comfortable being so far from the control center of my own life. Waxing philosophic, finding no answers forthcoming, more aware than ever of the insistent nagging in my brain begging *I need drugs*. *I need*..............*self-restraint*. I light a cigarette instead.

Echeles disapproves.

"We're all addicted to something. What do you want from me?"

"Be on that plane tomorrow morning. I expect you to take my advice."

"Can I expect your advice is qualified?"

Showing me the door does not convince me.

Chapter Eight
Rehab

Now that I'm relaxed, however temporary the condition, the advantages of doing this rehab stint floats through my idling mind. *A little R&R never hurt anyone...improving my golf game will give me a competitive edge and I am partial to excellent resort food....eating well and relaxing can't be the worst way to spend too much time on my hands... even if I do have to attend a few of their insipid meetings.*

By the time I deplane, I'm bad on booze.

This is disgusting. I shrink from the damp air that gets stickier. Two Pillsbury doughboys, with marshmallow butts, are leaning against a urine-colored Mercedes with *OBGYN license plates. Figures.* Dropping my bags at their feet, I point to the sign with my name on it. Slamming back a reserve mini-bottle of booze, I smack my lips and burp loud and long, for a nice effect. After wiping the sweat from my brow, I conclude my introduction. "What fire and brimstone swamp did I land in this time?"

"Nice to meet you, too. I'm Tom." Tom turns his head away; the scent of booze must make him nervous. "Ya'll shake hands with Mick."

In my best southern accent, I declare, "Don't *you* fret none about shaking *my* hand, Mickey boy. Sweat never hurt anyone. I should be worried about shaking *ya'all's hand.* I heard Klan boys wipe their asses with that hand. Now that we've become acquainted, I'd be much obliged if you two pussy doctors would get the show on the road. I'd like to shoot nine holes before dinner."

"Slow down, cowboy."

"Like my boots, do ya?"

"Hey, Mick, the brain cuttin' boy is under a considerable delusion that he's here for a resort holiday or he's in denial. Check out these fancy clubs. He's definitely in denial." The careless way they throw my golf clubs in the trunk pisses me off.

"Denial? C'mon. The entire fucked-up world is in that river in Egypt. Take off, there's no way I'm going with you. Who are *you* to be insulting me?"

I jump into the back seat of the Mercedes. "Get out of here! Go! Make tracks!"

A thunderstorm out of nowhere and a lighting bolt out of the blue split the tree right next to where I was standing, in half. I felt electricity's grip.

"That *absolutely* means something!" Mick's knuckles are purple around the steering wheel.

"What a genius! It means you should put some lead in it!"

Dragging off two cigarettes hard, I'd light a third one if I had an extra hand. From the look of repulsion on Tom's face, I'm probably a shade less menacing than the thunder ripping the sky apart.

"That's a sign that some of us better start praying for our sins."

"Are you positive you're scientists?"

"We aren't, but there are Scientists among us at the Center."

Dumb ass. I close my eyes. I have nothing more to say.

When the sun's brilliant debut illuminates a Swiss chalet, the expected dungeon dissipates. *This shouldn't be too disagreeable, now that I've lost the white trash. Someone around here will be decent enough to golf with, even if I don't speak the native tongue.*

Igor, the intern, ignores my misinformed ideas about where I'm at and who *they* are. He stows my golf clubs in what appears to be a repository for lost bags and packs me off to his office.

Already on my wrong side, he annoys me further with dull medical questions. "Did you ever have liver disease, kidney disease, syphilis, or gonorrhea?" When he adds, "When was the last time you took a drug or drink?" to his repertoire, I brighten. "I could use a double vodka on the rocks with a splash of soda and a lime. Don't exert yourself; just bring the bottle and a straw." I lean back in the chair anticipating his return.

He brings me Xanax, an anti-anxiety/anti-seizure medication. "If this is what you call southern hospitality, I'm disappointed." I peer at him. "Five milligrams. Can you spare it? I'll need a few more and whatever else you have to kick it up several notches. This stuff is boring on its own. You're not taking your job seriously. Isn't an addictionologist akin to a mixologist?"

"This is a rehabilitation center, not a psych ward."

"So, what are you telling me, there's no Friday night wine tasting seminars? And there's no golf, right?"

He hands me a brochure listing course titles: Getting in Touch with Your Real Self. Remembering and Loving Your Parents and Addiction as a Disease. I stop snorting in my tracks when I hear *Amazing Grace* sung beautifully somewhere on the premises. The soulful voice calms me until a rather large person called a Regulator deposits me in substandard living quarters.

"How can anyone relax in this dump?" I kick the blankets from the bed. "Didn't you hicks ever hear of down feathers? Where's the phone? I'm hungry." I shove a horrid pillow at him. "Get me two down pillows....will ya, please."

"I'll take you to the cafeteria." He flings the pillow back on the bed and runs out the door to assist staff bullies wrestling an inmate, with a few ideas of his own, to the ground. The Hickman catheter the guy hooked up to his subclavian vein is disengaged. "An anesthesiologist can easily hook himself up." I inform the spectators, as if they didn't know. "At Northwestern there was an anesthesiologist who would take the fentanyl meant for the patient and hook-up the patient to a saline solution. A cruel reality for all involved. "Take it easy, man," I call out to the hysterical anesthesiologist as he's carried from the premises.

At least the beautifully paneled in walnut and elegantly furnished dining room is up to standard. I can't say the same about the food. It immediately triggers my gag reflex. I wouldn't eat this crap with someone else's mouth. I want a two-inch New York strip steak grilled to perfection, but I know I won't get anything with the N letter in it. Anyways, I'm not breaking bread with stoned out descendants of racist red necks.

Deposited in group therapy, I snooze with one eye open. Among Southerners, someone's bound to do or say something eccentric. Who would have guessed the shrink would be the first to get weird.

"I ran drugs and guns in South America. I slept with too many women and I slept with men of all sorts, too. Not that I was gay… it's just that it happened. My life caught up with me the day I was brought to my knees at a murder scene. Fatally fucked up, I was busted holding a semiautomatic weapon. Three years of hard labor made me religious."

"Aren't you profound. Once you got religion, *have mercy*, you became a healer. *I* had to go the traditional route and attend medical school. Your dodgy criminal con lifestyle makes me shudder. I couldn't stomach your existence for five minutes."

"Bernard, please lead us in The Lord's Prayer" is his reply.

"I don't know it, but if you hum a few bars I'll fake it."

Someone in the know does the job.

I resume my sleeping posture.

After a dreamless night, my body endures the brunt of having slept in a horribly uncomfortable bed that I don't have the vaguest recollection of having gotten into. Listening to addicts profess a desire to grasp their higher powers first thing in the morning, and they aren't anywhere near convincing, is more than I can bear. What happened to their souls? Pulling my cap over my eyes and ears, I keep my refrain to myself. *What good are my healing powers doing anyone when I end up in a place like this. These phonies aren't devoted to patients. Their pretense make me want to puke. Why didn't my accusers take me out back and shoot me? Because, Bernard, you idiot, they're going to crucify you, it's more painful that way!*

On the third evening, a bunch of wimp doctors sitting in a circle holding hands look ridiculous to me. I keep my arms firmly crossed over my chest. Dr. T opens the session reminding me, the way he claps his hands, of a kid playing patty cake. "Each physician, in turn, will state their name and drug of choice. We will begin with B...Bernard."

"My name is Tommy Tuna and they're all my drugs of choice."

Just as I was getting into the swing of things, a former inpatient crazed on I.V. opiates bursts into the room. The guy's name is Jerry and Jerry's pissed. I move out of the way to make room for his anger. He's spewing, "I spent over thirty thousand dollars and three months on this rip-off scam joint and for what?! The first thing I reached for when I got out of here was drugs. All I really want to do right now is blow this damn place up with you in it, Dr. T."

"You tell 'em, Jerry. Good for you. Your monologue is refreshingly honest. What do they know about what you've been through? What do they know about your suffering, you poor bastard."

Dr. T punctuates the drama. "We will pray for you, Jerry."

Jerry slumps into a chair, exhausted but still furious. I don't blame him. Trustful, he put out a small fortune expecting sobriety in return. Jerry, like so many before and after him, is still an addict seven days a week.

On the seventh day, I decide to give it a rest. With my bags in tow, I confront Dr. T. "I disagree with your methodology. It's incomprehensible to me that you've worked out your methods or anything you're doing to it's logical conclusion. Maybe you're a whole lot smarter than I am, but I doubt it."

He regurgitates his Sunday best jargon.

"My will and my life are not going to be turned over to God….not as you people understand God. I don't want to be an inmate of this nuthouse or any other institution. Without further ado, I bid you farewell."

"If you don't complete rehab you may very well wind up in prison."

"I thought about that. My suspicion is I would be more at ease anywhere than I am here."

"We will pray for you, Bernard."

"Who listens to phonies that don't care about their profession. It's all I, I, I, in this joint. You're not doctors… you're puling infants. Don't forget to burp the babies after you've blown them up with all that hot air. Gesundheit and adios."

The institution's baseball games were the one event worth participation. Even Bridget, a deposed pharmacist, sliding provocatively into my bases with her state of the art body wasn't enough to keep me playing ball. Always willing and wanting to be helpful she goes for my crotch and offers to take me to the airport by way of her house.

I sidestep her. I know all about Bridget. The cops literally chased her into the center with drugs in hand. She spends her days brutally renouncing her *past* addictions. For this, after thirty days residency, she earned the privilege to live in an apartment with two other women, which I happen to know is snug with alcohol and drugs.

"My boyfriend is out of town." She licks her slick red lips, making a perfect circle around them with her tongue. "I have a stash of ludes and Halcyon. I don't want to be a bad influence on you. If you don't want to get high, we can jump into the hot tub and you can fuck me until my mind blows."

Imagining her, her drugs, and her hot tub, I contemplate what I could say to doncha, if I canceled my flight. *What if her boyfriend comes home? Asshole Hockstrap might be waiting at the airport with a bottle for me to pee in. That would end my probation in a heartbeat.* Putting aside my desire to get fucked-up, as opposed to fucked, I play it straight. "Thanks for the invitation but I have to pass."

Jumping into the taxi, I implore the driver, "Get me out of here, quick! Step on it!" I take a long last look from the back window at that luscious derriere and those long, long legs on those high high-heels. "Damn. How much? How much should a man be willing to give up?" I hear doncha inside my head. *I don't know, you tell me.*

Navigating my way to the gate via watering holes downing doubles, I board my flight adequately inebriated. I pass out and I don't wake up until I'm back in the Chicago. In spite of everything, it's still my kind of town.

Chapter Nine
The Rat and the FBI

In the crowded airport or anywhere on earth, my redheaded woman catches my eye. To tell the truth I'm a bit nervous. Witchy woman might have sensed my libido made me take a long hard second look. A stay of execution; doncha is a miracle of loveliness in the gauzy green and gold sari I bought for her in India, and she's smiling an I adore you Bobby smile. Fortunately, she's exquisitely blissful; a jealous goddess is a terrible thing to behold. I caught on quickly - forgetting a stray thought now and then - that I cannot play with a true heart on fire, *after* she scared me monogamous. Her quixotic acts of jealousy are crystal clear signs that she loves me. High drama satisfies me, but not as much as the oozy wild love she greets me with. Kissing every inch of my face, she moves on to ravage my neck. The tigress is hungry for love.

"My love, where's your tan? No golf?"

"It was rainy."

She rushes on in between kisses. "I missed you, my heart." She rubs my bottom; her very own crystal ball.

There is a disruption in our magic circle.

"What's the matter, darling?" She follows my eyes, latched onto Agent Hockstrap, the most infuriating and irritating ignoramus of the century.

"Here comes the lunatic who chain sawed my life and career for kicks." Unable to unclench my teeth, my chest is tight. "Agent Hockstrap, how nice of you and your sidekick to show up here with your government license to mutilate with impunity."

"Couldn't complete your rehab could you, you fucked up addict. The judge will want to know about this." He crosses his skinny arms over his narrow-minded federal chest and thrusts his puny pelvis forward.

"Very impressive." doncha comments on the body language. "Who was that character in the corner with you? You looked cozy together."

I side step him, anxious to leave the airport before there's a regrettable scene.

Not accepting well-defined boundaries, doncha compromises; borrowing a tambourine from a group of Hare Krishna's and a handful of Krishna literature, she dances around the G-men singing, *Hare Krishna, Krishna, Krishna...* Handing literature to Hockstraps's entourage of agents, *nonchalantly* hanging out, she lets them know that we know they've been tailing us. "Study up boys. Nice day. Namaste." She returns the tambourine with a donation and another namaste, smiling at me, angelically.

"I asked you to ignore them. All I want to do is leave the airport in one piece and see my lawyer."

"I'm going home to smoke a joint. I'm not in the Gulag. Not yet. We should have stayed in India, where you were appreciated and we were happy."

She drops me off. I know she's thinking what I've heard her say before. *Our lives will never be the same. This country rids itself of heroes. They may not murder you, Bernard, but you're losing all the joy you ever possessed. The powers that be, the supposed authorities, are too shockingly stupid for words. How could you buy into what they're doing by coming back. They're going to crucify you. It's terrifying.*

Julius Lucius Echeles' uncanny resemblance to Hemingway reassures me. *All this crap dumped on me will soon end. The stink will come to surface and be cleared-up with one cast of his line.* Today, being in the office of this high-powered attorney inspires confidence until, without so much as a *how do you do*, he nearly feeds me a stack of prescription triplicate pads. "Sixty prescriptions written over a four year period, Doctor, to equal one hundred and twenty counts of felony. Two counts for each prescription written, some of them written to dead people. Who writes prescriptions to the deceased?" Bringing the drama of the stage to his voice, I'm addressed in a full courtroom baritone.

"If they were on my service they wouldn't have boxed."

He releases hot air through his nostrils. The prize bull is ready to charge me more money. It's transparently obvious that you're in dire straits when you're attorney wants to take you down. "I have also been made cognizant, Doctor, that ten living breathing souls returned medication to you from their prescriptions. Although the counts are duplicitous, the possibility of a one hundred year prison sentence is not remote, if you're convicted on each count."

"Sounds excessive to me."

"The government spent over a million dollars to bring you to trial. They're not playing; they're serious."

"Come on Julius, I'm not a criminal. Agent Hockstrap, on the other hand, obviously has leanings in that direction. He showed-up at the airport today with a rat that I was unable to place, at first. Later, I remembered that rodent called me at a holiday line-party, given by one of your attorney buddies, not last Christmas, but the one before."

"Get to the point, Doctor."

"That flea infested Mickey Mouse tried to sell me a half pound of cocaine over the phone. Pressing his agenda, he showed up the next day at Northwestern, flashing a handgun and a DEA Special Investigator's badge around my office. I told him I'm a neurosurgeon, not a drug dealer."

"Of course. Why then do you think this character contacted you in the first place?"

"Probably to set me up after Hockstrap's case against me, whatever that might be in his deluded mind, didn't turn out as he expected."

"Let me get this straight. Hockstrap, being a disappointed lad, having nothing on you after he followed you around for a long while, had a small gnarly mammal contact you with a view to entrap you?"

"I notified the FBI. They wanted me to help them bust the creep."

Julius leans back in his throne and places his fingertips together. "Doctor, I don't recall ever hearing of a physician of your caliber who lives near such an extraordinary life. Shall I assume undercover work is a relatively new undertaking; a second career choice, perhaps?"

"I'm not in the business of playing with lives."

"Naturally."

"Smith, that's the rat's name, showed up at the hospital whenever the whim hit him. He said he was checking up on me. I told him if that's the case he better live in scrubs because I live in the OR."

"How were you able to perform?"

"*This* was not the pressure of the OR where I'm organized for every event. There are no surprises for my patients. These people: Smith, the FBI, and whoever else is in on this, don't give a damn about me or my responsibilities."

"That is the way of the world."

"Not *my* world. Anyway, I drove to Smith's business wearing a wire, tailed by the alphabet boys. One of them tried to pass me a handgun, which I refused to take. I told him you guys are here for that."

"Absolutely, correct."

"It was dark and silent when I walked into Smith's place of business with fifty thousand dollars in marked one hundred dollar bills. Smith's gun was on the table. He did exactly what I wanted him to do. He refused to take the money."

"He knew something was up." Echeles taps his pen on his desk.

"I got into all of their heads."

"Well, Doctor Lerner, that's because you're not the run of the mill target."

"I met up with *the Alphabet boys* at the designated rendezvous place, a seedy pancake house. When I handed over the paper bag with the government's money, the head honcho said I did a great job, maybe too great.

"Another word about this and you can arrange different counsel for yourself."

Shown the door, I have the most sickening sensation. My future hasn't unfolded, nevertheless it's a tale that's been told by idiots, with much sound and fury.

Chapter Ten
Before the Trial

Realizing how precariously the sword of justice hangs over my presumed guilty head, I attempt to elicit a straight answer, regarding what's *really going on,* from a charging-by-the-second bullshitting attorney forever demanding more money, and it's all for nothing. I pop another antacid.

Echeles feeding me a daily diet of "Do you recollect this prescription, Doctor," makes me cringe. I recollect sixty prescriptions; the details of each case pried from dormant memory files, without any anesthesia, drugs or booze to bolster me. "This was the case of…" and "No it's not too much medication to prescribe after a burr hole is drilled in the skull to raise a flap of bone, and that's just the beginning."

"Irrelevant," Echeles barks, before going into another snore of a monologue.

"Why is all this time and money being wasted on me? Why don't they go after the tobacco companies; they're rolling up toxic waste for profit."

"Stay on track."

"Grave consequences transpire when government henchmen can't separate criminals from commoners, even if the commoner is uncommon."

Echeles flings another prescription my way. "That's not relevant."

"I think it's relevant."

Out of patience with me, my attorney bolsters himself with another lobster cocktail. Delivered by the half-dozen to his office, he's constantly cooing to crustaceans, when he's not billing sharks, or me.

Take care to do it perfectly. You really know what's important, you blowhard. I visualize a monster-sized lobster claw grabbing Echeles' face as Harry Belafonte sings the *Banana Boat* song. *Daylight come and he wan' go home...*

"Won't you partake?" Echeles interrupts my reverie.

I refuse the bait and the last of the triplicates he expects me to chomp-on and return to speculations that are more germane. *Why am I in a criminal attorney's office? Who in the hell do they think I am, Bernard the Badass. I'm a great neurosurgeon. Meanwhile, phonies sitting on their bony butts in ivory towers have residents, who can't cut their way out of a paper bag, write rehashed papers, that are useless, for publication. I've written dozen of useful and original articles, myself, based on reality. All I want to do is tune out of my own head and work inside someone else's head, intervening with surgical instruments. I want what I had. I want my life to return to normal.* Fishy smells brings me back to reality and Echeles offering me another scrap.

"I've had enough. Goodnight."

No sooner out of that stinking situation than I'm trapped in the elevator with a smoker, smoking a cheap cigar. Convinced it's impossible to escape the repellant, my head spins from atrocious smells and horrible thoughts.

"You want to get off?"

The man's clairvoyant.

"This is the third floor." He tells me, believing I'm confused about that.

"No, I'm going all the way down. Once you've been as high up as I've been only rock bottom breaks the fall."

Chapter Eleven
The Trial

Like the chorus in Greek Tragedy, on this day - the day of trial, We the People ask, Whom did he murder? Whom did he harm?

Do you want the Truth? The chorus questions.

Yes, the People answer, we want the truth.

The truth is we are captive to a bogus charade performed by the misguided, the misinformed and the misdirected stupidity of dumb power.

Mr. Burner, the Prosecutor, narcissistically infatuated with the sound of his own voice, maliciously sets out to trash compact my brilliant career. The reason for this hardhearted deed is simple. Burner intends to leave his government pit of a job to pander privately. Inaugurating his graveyard campaign, he defames others.

We the People are witness. We hear his claims, in the vein, that the Doctor is an evil man, an inhabitant and a conspirator of a forbidden, illegal drug world. His true friends are the dregs of society. Doctor Lerner lives a double life, dark and dangerous. He associates with pimps and prostitutes, dope fiends, and women who sport three-inch fingernails and five-inch stilettos.

Echeles lets out a dismissive snort. "Does anyone question how the Doctor manages to come up for air from this nefarious underworld, no matter how glamorous, to perform incredibly intricate neurosurgical procedures?"

The jury looks numb. Could be they're stunned. It's not often one finds oneself in the presence of a Clark Kent super-surgeon crossed with a Dr. Jekyll and Mr. Hyde. To arouse them Echeles drops a heavy book on the table. "Doctor Lerner does not have clandestine meetings. He does not meet drug dealers on the street corner." Pausing dramatically, his eyes dart around like a thief in the night; he slyly slides an imaginary procurement into his pocket, before he slinks off a distance, profiling a villain in a second-rate silent film. Turning back, he crescendos "This is *not* how it was done. The Doctor simply wrote a prescription to his patients and received medication in return; medication for legitimate pain... but medication is addictive. His methods were sometimes extreme. No doubt, he was carried away when he wrote prescriptions to the dead. He owns that.

Doctor Lerner is an unusual man. However, not in this regard. The medical profession, whether we want to be on familiar terms with the truth or not, is a highly addicted community, Ladies and Gentlemen." Pensive is the counterfeit expression the faker pulls out of his bag of disguises and tricks; an illusion to say how terribly unfortunate reduces the truth to an absurdity.

Statistics prove twenty-five percent of all medical professionals suffer from substance abuse. This number, derived from a small fraction of the addicted, can hardly be representative. Fear of damaging hard-won careers prohibits many suffering the disease of addiction from owning the truth. Reflect on this pertinent information before you judge, Ladies and Gentleman of the Jury."

Depleted from his efforts, poor Mr. Echeles slumps into the chair next to mine and pops a hand-full of opiates. After a sudden medical intervention, he too needs relief from pain that doesn't quit. I have to wonder how much his over-medicating himself critically affects him and screws me, and this screwed-up case, in turn.

Testimony is next. My patients take the stand as witnesses. Ten individuals under oath, in succession, swear, "Yes, I gave Doctor Lerner medication from my prescription. No, I didn't think it strange or wrong. You know," each of them contribute in one way or another, "Doctor Lerner was always extremely busy. We were going to the hospital pharmacy anyway so he doubled the prescription. We brought his half of the pills back to him. We didn't think it was going to be a major ordeal."

In order to hold the ground he lost, Burner pulls an ace from his sleeve and swears-in Henry-0 Daley. "Mr. Daley," he smirks, "please be so kind and tell the jury in what capacity you know Doctor Lerner."

"Doc is the man. A good friend of mine….a real bro."

"Have you ever engaged in illegal dealings with the defendant?"

"Yeah, man, the Doc's the man. I already told you that." The witness stares vacantly over his sunglasses.

"Mr. Daley," the Judge instructs the witness, "remove your sunglasses. The sun is not shining in this courtroom."

"Tell me why that dude over there is wearin' shades? Are you discriminatin' against me?"

"Mr. Hockstrap, you, too, shall remove your sunglasses."

On cross-examination, Echeles asks the witness, "Has Doctor Lerner ever given you medication in exchange for cocaine, Mr. Daley?"

"Oh yeah, we do the exchange thing all the time."

Flabbergasted by the lies the liar in pink leisure suit and twelve pounds of gold jewelry is telling, I jump out of my seat. "What do you people think you're doing?"

"Control your client, Counsel."

The witness's eyes instinctively stray in my direction.

"Mr. Daley, are you currently on probation?"

Echeles taps his foot, impatient for the answer.

"Answer the question, Mr. Daley."

"Well, sort of."

"Yes or no, are you currently on probation?"

"Yeah, I am; so what?"

"Isn't it true that you have been offered a sentence reduction in exchange for your testimony?"

"I better get what they promised me."

"One final question. Keeping in mind that you're still under oath, with penalty of perjury, tell me, did you and the accused exchange drugs or partake of them together? A simple yes or no will do."

"What's up with this? Damn. No." His head hangs low.

"No further questions."

Mr. Daley's change in his testimony was due to an inadvertent glance at me. A code of honor was at stake the minute he recognized me. In his *hood* no one messes with the Doc, and I believe he's no exception. Everyone he knows knows *Doc takes care of the people.* Otherwise, it's possible that Echeles hypnotized him with his pocket watch. Rumor has it that he did that very thing during the Charlie Marazano Purolator Robbery trial.

Agent Hockstrap escorts Chelsea Teasdale to the witness stand. Burner's there too, vying for Ms. Teasdale's attention. She's sworn-in, with the two of them nearly nestled in-between her unstinted breasts. Burner hisses, "Sit down, dog!" Reluctantly, Hockstrap mopes back to his seat, led by his dick. Pleased with himself, jerking his head, as *if* he could ever get the kink out it, Burner fusses with his belt, and persuades. "Ms. Teasdale, please tell the court, have you received prescription medication from Doctor Lerner?"

"I don't take drugs. I swear it. I gave them to my sick mother." She rearranges her snug sweater. "I'm healthy!"

"Doctor Lerner gave you drugs for your mother's medical condition?"

She brushes imaginary specks off her chest. "Yes, we're good friends."

Burner is a fast sweet talker. I've never seen that woman before.

"Did you and Doctor Lerner get high together?"

"Oh, yes."

"Thank you, Ms. Teasdale. You may cross examine the witness, Mr. Echeles."

I know what's up. It doesn't take a genius.

Attorney Echeles snorts. "What do you do for a living, Ms. Teasdale?"

"I'm a massage therapist."

"Are you licensed?"

"I mean I'm an interior decorator."

"Are you licensed?"

"Oh yes, I forgot…I have a driver's license." She giggles.

"Ms. Teasdale, please tell the court what you *really* do for a living."

She turns to the judge and pouts. "Do I have to tell?"

The Judge nods a bored affirmative. "Yes."

"You can go to jail if you don't tell the truth, you're under oath. Answer the question truthfully. "

"Do I have to?" she asks the Judge, again, not at all clear how Echeles knows she is not an interior decorator.

"You're under oath."

"Are you and the accused friends?"

"Sort of."

"Perjury is…"

"Well, not exactly friends."

She looks in Hockstrap's direction. To give Echeles credit, he blocks her visual path.

"Ms. Teasdale, how do you earn your living?"

"I'm a whore, I'm a whore." This young woman, with the street not yet defined in her face, cries out. "I lied because they told me if I said what they wanted me to say I wouldn't go to jail. So I'm going to anyways, right?

"I don't know. Are you licensed?"

Are *We the People* incredulous, stunned, dazed, or even remotely taken aback when witnesses bullied by unscrupulous lawyers are encouraged to commit perjury? The impression that this staged transgression failed isn't significant. Nothing matters once the fix is in. How else could the lowest rank climb the food chain?

Personally, I'm horrified. My imposed demeanor demands straitjacket restraint. This political swindle has nothing to do with my performance as a surgeon, or my two-fisted addiction. The sword of justice will sacrifice me to satisfy the perversity of the insatiably cruel.

On the fifth day, there is one less juror. I hypothesize that a twinge of conscience got the guy in the gut. Regardless of the outcome, I have to say good for the man that possesses reason and honor enough not to participate in this disgusting travesty, if that's the case.

Given the opportunity to restart the grill, I waive my rights and agree to eleven jurors. Only a fool cares if his assassins are lessened by one.

The prosecution in closing points out that I drive exotic cars. Does that diminish the fact that I'm one of the very finest neurosurgeons in the field? Addicted or not, my addiction never harmed a patient. In addition, what about the patients not seen in the courtroom, who I operated on… never caring about money. (I invented surgeries for which the insurance companies had no codes; therefore, they did not pay me.) I did not expect patients, without the means, to pay out-of-pocket. Changing the status quo is a feat in itself. Being owed a million uncollected dollars didn't stop me from saving lives.

The A-listed companies paid me after doncha explained how my surgeries replaced procedures that had to be redone and therefore weren't even cost effective. I was proud of her when she called a board member to notify him that a policyholder wouldn't have surgery *for free* when his company refused to approve the surgery. A check was hand-delivered in the morning. Of course, I'd operate whether they paid me or not. I don't want anyone to end up in the wrong hands. I've seen enough garbage can backs. Not all surgeons graduate at the top of their class. The doctors at the *very* bottom half of their medical school class had a sloppy attitude toward their professional studies. Would you *knowingly* want them to open your head or spinal cord?

After spending the week napping the remaining jurors are delirious for closure. I expect they are clamoring *off with Lerner's head, let's take him out in the back and string him up. There's a limb on an old oak tree. Naw, we can't do that. Let the law have some licks. Let the law kick the daylights out of him.* These aren't Southerners and the rest of the country, even when they are rednecks, aren't so hands on, even in hard-hat cities like Chicago. They simply say...

"Guilty."

Now that that's settled and I'm humiliated and dishonored, labeled a low life convict, I'm handcuffed and hustled out of the courtroom. Not knowing who I'm supposed to be, my one consolation is that doncha isn't present. I told her this was going to be a closed hearing. I had no idea at the time how correct I was.

Negated, placed in the custody of a prepubescent probation officer, there is nothing left to be sure of ... except the man's unable to grow adequate facial hair to cover the evidence of a pockmarked face. One of the injustices of youth has scarred him for life. It's hard to determine which of us is more painfully self-conscious passing through this institutionally sterile vastly oversized room with glaring lights, the path he must follow to reach his pen.

After an attempt at élan fails, Fass, the ass, hoists himself onto his desk. Kicking his heel against the metallic furniture emits sounds as hollow as the voices heard in the courtroom. In a trance, staring at his drooping socks, I notice he has conspicuously pink and horribly skinny ankles that can't possibly be of human origins.

I feel nauseous. Pointing to the plastic and aluminum chair, he grunts, "Sit." His stingy lips blossom articulating "Punishment, not rehabilitation is what you'll receive. Any questions? But keep it simple, stupid."

Squinting guinea pig eyes, narrow like his mind, I become fully conscious of how he compensates, needling me. Concealing the agony I feel from today's events, unable to analyze or imagine the extent of my wounds, I'm not confident of how my voice will sound or what I'll say. Surprisingly, "How about letting me go to Florida? I deserve a break," comes out loud and clear.

Fass hands me a specimen cup. "Take care of this, wise guy."

In my absence, my probation officer.......... yes, I Bernard Lerner, an outstanding neurosurgeon, has a probation office, who, in a matter of minutes, cultivated a curdling sweetie-pie voice to ask me, "How do you feel about your trial? Was it fair? Is everything okay?"

The absurdity of the situation prompts me to answer, "When Galileo faced the Inquisition did he know what to expect? Does anyone expect the Inquisition? Altogether, it was an experience, the likes of which I'm not soon to forget. Now, what about that trip to Florida?"

Chapter Twelve
A Not So Spring Break

Sunning on the beach, I draw up two lists. Robinson Crusoe did this exact thing when he was lost. He made one list for all things bad and the other for the declaration of the good.

The worst thing: A jail sentence ends my hard-won career, denying patients the advantage of my exemplary services - altogether a pitiful and criminal waste and totally out of my control.

Good thing: I have a few days to try to figure it all out. Never mind. I think I'll just unwind in the sun and leave Pandora's Box alone.

Bad thing: I look like I've aged a hundred years.

Good thing: I'll rest and, if it's possible, I'll recuperate.

Bad thing: I won't be able to cut for I don't know how long, if ever.

Good thing: No longer will I have to deal with the never-ending hypocrisy in the world of medicine. To tell the truth, I'd put up with anything to operate again.

Bad thing: My name will be mud in the community.

Good thing: The community I was in sucks mud; I'm finished with them.

Bad thing: I won't be able to live my life, the only life I know...and love.

Good thing: My head goes south and catches up with the rest of my body. Trepidation and anxiety melt in the forgiving Florida sun. Everything unpleasant, swept away with each ocean-warmed breeze, leaves doncha alone next to me, deliciously golden and scented with suntan lotion and sex. I close my eyes. A peaceful life with her is all I want. Nothing more.

Bad thing: Conscription comes instead. No one but doncha pays attention to my desires or wishes. I just want justice. A consummate conflict of interest to be sure; I'll wind-up with the fuzzy end of the lollipop, one way or another. Makes me want to spit... or cry.

Chapter Thirteen
The Sentencing Hearing

In court, at the about-to-execute me sentencing hearing, Echeles leans into me. His geriatric whiskey breath stinks like a found week old corpse. His brain is atrophic with razor sharp temporal lobes. He's lost all worthwhile neurons. As the neurons pouf, pouf, pouf, disintegrating into iron filings, he insists I take last minute advice from him.

After the pimp and the prostitute confessed the government threatened them with prison if they didn't lie about me, Echeles' advising me "Astound the Judge with your contrition or I'll do it for you" is where I draw the line. "I'm fully capable of speaking for myself... I should never have listened to you and gone to trial in the first place."

His withering glance evaporates when he hears the "All rise for the Honorable Judge Marvin Assbern" bit. I'm not standing up for a judge who is so desperate for everyone to think he's not partial to his people he'd re-incarnate Hitler to prove his point.

"All rise for the Honorable Judge Marvin Assbern" is announced again for my benefit alone.

"Is there a law that says I have to stand? Are we about to say the Pledge of Allegiance?"

Miffed, after not getting a standing ovation from me, the Judge decrees, "Bernard Robert Lerner you have been charged with and found guilty of possession and distribution of a dangerous medication. You distributed sixty prescriptions, two counts each to total one hundred and twenty felony counts for narcotic analgesics. Do you understand?"

"I understand the legal charges in regard to this action are ludicrous and the distribution charge is over-the-top rubbish.... and you know it. The fact that my patients needed medication has not been disproven. The medication given back to me out of their prescriptions was a courtesy and solely expedient. It was easier to increase their prescriptions, when they were on their way to the hospital pharmacy anyway, than it was for me to go to another doctor. The medication patients returned to me, I took for pain. Not unless this inquisition has exhumed the dead, that I wrote prescriptions to, and forced the corpses to admit complicity do you have a case against me. It's easy to judge, Judge, that you have the wrong person. May I leave now?"

Banging his gavel and contorting his face, his so-called Honor, looks like he's about to take a dump after an eternity of constipation. "Silence in the court! This is not a laughing matter. Mr. Echeles, control your client."

His honor's hemorrhoids are not honoring him and the asshole is taking it out on me.

"The Doctor requests to speak on his own behalf, your Honor…"

"Damn straight. Someone around here has to speak the truth."

Trying to silence the amused and bemused observers, Judge Assbern bangs away. "Where is your support group, Doctor? Where is your family? Where are your friends?"

Where is your brain? "Why would I subject them to these fascist practices and needlessly contaminate them. Out of consideration to them, I told them this was a closed hearing. Everyone's mind is closed and no one is hearing."

"One more outburst and you'll be in contempt of this court."

"I am in contempt of this court."

"Doctor, you have been given a gift by God, a gift that you have abused. A jury of your peers has found you guilty. You remind me of the main character in Tom Wolfe's latest novel *Bonfire of the Vanities*. At the top of his world, too, the character makes bad choices…"

"If I were you, I wouldn't draw a public comparison between a fictional character used as a political pawn and me. Especially, when it's so obvious that's exactly what's happening here.

Persecuting me with a felony, punishable with a lengthy prison sentence, to advance political schemes *is* criminal, not to mention immoral. And, may I remind you, this isn't fiction, it's *real* life. I'm positive there's enough corruption in the world that you don't have to manufacture the crap."

"Doctor, do not…"

"I have the floor now. I want to know why it is that one doctor, out of millions taking narcotic analgesics for pain, is put against the wall…and don't make me laugh calling malicious misuse of the legal system justice."

"You show absolutely no remorse. You might as well have been standing on the street corner handing out bags of drugs."

"That's not true and you know it! I *would* be guilty if I spent my days doing that, chiefly in my position…. if I have a position in the medical community, or with my children, after you clowns draw this carny-spectacle to a close."

"You should be ashamed…"

"*You* should be ashamed. I admit to feeling shame, too; I know I should have handled the situation better, but for Christ's sake, where's the criminality in it? Wasting taxpayer's money with ludicrous million dollar proceedings to advance political schemes and turning people into criminals has become a national past time. For that, I express sorrow on behalf of a system steeped in its own excrement."

Assbern's hatred for me oozes from his pores. "You're familiar with the City of Rochester. You trained in neurosurgery at The Mayo Clinic, did you not? Well, I am sending you back to Minnesota, and Mayo is not on the itinerary. Your sentence is three and half years at a federal prison hospital in that same city. You need psychiatric treatment. "

"What are going to do, have me lobotomized?"

"I'm warning you!"

"Listen to me…. for close to twenty years, my life and all of my energy and resources were devoted to medicine. You people have mutilated my illustrious career and denied my incomparable service to humanity. A trick, like a house of cards, with a sealed indictment, investigation, and a bogus trial are not justice. It's contempt for justice that motivates twitchy tribunals. Get me out of here! I have absolutely no respect for any of the proceedings or the people involved in this reprehensible spectacle. I would prefer to start my sentence immediately and get on with my life. At least I'll be free from the stench of this courtroom."

"Bailiffs, get the prisoner out of my sight. Turn this reprehensible creature over to the U.S. Marshals. Let him begin his sentence immediately at the Metropolitan Correction Center. See how he likes that!"

The scandalous criminal, the infamous villain in handcuffs was, not so long ago, a world-class neurosurgeon. On my way out of the courtroom I express a final thought. "So much for the criminal justice system or excuse me, do you first have to be a criminal to receive justice? Justice... you know...a fair, impartial, morally correct application of the law. All I've gotten is screwed, glued, and tattooed."

Chapter Fourteen
MCC

The Metropolitan Correction Center, situated among some of Chicago's finest architecture, is a cold bleak featureless triangular-shaped tower. Numerous narrow medieval slits replace windows. Sunshine does not shine on the one thousand detainees. There is only one way in and one way out and that is behind dense bulletproof doors. Once inside, a cavernous space opens likes the jaws of a beast in a 1940's science fiction comic book, except no one's laughing.

Initiation begins. My life is confiscated: I'm inventoried, numbered and scarred like a Jew in a Nazi camp. Examined, I'm ordered, "Spread your cheeks, asshole," and I'm reinvented.

A lost man, I'm deposited in a five by ten foot cell with a stainless steel sink and latrine in the middle - no toilet seat; I suppose it's better than a hole in the floor. The only object in the room besides me and the plumbing is the bed. Mentally and physically numb, I lie down and listen to the moans and groans of the numbers around me. For the first time, I can do nothing to mitigate the pain of others.

Attempting comprehension from a prison cell, lying on a two-inch mattress with no sheets, no pillows, and so many slits in the plastic mattress where previous prisoners hid whatever contraband there was to hide, is as impossible as it is to find comfort. Figuring out what has happened to me wasn't promising before, and I hadn't come this far.

Hearing someone call, Doc, I look out of the two by four inch window and see nothing. "What is it? Who's calling me?'

"A neighbor. Look under your door. I sent you a kite."

A rolled up piece of paper attached to a piece of thread is out of my reach. The only available resource is a cover of the Bible, which helps me retrieve the message *Welcome to Hell. How are ya doin'? You look better in real life than on TV.*

Just in time, I flush the note. A guard with a flashlight is taking count, staring at me through the window. I form a picture in my mind of this hulking Neolithic charmer plastering a fixed smirk on his face readying himself for his paid with perks job. No different from any other discriminating tormenter, when this barely employable pertinacious form speaks, it's guttural. Basking in the muck of bully heaven, other cloned prototypes with ancient malevolent historical roots join him. Genetically identical organisms stride through the area barking, "Get up, you lazy sons-of-bitches, it's time for count. Mooovvvee It!"

Expected to respond to a number, I respond like I'm an amoeba responding to light; a ritual performed four times a day, every six hours to ensure that all guests remain for the duration. Tallies, reported to the Central Bureau of Prisons office in Washington, D. C., are mostly coveted for the almighty dollar they represent. Prisoners are currency of a big business…that's why there are so many of them.

For one hour following count – no more and no less - detainees socializing in a common room prove their innocence, "This load of dung is a mistake." "Duh." "I shouldn't be here." "I was just helpin' out a friend. I didn't do nothin'." "What the fuck, what's the beef." Versions of recurring themes that is not music to my ears. In an effort to remain inconspicuous, I back into a corner, but I can't back up far enough. A man who looks like someone I might have known before incarceration corners me. "What's up?"

"To be honest, I don't want to speak with anyone named Louie the Lunatic, Marty the Marker, or Wild Willy who can't let go of his balls and is not the least bit communicative in the English language."

"My verbal skills are excellent, Doc. My family paid up the nose for my education."

I give him a once over. "So what you're telling me is that you're not a jive talking rapper." He's a husky six-foot tall, black bearded, baritone, burdened with a paunch, in addition to his other setbacks.

"They call me Mike the Gaffer. Gaffer means boss."

His sparkling steel blue eyes on closer inspection encourage me to withdraw. I suspect I might be stabbed in the back if I'm not careful in this concrete jungle. Besides all well educated people aren't trustworthy; engineers built gas chambers, doctors can definitely be assholes, and attorneys and judges are known bottom dwellers. To indulge my need to be in touch with other humans who exceed the law, and aren't indisputably Neanderthal, picking parasites off each other, I calm my overly active imagination and listen to Gaffer.

"I heard the judge set you up for some diesel therapy. Why do you looked surprised. They do it to soften you up so you'll roll on the other guys involved in your case." The Gaffer may not understand my predicament; in spite of that, he's unusual in owning his own guilt. He tells me about his cocaine arrest at a major international airport.

"Fascinating."

"I have better accommodations than this dump waiting for me in Duluth. It's the travel arrangements that I disapprove of; I've already been through: Terre Haute, Indiana, El Reno, Oklahoma, Talladega, Alabama, back to Terre Haute, and now here…just one more stop along the way."

"I like Lake Superior. There are a lot of Native Americans up there."

"Traveling on a bus with criminals sucks, especially when murderers sit next to you grossing you out with the gory details of how they did their victims in. I don't feel comfortable shackled in leg irons and handcuffs with violent assholes sitting next to me, even if they do have two sets of handcuffs on. They tell you the most amazing things like…."

Envisioning a criminal Houdini getting out of his chains and choking me to death, I'm saved; Gaffer starts going over particulars that aren't life threatening. "There are periodic stops for relief of function and food. You'll eat with your handcuffs on, feeling like a chipmunk that eats fast food. Complain and you won't eat at all. That's how it is. The bus always stops before nightfall at a federal prison or a county jail, whichever is on the trip plan. We're separated from the resident population for safety reasons. Some of our brethren can be incredibly hostile, and sexually imprudent. Watch out for them. Bathing, once in awhile, is communal with guards and guns in attendance. After a few days, most of the guards and drivers can't stand the smell of the accumulated sweat. The cruder among us actually shit their pants and the meanest guards will leave them that way. At least you're not going to a level five joint."

"I'm not sure."

"Five is maximum security and level one is a camp. Two to four are in-between behind the wall joints with nasty ass guards ready to shoot ass. From what I hear, where I'm headed is a country club."

"Maybe I'll end up there." *I wish it were true.*

"Let's go, assholes. Move it." The guard blows his piercing whistle in our ears. Shaking my hand the Gaffer comes in close. "Don't let anyone know you're a Doc, more than ever because you're a neurosurgeon. These guys are jealous sadistic…"

"Shake your ass, lover boys." We're shoved into a separate groups of funky smelling men.

Alone in my cell, a siege of convoluted thoughts plague me. Near sunrise, I sink into the darkest despair of my life before I fall into a fitful slumber. Sleep offers no reprieve from the nightmare I'm living. I dream I'm on a hospital ward. The medical men are gruesome, with elongated calcified extremities. The most horrid of them directs a daggered finger at me. "Did you notice Lerner has pin point pupils? The whites of his eyes are electrifyingly red. I do like that."

"He's scratching himself with that hair shirt he insists on wearing."

I don't see how I can scratch anything. My movements are restricted.

Another foot long hypodermic is waved in my face. "Curare is indigenous to South America. Natives use it to coat arrows and darts. You haven't forgotten that trip, have you, Doctor Lerner?" Before I can remark that I've never been to South America, the alien consultants vanish. I turn to the man next to me in a straight jacket; straining my larynx is all the effect I produce when I try to speak. When I try again, random letters inside cartoonish bubbles float from my mouth.

An emaciated man fastened to a gurney laughs shrilly. "You're an inmate in an asylum, you're the loony in the loony bin, and you're about to be lobotomized. Ha ha ha ha-ha..." His mandible clatters and the bubbles, that might have contained a message, burst.

The spaced-out medical men race to my bedside. Hovering over me, they discuss the next group of letters that won't form words. "That's it, we gave him his chance." Drills, hot from friction, nearing my head, follow the Chief's pronouncement. Recognizing my terror, a psychosurgeon with strangely compassionate eyes leans in close. "Tell me what to do, Doctor."

My tongue is heavy. The words are slow. "Shave... my... head... in... a... tonsure. I'm... going... to... be... a... monk." I am hopeful of a reprieve, now that someone understands me.

"Sorry.... Doctor, that... isn't...possible." He mocks my impaired speech. "You're... a...Jew."

I wake up in a cold sweat. A guard is shaking me hard. "Get up dirt bag and come with me. Get your lazy ass out of that bed."

I obey the gun.

They're going to kick the shit out of me is my primal instinct. *No, that's not it. They're going to execute me. I know it. That's what this is about.* Shuddering with resurging fear, silently I pray *Shema Yisrael adinoi alahenui adinoi echoi.*

Taken from the hellhole, where time is never replete, I'm warned, "You'll see and know what we want you to see and know." A U. S. Marshal stands by as they shove me into a car.

We stop in front of the Federal Building; the same building they marched me out of in chains less than twenty-four hours ago. Reversing the procedure, the guards escort me back in; this time I'm deposited in a room that has *Judge's Chambers* written on the door.

Judge Assbern shakes his head. "You are an arrogant man, Doctor Lerner. You caused me to lose my temper. However, I will not lower the federal government's high standards; you will serve the next three and a half years in the federal prison system, at a level one camp. I'm permitting you to self-surrender two weeks from today. God protect you."

I have to bite the inside of my cheeks not to bow and say thank you your Excellency. After one night at the MCC, I restrain myself admirably.

Even when he remarks, "That jumpsuit looks stunning on you; you've always been a hallmark of fashion," I hold my tongue. Told, "I forbid you to speak to anyone, including newspaper reporters and TV news reporters. You are under the jurisdiction of the Bureau of Prisons and under felony conviction and therefore you enjoy no rights. Is there anything you would like to say?"

I say nothing. I leave the building, silent as the grave.

Chapter Fifteen
Leaving doncha

The period of grace before incarceration begins is not, in my estimation, a bonus. "Penal interruptus," I snort, "two more weeks of agony before I face the heat." Blurting out my anguish to the bartender where I down doubles in the middle of the day, I give the man more information than he needs to know.

"Funny, Doctor Lerner." Two football games blasting simultaneously from two TVs distract him.

"My take on the situation is different. The possibility of coming out whole is unlikely. It's easy to tell after a few layers have been peeled off, layer by layer. Public humiliation is excruciating. They want their pound of flesh, and quite honestly, what they're weighing it against remains a mystery to me."

"That sucks."

Using my free time to do small things, I buy a good watch with an ironical appreciation for the play on time. Items on a list are collected and stowed; it amazes me how little is allowed to launch a new existence.

In an agonizing farewell, embracing doncha, gently stroking her hair, I whisper, "My love, please listen…" She entices me with her siren song. She hopes to drown me in the seaweed of her sheets.

"You're not going to the airport with me" is all I can manage to say. I rise from the bed resisting further temptation. She prays the power she felt animated her goes with me, an offering from her soul. I walk out the door bound to my destiny like Odysseus, bound to the mast of his ship.

Chapter Sixteen
Traveling to Camp Walkaway

A singularly strange journey begins with a repetitiously deadening voice, inside my haggard head, conjugating *you're going to prison, you're going to be imprisoned, you're to be a prisoner.* The significance is elusive and mindless as any echo. In case that isn't enough, Jealously - serpentine tormentor - strikes and she is wicked. Think of doncha's lovely body. Suspicion intermingles with insinuation. How long will it be before *my woman* falls in love with another man? I slam down another double. An explicit vision puts doncha in the iron maiden and chains me to the rack.

One drink follows another in the last rerun of my first-class life style. Numb, I disclose to a sympathetic flight attendant that I'm on my way to the joint. Enticed by the sensual vulnerability of a grieving man, she embraces me. And then, goddamn, she kisses me. *I'm good at this, better than doncha will ever be,* I congratulate myself.

The pilot announcing the sighting of the airstrip sobers me up. *The Metropolitan Correction Center was horrendous; this place will be… unimaginable.* The plane hits the pavement. The conviction that I'm about to enter the ninth circle of the Inferno unnerves me in degrees I didn't know I had the depth to realize. The plane screeches to a bone chilling halt.

Mesmerized by the aircraft's shadow on the ground, I half-listen to people speak. Everything sounds like gibberish to this male Alice about to enter winter hinterland. Falling, going down hard, I land on my ass. Lying back in the snow, I make angel wings and yell into the bluest sky I've seen in a long time, "How far has Lucifer fallen this time?" The frigid air slaps my sorry face as a veteran cabbie jerks me to my feet and cuts to the chase. "Going to Camp Walkaway?"

"For a short visit."

"I'll bring you over there, before you freeze to death."

"Take the scenic route; I need to case out the joint." I suspect any self-respecting jailbird would do the same. "Drive the perimeter of the grounds. I want to know exactly what I'm up against."

Stationed on a hill, I survey the set-up: No fences, no towers, no guards, no guns - nothing more than rows and rows of barracks. Forget my expectations; I'm relieved to find this isn't a Sing Sing/Alcatraz lock down behind the wall penitentiary prison. Neighboring an active National Guard Air Force Base, it's convenient for escape, if you know how to fly a jet fighter. *Damn.* I always intended to learn how to fly. I flick the butt of my cigarette in the direction of three F-16's taking off in succession and return to the cab.

The cabbie shrugs. "From what I've heard the camp's not too bad. I've been told the food is really good and there are a lot of activities to keep you busy. The worst thing about the place is the weather. It's colder than a witch's tit. I guess you already figured that out. Incidentally, what did you do to deserve the honor?

"I did what wasn't allowed."

"Most of the guys inside did likewise. Don't think twice about the alcohol I smell on your breath. I've seen guys brought in in wheelbarrows. Hey, if you don't like it you can walk away. They won't chase you. That's why they call it Camp Walkaway. Defectors end up in the Big House, *if* they're caught. This place is a country club in comparison. If you ask me, as a taxpayer, sending guys up here is a waste of time and money."

"Prisons are big business; that's why they're packed and there's so much variety. Too bad public education doesn't inspire the jerks with the deep pockets."

Stopping at the electronic gate crossing the road, unflanked by fences, minus armed guards, a voice calls out over an intercom. "Who goes there? Identify yourself."

"Bernard R. Lerner, M.D., at your service,"

The cabbie chimes in "Doctor Lerner is a new guest." He hands me his card. "Here you go; call The Midnight Special if you ever need a lift."

The frozen stiff gate opens slowly and snaps shut. I feel paralyzed. The driver opens the door, sensing I'm incapable. It's all slow motion. I pay him. He hands me my bag. I receive moral support in the way of a handshake. With one last look around, I shake my head in disbelief. Lighting a cigarette, I step over the line that ends my life as a free man. Fuck all of them. I sing:

> *Now if you're ever in a Houston,*
> *you better walk right*
> *you better not gamble boy*
> *Boy you better not fight.*
> *Cause the sheriff will arrest you*
> *and the boys will pull you down*
> *and then the next thing you know is*
> *you're penitentiary bound.*
> *So let the Midnight Special*
> *Shine her light on me*
> *Let the Midnight Special*
> *Shine her ever lovin' light on me.*

The greeting hack is a sadistic prick. They call him Buckaroo. Every time someone says fuck you, he confuses it for his name. While I sing the blues in silent dejection, Buckaroo baptizes me with a slur of obscenities and a number. Membership demands a signature. I sign in. Buckaroo crosses out the M.D. after my name. "Forget that, phony bullshit!"

Another hack (guards are called hacks) is a safer bet. He reads from note cards. "You are going to be examined and interviewed by a physician. Blood will be drawn and assessed for various diseases." John, the hack, looks up from the note card. "Your next interview will be with Dr. D. Maybe he won't hurt you and you'll be out of the medical center quickly without any problem."

"I hope the accommodations are as good as reported."

"They are....in the honor dorm."

A physician's assistant recites all the basic medical mumbo jumbo. I could tell him I have highly infectious meningococcal meningismus and he would check off some point on the paper. He isn't listening. Not wanting to spend my first night, or any other night in solitary, I go through the motions and answer him.

Dr. D finally shows up. Hiccupping, skipping a beat, he slurs, "Nooo practicin' here." He shakes his finger, warning, "I'm keepin' my eyes on you. Roll up your sleeve. I'm goin' for blood."

If his eyes were superglued to his occipital cortex, he still wouldn't be able to focus. "Is your tremor from a stormy evening or is it a true extrapyramidal disorder?"

"Stormy evening, ha, ha; what are you really, a poet? My tremor isn't irregular. I shake in rhythm."

Following one too many nerve-racking jabs, the man no longer practicing medicine advocates practice to the one licensed to do so. "Buy one of those kits distributed in medical schools. With direction, you may be able to hit a vein. Hold the syringe at a forty-five degree angle. Bevel up...good. Now, palpitate the vessel under it. Okay, steady...steady....stick it in. Take it easy. Pull back to draw blood. I know you'll do well with the rectal examination. No doubt you're an expert with that part of the anatomy."

"Hmm, what?"

When Dr. D. concentrates, he reminds me of a cadaver I worked on in medical school. The one noticeable distinction is Dr. D is almost able to walk and talk but that doesn't stand for much.

Waiting forever with the specimen cup at the designated toilet, wanting a slew of things, I look around to see what I can do. Finally, the bathroom door swings open.

"Forgive me for taking so long, gorgeous."

I speak into the face so close to mine I spell perfume and cosmetics. Not knowing what to say, I say, "Your lipstick is smudged." I pull my head back; I don't want *him* to kiss me.

"It's a delicious color and the perfect shade of orangey-gold to compliment my honey-toned skin. Wiping it *all* off is out of the question; I'd look dreadful. But my pussy is clean for the cavity search."

"I see."

"Go on in, baby. You can't hold that thing all day. Hey, what's your name, handsome?"

"Bernard."

"Enchanted. My name is Rainbow."

My second acquaintance, The Quarter Master, sporting a Hercule Poirot up-turned waxed mustache, deems anyone wearing ill-fitting attire offensive. This idiosyncrasy is most noticeable when he crosses his arms over his chest, turns up his finicky chiseled nose, and taps his foot. Criticism is not without remedy; tailoring is inclusive. Imagining himself a first class tailor in the finest establishment, his desire is for everyone to look smart in khakis.

"Sorry to keep you waiting, Doctor Lerner, please excuse me. I am Juan of San Juan, at your service to furnish all of your clothing needs. I have to say, you look like a million dollars in that suit." Juan has sized me up, puffing on a cheroot held between his thumb and index finger. He extends the opportunity for me to do the same sizing up with him, telling me about how he sold a truckload of marijuana to a federal agent in Puerto Rico. "That little fiasco entitled me to five years of government hospitality."

"Too bad you got caught." No further information forthcoming, I assume financial gain was his motivation. But who knows. He might have left a life of poverty behind. Bread crumbs instead of bread. He wanted the dough, is my guess.

Juan smiles a photographable load of excellent dental work. "May I suggest a lined overcoat? When I'm finished you'll swear it was custom designed for you."

"I'll take the standard outfit and pick up the extras after I open my account. Presently I am without funds. I can't wait to spend the big stuff."

"What's the deal?"

My answer, "I heard we draw out our money in quarters," disappoints him.

Displaying army surplus the way high-end retail employees display the latest fashions, he runs his hand over the merchandise. "Tres chic and I don't think you'll have any trouble matching tops with bottoms." Sizing up my feet, he hands me a pair of army surplus shit-kickers with steel shanks. "Take these with the complements of your Uncle Sam." Before I can say goodbye, the awaiting hack wakes up and rushes at me, moaning like an overtired child, "Get goin', get goin'. I ain't got all day."

I know exactly where I'd like to fasten this well-made but entirely unrefined boot. Treated like a juvenile delinquent at an overnight camp, I'm shoved the distance to my accommodations, an army barracks dorm. There's no honor in it.

"You'll occupy that top bunk. Keep all your stuff in the basket. And don't go lookin' for trouble, if you know what's good for you. On the sign-out sheet next to the door, sign your name, number, where you're goin', and the time, whenever you leave the building, until you have a job. Got it?" My chaperone carelessly flings a map and a letter at me. "From the Warden…read it *now*, aloud, to me." In the middle of the first sentence, he walks out. Off to some crusty corner to finish his nap, no doubt.

Wandering outdoors, I come across a substantially large cabin down the road. Seeing that the door is unlocked, I invite myself in. The instruments in the Music Room, beginning with a piano, are well tuned. I end up with the sax.

My eyes shut, I listen to the voice, faithful to my mood, sing, *"My Valentine, my funny Valentine…"* Rainbow has joined me. She plays the piano as I play the sax. Lonely for the life and the love we left behind, our tear-stained faces betray our grief.

I play until I'm numb and I hear *Love sees not with the eyes but with the mind.* It's doncha's voice that I follow back to the dorm. Crazy, I almost expect her to be there.

Gazing absently out the window from this dismal barrack facing the north woods, which seem accessible in winter by dog sled alone, a tremor from the chilly late afternoon enters the empty places in my exhausted detoxifying body. Fearful and incredibly bewildered, my presence in this puzzling world outstrips my comprehension. I climb into the top bunk bed, loathe as I am to do so. My body doesn't warm under the awful wool blankets. Cold and depressed, I listen to the sniveling misfit taking the bunk below mine.

Schlmo, a slight, young pharmacist, involvement in a drug ring would be thorny to picture without honey, a high-maintenance JAP (Jewish American Princess) in the scenario. After he repeats, "I can't stay here for six months without my beautiful young wife" for the hundredth time, I've had enough.

"Look, Schlmo, there are no fences here. Take the time like a man, or take off. I need some shut eye." The young man twirls his wan beard and whimpers, "Maybe you're right; maybe I should take off. She'd never move up here."

I offer him a cigarette. "You'll be out in no time. It might have been a lot worse."

"I don't see how."

"You could have been sentenced to six months in Montana, with your wife. That would have been the longest six months of your life. Think about it. Shopping for clothes can't be in Montana what it is in New York, and where would she lunch, without *the girls*."

Mercifully, he laughs and then he's quiet, until I hear him snoring.

Diminutive and less dejected, Jake's voice reverberates in my pounding head. "Schlmo, over there and I are friends. He was also my business partner, before I snitched him out... but he snitched me out, too."

"A brilliant government official rewarded the pair of you with shortened sentences for your disloyalty. How nice that you birds remained fettered together. That's what I call a successful flea bargain."

Afflicted with malevolent pain and every other wicked sensation that descends upon me, approximating harpies seeking vengeance, the fiends finally cease pecking when they hear "Doc."

"Yes."

"My name is D.C. Don. I'm up here from Washington, D.C. for pedalin' coke and pimpin'."

Feeling more or less like a stranger in a strange land, with an ear for tall tales in short doses, I listen.

"I got a year on a rap. Nothing to it, I need the rest and I can recoup business the day I'm out of here."

"Wish I could say the same."

"Things are *always* hot in my field but they have a tendency to catch up with you. This isn't the worse place to relax. Great recreation center, three squares a day of super fine food; I'm tellin' ya, a year will do me nicely. If I need anything, I know how to get it. Check out my business card."

D.C. Don for Drugs and Ho's. When you fuck with D.C. you're fuckin' with the best is written in bold-faced red on a shiny black surface.

"Impressive. Do you mind if we continue this conversation later?"

"Sure, Doc. Later. I'm not going anywhere."

I accept 1000 milligrams of Motrin, handed out regularly by the hacks. I'm pleased to discover they have a decidedly hypnotic effect.

Chapter Seventeen
The Joint

Numb to the sensation that I live and breathe, it takes time to realize my surroundings. Not exactly in the pink, I warn Schlmo, "Don't speak another word!" He started in from where he left off last night, grinding down what's left of my shot nervous system. Staring at the ceiling, I light a cigarette with trembling hands I cannot conceive to be my own. A shattered voice inside my hammered head begs *Shoot me; my fucking body is fucking killing me.* No sooner do I register that disgusting thought before others, equally desperate, crowd in to kick my wretched ass. *Never mind that. You need to work.* I robotically maneuver into army issue, aching in places I did not think possible. Studying the alien in the emptiness of the mirror, I look hard to find a vestige of my self. *Time to face the day, loser.*

My instinct is to follow an aircraft headed in the direction of the airfield to see if the spaceship that dumped me has returned to rescue me from this frozen reel of a nightmare. Visualizing myself before take-off, shutting my eyes tight against the too bright sunshine, I suppress raw rage lodged in my throat pounding out grief like Morse code. *Where is everyone when I need them? Why is no one on my side? I was there for anyone who needed me!*

"Now what?!" Back on earth, I find myself in the big bear paws of Gaffer, the informative man from The Metropolitan Correction Center in Chicago. He pulls me close with a generous hug. "We've been expecting you for days. Professor Einstein intercepted a BOP memorandum that said you were on your way. Here you go, Doc, a welcoming gift from some of us guys. Ain't we sweet!"

"Thanks." I shake the box.

"Just some cigarettes and shaving stuff, useful things like that."

"The first time I saw you, Gaffer, I thought you might stab me in the back and leave me for dead. Now, I find you're the man of my dreams."

"And, visa versa. We're damn lucky that you're vacationing with us at this Club Fed. Come with me; you need to eat. You're probably starved. You had no dinner last night, and all the other hassles you've been through sucks. Look at that asshole over there. Trust me, Doc, stay away from that creep. He's totally fucked up."

"Really? Why?" I like this gossipy man even more than I did before. We do the male bonding thing. Identifying we're on the same page, we talk about whomever and whatever comes to mind.

Coming through the door of the mess hall, Gaffer announces, "Three hundred of the eight hundred men in this camp are accommodated at a time. I like colossal. We'll have a spot of breakfast."

In the middle of the mess hall's thunderous racket, seized with panic, I envision a knife in my back or a racial slur that provokes a riot. Gaffer encourages me. "Come on, Doc, the natives are restless but they're not cannibals. It's like boot camp. It's not like MCC."

From now on, no one will know what goes on inside my head. Surveying the cafeteria line, feeling out of place, I say something stupid like "I prefer a sit down meal." Meanwhile, I stand in line with the rest of the untouchables.

"I hear ya. I prefer fine dining, too; preferably with beautiful women serving me. And then, after eating too much, I like to smoke a humungous fatty and fuck."

My wired for sound nervous system plays a mellower tune while contemplating food. I choose flawlessly cooked eggs, whole wheat bread - perfectly toasted, crisp dry bacon, great orange juice and coffee that stands up for itself. Now we're talkin'. Gaffer and I join ten other reasonably intelligent men. Although unanticipated, in the process of savoring a delicious breakfast, a pleasant chord chimes resonating with an officer's mess table.

We return our trays to the six-foot by two-foot rectangles in the wall called the car wash. Hassle free and smooth from beginning to end. No stabbings. No brawls. Everything is copacetic, so far.

When a tall civilian, appearing harmless in a rather good-looking suit and unremarkable tie, approaches *me* Gaffer takes off.

"Doctor Lerner, my name is Warden Warden, the same both ways."

To be courteous, I shake his extended hand. "Missing your title you can always catch your name."

"I'll tell you straight out that I'm glad to have you here. This is probably the finest camp in the country."

"I'd never meet you under any other circumstances."

"Please accompany me to my office."

"If you insist." *What could they possibly do to me now? I bet that prick judge changed his mind again and they're going to ship me out of here. No that's not it.*

The Warden points out some of the sights along the way, but I'm scarcely listening.

Removing my parka, my theory that clothes make the man kicks in. Exposed in imposed prison attire, self-conscious, I walk around the Warden's office, looking at the photographs on the wall: The Warden with the Chief of the Bureau of Prisons, the Warden with the Secretary of State, the Warden with President Reagan, and the Warden with the Pope. Suppressing an urge to laugh, I sit down. It's better to get this over and done with before I crack up.... one way or another.

The Warden offers me coffee. "I have a difficult situation and I'm anticipating you are the solution."

"Incredible."

"Thirty percent of the men at this camp have been convicted of a grave error in the eyes of the law, but most likely they will never do so again. I'm speaking of: lawyers, bookkeepers, government officials, bankers, white-collar crimes. For another thirty percent of the population crime is a way of life. Those are: the bookmakers, professional criminals, tax antagonists and so on. The remaining thirty percent of the men are serving the final two years of much longer sentences here, to reverse the affects of institutionalization from being in high security prisons. The others in-house are poor drug dealers from the inner city who never had much of a life. Some of them say they never had it so good."

I light a cigarette and take a long drag. "What has any this got to do with me?"

"I have an embarrassing predicament on my hands. This camp has the lowest percentage of men able to pass the GED in the entire country. Mr. Chiller, the head of the Education Department, threatens to send anyone who fails three times to a behind-the-wall prison. I would like to avoid that. That's why I want you to consider heading our Education Department."

"Why me?"

"This feat calls for a leader of unique capabilities."

"It took unique capabilities to land me in here in the first place. Now you want to capitalize on that. Actually, I had planned to check out Unicore. I've heard they make *the* perfect ashtray. If I don't take you up on your offer, are you going to have me tortured, or what?"

"If that's the case, we never had this conversation."

Chapter Eighteen
First Impressions

Whistles shriek non-stop on these premises where suffocating dust, grinding nerve-grating machinery and backbreaking punch presses have no mercy on the three hundred over-dominated campers toiling in the inferno called Unicore. Whatever I was thinking has escaped me, but it wasn't this.

I can't stand watching workers, resembling androids, place one screw into one object at a time, while guard-dog-mad hacks growl brutalities at them.

If I'm going to be my own boss in the Department of Education, I'd better escape before these vicious bastards chain me to an assembly line. The limbic lobe, responsible for fright and flight, twitches. *Slip out the back, Jack. Make your new plan, Stan.* I disappear into a darkened exit like a ghost. I'm spooked.

Breaking away from the crudeness of Unicore, and all its contingent subjugation, sweat and grime, turns a breath of fresh air into holy nirvana. *Meaningful employment will be my saving grace. The fellows over at the Department of Education will welcome me with open arms. After all they need me.* Besides, *a man's gotta do what a man's gotta do. The rest will fall into place.* With that in mind and extra zip in my step, I head over to tell the Warden I'm ready to head his new GED program. I'm a professor, I can manage anything these men need to know.

Fantasy and reality collide. I have not arrived at a Mecca of learning. I can't even orchestrate my thinking. Disco reverberates from several boom boxes simultaneously. *Jail House Rock* or *Folsom*

Prison Blues would be better choices in music. Dodging a flying object, I nearly trip over men throwing dice, spitting and cussing. To make matters worse, a jackknife comes into play. A menacing student body shakes me out of my ivory tower tree. Crashing back to earth, my inner turmoil, and my appalled senses, mentally straightening myself up, I recall my one advantage - *this is where the ability to walk away from Camp Walkaway comes in handy.*

Let them send me to the nut house -- if they catch me. At least psych wards medicate their nut jobs. Beats being knifed in this joint. They don't need professors, they need prison guards. Arrested from sinister thoughts; not entirely believing my eyes, the possibility that I'm dead exists... I'm already seeing a holy person.

Patting my arm, sympathetic to my distress, a nun named Sister Mary explains, "I'm from the convent. I try to help the men out as much as I can, but I'm afraid they're a little out of control... well maybe more than a little. I have faith they will improve now that you're here, Doctor. Please follow me; I'll take you to our supervisor. I must tell you how truly thankful I am that you are here with us. You are a gift from the Lord. I prayed and prayed for your arrival."

"If anything can happen, which it can, there are places I'd rather be, Sister."

"The Lord knows best."

It's impossible for me to tell her that I'm on my way out.

"Sister, when was the last time you had your eyes examined?"

"Maybe ten years ago."

"You must have your eyes tested again, soon. It would be helpful in navigating your environment more efficiently, dear."

"God shows me the way."

She leads and I follow.

Tapping gently on Mr. Chiller's door, the man in-charge snaps from the other side, "Come in, if you have to, and be quick about it."

"Mr. Chiller," Sister Mary nearly whispers, "I'd like to introduce you to Doctor Lerner."

Chiller is engrossed in a manuscript that appears to have a tormenting effect on him. I can say his office is nicely decorated - a glaring contrast to the rest of the non-entity architecture.

Condescending to speak, he recites what might be my ten-digit identification number, adding, as though M.D. followed the number, "You're not a doctor anymore. You're a piss poor prisoner."

"Considering my new name/number is unusual, I'm flattered you remembered it. It's kind of secret agent man; they give you a number and take away your name."

Peanut man scratches his slash of a black mustache and slicks back his greasy dyed-black hair. Mentally zeig heiling the little fuhrer, I shove my big black boot up his lily-white ass. Drawing a permanent line in this ghetto, I wonder what, in this land of schemers, possessed the Warden to give a liberal Jewish prisoner like me authority on Adolph, Jr.'s beat.

"So, you're the chosen one that's supposed to save the GED program. What a joke. You people are the scum of the earth and these assholes," he assaults a stack of files with his furious fist, "have absolutely no idea what an education is. All they care about is getting out of here and getting high or ripping someone off."

To begin again, with territorial divisions in place, my professional side dominates. "We need a program to provide these men with better options. To begin, they must have a GED..." Chiller clenches and unclenches his fists. *Let him take a swing at me; I'll knock that silly toupee sideways.*

"Who in the fuck do you think you're kidding? No one's going anywhere but behind the wall." Shoving a stack of folders at me, he snarls. "Keep to my schedule, Mr. Nobody; it's right there, on top. Take off, you..."

He meant take off, Jew. I take up the gauntlet. My adversary slams the door behind me and startles Sister Mary.

"Don't despair." She smiles sweetly and pats the folders. "You can help these fellows, they're rather nice... really they are."

"Sister, *please*. In case you haven't noticed, there are only convicts here."

How are you going to manage convicts? is the next life-sized question. My mind races until I hit the winning mark. *I'll be the shining star on the dark side of this lunar landing. I have to be the best. The best what? The best part of my most awful self, of course. What else could I be? I'm in the joint.*

"Show me some of the better sights, Sister, and don't be sad. That jerk doesn't mean a thing to me. You've got the right idea; things are going to improve around here."

Chapter Nineteen
Education Department Staff

"This is our computer room." Sister looks disappointed. "Einstein is the only one to use the computers on a regular basis. Have you ever operated a computer, Doctor?"

"Anything controlled by a mouse does nothing to inspire me."

"What about art? Does art inspire you? Picasso is our resident artist."

"I like Picasso's blue period....especially now."

"Good call, Daddy-O. Good morning, Sister." A beatnik in a shabby beret shoves a paintbrush into a knotted goatee and locks hands with me. "It's really cool that you're hangin' with us. An awesome life, most excellent Doctor, is comparable to kickass art. In the joint that means art is the upshot, not the downside of down time. Keen perception, constant vigilance, and insight are mandatory. That's why I'm informed of who's who and what's what around here before it happens. You dig?"

With pointed curiosity and a twinge of superficial doubt, I arch my eyebrows. "I have those exacting talents in neurosurgery, not in life."

"Don't worry about it. Around here, you're covered. Our Einstein has doctorates in physics, electrical engineering and computer science. His vibrational connections with the main computers servicing this camp benefit us enormously. If Einstein knows, Picasso knows. Dig?"

"I dig what you're sayin'." *Actually, I'm clueless.*

Back at the canvas, Picasso gazes at me with perspective. "That information, my man, is to be kept under raps."

"Natch."

"Your fine reputation is the buzz of the beehive. Now that you're the queen bee of this department...."

"For your information, I'm a drone, not a queen."

"Right on. I'll pass on to Rainbow that girlymen are not your handbag. We're all groovin' that you landed on our planet. The best news is you're the real medicine man in Dr. D's Death Valley. I'm here to tell you *that* ain't no walk without a tomahawk."

I smile. "How do you know?" One remaining advantage I have in life is hearing about me. Just don't talk about my dark side, if you want to be my best friend. I've only taken first steps acknowledging I have a dark side. A small encouraging voice inside my head insists I take others. I prefer to take my time in unchartered territories.

"Knowing you're an upright super-trustworthy, I'll turn you on to my latest reproductions, ready to go when I blow this pop stand. They'll flip your gourd. I counterfeited quite a few of the great American heroes. It was a drag havin' my career messed with at its pinnacle. Time is smarts. I got eighteen years worth. My last three aces will be played hangin' in your good company."

"Even though I'd like to see your work, I don't want to earn bonus years."

"In a system that cavalier we'd all be lifers."

Desire is irrelevant. "Maybe later" doesn't mean later, it means never. The system is cavalier enough for me.

"Cool man. Later. Sister, I see you're into my latest. *Separation of Church and State*."

Standing silently before the canvas, I take in a pope figure praying before an immense cross. What's odd is: his eminence is not only behind bars… he has an uncanny resemblance to me. Sister smiles sympathetically. "We're running behind schedule, Doctor."

Picasso escorts us to the door. "See you around, Papa. Be cool, Sister."

Walking through the noisy hallway, Sister confides, "Picasso has been institutionalized for such a long time, Doctor, that he's developed a rather bizarre sense of humor." We stop outside another classroom. Opening the door disturbs dust particles drifting like dreams, but our presence doesn't disturb the student betting his three aces beat a bluffed full house. The less motivated roll dice. The last two, who are not comatose, trade treats like grade school kids, but the mainstream snooze.

Sister Mary guides me to the faculty table, substituting as a bed. "Zee." She taps gently on the shoulder of a man curled into a fetal position, careful not to startle him. "Doctor Lerner is here. Please try to wake up."

Sleepy-eyed, pudgy and scruffy, Zee floats into consciousness. Yawning and confused, he finally notices me. "I didn't expect you until eleven." Finding his bearings, he picks up his pillow, a book. "That's me, Rip Van Winkle. As lazy as Rip, I plan to stay that way,"

"What's happening here?" I indicate the entire room.

Sleeping on a work of fiction is an alternative way to become acquainted with its virtues. My students are in the process of mastering the technique. Osmosis is an innovative method for assimilating material. Don't you agree, Doctor?"

"At present, it's difficult to evaluate your students. Tell me more about yourself."

"My Ph.D. in American Literature kept me quite usefully employed; although it didn't do much for my lifestyle. Sleek women love cuisine, which they don't eat, and sleek cars, which are the only type they'll get into. When my briefcase - stuffed to the gills with coke - was confiscated, I got five long years. I planned to sleep off ninety percent of my sentence. Disagreeable threats convinced me that working here with these men was the way to avoid hard labor elsewhere. The word is, it's impossible to sleep all day in a high security pen. Perfecting the art of compromise, I catnap on the job. If you'll excuse me, I'll return to another short nap on what I hope to be a prophetic short story. Maybe when I get out of here America won't be so uptight. The conservatives make me break out in a rash. I'll sleep until enlightened people give me a reason to wake up. By the way, Einstein is *dying* to meet you."

"Why is that?"

"If you don't save his ass, I'd like to know who will. You don't happen to have any sleeping pills on you?"

Not to intrude, I observe Einstein in action from the hallway. Shaggy contributes to the intelligentsia mystique. Pointing to a map, he giggles. "Miami, the one in northeast Nevada, prides itself on a whore house called *The Top of the World*. Dating back to the mid-eighteen hundreds, it is the oldest whorehouse and organized gambling casino in Nevada. This little mining town has more bars per capita than any other city in the United States. Violent crimes are rare in comparison to the eight other cities we studied." Einstein acknowledges us with a nod. "Excuse us, class. We'll be back in a jiffy."

For a heavy man Einstein moves quickly. With his hand extended, he joins us in the hallway. "How do you do, Doctor? We're glad to see that you met Sister Mary. In case you're curious about our methods, we've been attempting to inspire enthusiasm for the subject matter."

"I admire your success."

"It's our contention that the new and improved education department headman…that being you, should permit the instructors…."

"Let's talk about what you have to offer at another time."

"We look forward to it, being in desperate need of your expert medical opinion."

"I'll see what I can do." Satisfied, he says goodbye to Sister Mary and me.

"Einstein, *sometimes*, speaks as though he were two people."

"That's nothing, Sister." Hearing him speak I look back to where he's standing; the Professor's conversing with someone I can't see, but he's seems quite engaged.

On a superficial glance, the disorganized library has a haphazard offering of newspapers, archaic cowboy and detective books, pulp fiction, romances, and other throw-aways left over from the Salvation Army. Searching for a smattering of decent literature, I address the librarian, following me around like a puppy dog. "Charles, let's get together first thing tomorrow and pull this place together. What are you humming?"

Charles' cheeks color pink and puffy. "It's what I'm hearing… musical instruments…and voices singing… in my head. Has that ever happened to you, Doctor Lerner?"

"Tell me what you hear in your inner soundscape."

"I hear an entire orchestra; but, I can voice only one section at a time. I've been trying to synchronize this piece for years."

He hums a simpler tune.

"What is it? I can't say I know that one."

"The Carpenter's *Close To You*."

"Of course, I should have recognized it."

"I'm always alone in the library. No one comes in here. Maybe no one likes me. Music is good company. It helps me to think of better days. I'm going to become thirty on my next birthday, in prison."

"That's too bad." I pat him on the back. I do not approve of Charles' taste in music, but I do feel for him.

His head hung low, he's signing.

"I don't understand sign language."

"I just said that during the Christmas rush at the post office where I used to work, I violated their trust in me when I put five hundred dollars in my pocket. Please don't think I'm a jerk. I'm not really like that. I don't know what possessed me to do it."

"Tomorrow, I'll teach you some new songs."

"Do you mean it?"

"I mean it."

Sister Mary hasn't stopped smiling. "Doctor, I want to tell you how much I respect the way you are with Charles. His parents are both mute and gentle people, like him. Mr. Chiller locks Charles in the library and forces him to re-type the same document, over and over again, for no reason at all. Mr. Chiller seems to be… you know… cruel. To see you so sweet with Charles, so truly Christian, I'm thankful to know you."

"Thank you for the compliment, Sister; however, I'm Jewish."

"Yes, dear, I know; and so was Jesus."

"Sister, would you like to have lunch with me and tell me why so many Christians are anti-Semitic when they worship Christ, who was a Jew."

"Thank you for inviting me, but I don't think it's allowed. I must tell you though, anti-Semites aren't Christians, no matter what they call themselves, they aren't Christians."

"I agree."

Chapter Twenty
Lunch with the Guys

"I signed you up for kosher, Doc." Gaffer joins me in the cafeteria line. "I'm famished." He's not kidding; he piles his plate high. "Kosher is the food to eat in the joint. Twenty-five percent of the campers who aren't Jewish turn Jewish at mealtime. Eat Mexican kosher; it's the bomb against assholes. Come with me; we'll sit with good people."

Still known as The Governor, Dan Walker greets me with a warm smile. "Really bad over there at the education building… the place is a zoo. Tired you out, didn't it?"

"I'm fine." I answer thinking *he's the same. Tall and thin, deliberate and distinguished, now in his late sixties, worse for wear, ex-Governor Dan Walker of Illinois couldn't be a criminal.*

"Naive is what I was, and now, I'm reduced to working for an inebriated defector from the Christian race. I wish I had retired. I'm not a businessperson. They knew that when they masqueraded me as a front for a car lubrication business scheme. When you're not a liar and a thief you aren't suspicious that others may be."

"Governor, I understand all too well."

"I knew you would. Be cautious with Chiller. He is without conscience, integrity or intelligence. It wouldn't surprise me if he received his degree in education at an institution advertised on matches."

"That weasel married the boss's daughter. I was a major player in the Chicago's Park District…do you remember me? Of course, you do." Alderman Jackson shakes my hand. "They call me Action Jackson these days. Part of my duty is pruning the lawns and hedges in front of the dick's houses. Would you like to know what I witnessed?"

"I…

"Chiller and his wife were beating each other up, until the cops were dispatched to the scene. The entire neighborhood heard her say cute stuff like, 'You better not come back or I'll finish the job and cut off your tiny dick and stuff it down your stupid throat.' Cute stuff like that."

The Governor shakes his head. Obviously high-quality material of a low nature disturbs him.

"What are you looking at me for?" The person sitting next to me balks. Hovering over his plate, he glances up. "I'm not saying anything. I don't talk unless someone pays me to talk."

"You must be an attorney." I make a good guess.

Gaffer, always willing to let you know what's up with the next guy, divulges a little of Rocky's unfortunate history. "Rocky added fifty dollar bills and his business card to pizzas before he distributed them at traffic court. After a pizza or two was eaten by a judge or two, Rocky's better business scheme went as flat as the pies and he was busted for bribery."

Nearing fifty, I would guess Rocky ate too many of those pizzas himself. Although overweight, he is extremely strong, thick and hearty like a bull. Recently implanted hair, at a first glance, looks like spiders are breaking through his skull.

Rocky, although not paid to do so, states for the record. "Most of the staff here are a bit bizarre, but Chiller is in his own class of stool. That's nothing new in the land of toads. My vote is for you to keep a low profile, but you won't."

Nothing But Trouble, a bookie, has the last word on my employment. "The Doc can handle Chiller. He operates on brains; he's not stupid. Let's leave it alone for a while. Incidentally, Doc, our camp football team plays against cops in the Snow Bowl Football Tournament. The word is you threw a mean ball when you played quarterback… looks like you're still in good shape. Why don't you see Whacky; he could use a good backup quarterback."

Gaffer pats me on the back. "I'm arranging for you to bunk in the honor dorm with me and the Whacker. Be forewarned.... Whacky's meticulous and methodical."

Alone, I go through the list of characters I've met, filed in my head like a medical chart. *Einstein: computer genius and bipolar personality disorder, giggles inappropriately, displays manic side presently and refers to himself as 'we'. Picasso: beat artist, counterfeiter, proud of his friendship with Einstein...needs exercise. Charles: boyish, hears music in his head. Parents are mute. He signs when nervous. Zee: literary, sleeps too much, needs exercise. Action Jackson: politician; answers his own questions. Sees a lot in his line of work, peeking from bushes. The Governor: what a shame, poor health, always the gentleman. Rocky: lawyer; life was shut down because of a better business scheme involving pizzas. Hostile. Immature hair implants. Nothing But Trouble: bookie; sensible and straightforward. Gaffer: bossy but affectionate, he looks out for his friends. I like him. Whacky: obsessively clean. Plays football and I'll find out what else, soon.*

If life at FPC doesn't keep me on my toes, I'm not worthy of my title. Basically, I intend to mind my own business; I'm already familiar with the crime of caring too much.

Chapter Twenty-One
The Beast Tamer

So remarkable are my results playing director of the new Department of Education that skeptics have accused me of spiking the water supply. Besides my personal magnetism and calculating plots, my real ingenuity lies in my ability to manipulate Chiller as my fool, like Hamlet with sneaky Polonius, or the usurper Claudius. Only this sometimes Hamlet will not be defeated.

With a masterfully set stage, I provide the disengaged campers with a focus. Notwithstanding it's all performance art, the purgatorial waiting to get out of jail has ended. Chiller unknowingly facilitated the transition without exertion on his part. There's nothing like an attentive audience to motivate this tenacious department head. Even so, my accomplishments up to this point have been mostly for show. I'll figure out the rest as I go.

Charles is the most authentically improved by my presence. He tried to fill his empty hours alone in library, BD, before Doc, as he says, making headway in a novel or two. Never able to read past first chapters so perfectly written he wanted to continue, but he wasn't allowed to - not with Chiller the Killer lurking behind the scenes.

"Now that Doc has taken over," Charles confides in Sister Mary, "I have a life. When I hear Doc's mantra *there's a lot of work to be done today, Charles,*"Charles does a perfect imitation of me, "I feel like a new man and Mr. Chiller can't take that away from me. Doc told me he's going to kick Mr. Chiller's... oh, excuse me, Sister."

Sister Mary sighs. "Mr. Chiller, I'm sorry to say, might be a better person for a little punishment....although I don't want to see Doctor Lerner reprimanded for inflicting it."

Charles hums *Night and Day* from his new repertoire of Cole Porter and pours perfectly brewed coffee, made strong enough for me. Before I can frustrate myself, Charles locates the papers I'm searching for in ever accumulating piles. I don't like to deal with *official* paper work. Important issues require my attention, like my first unscheduled appointment of the day. Before I close the door, I overhear Sister tell Charles, "You can learn a lot listening to the Doctor."

"Come on, Doc, fess up, it depresses you to be here." Rocky takes a seat and two cigarettes from my pack, one for his ear.

"It's strange how things work out. Life is seamless, even when it gives the impression of being torn."

"What the fuck does that mean?"

"I think it means there are considerations more profound than depression."

"Like what?"

"The soul Rocky, the soul is deeper than depression."

"Who taught you that hooey, your woman? I expected better from you."

He slams the door behind him.

I finish the session alone realizing I'm not a master among these men. I'm out of my league. Diving psyche deep, coming up on the dark side of the moon, I'm near drowning. *I'm going to pay for fucking up every single day. Playing amateur shrink really sucks. Why didn't the schmucks mind their own fucking business and let me medicate myself...or do a line, or pop a pill, or let Rocky give away pizzas with money instead of sausage and anchovies. Fucking fascists...I hate their fucking guts.*

Charles comes in with his radar engaged. "Another sweet roll? Some Motrin? Anything Doc, tell me how I can help." I might as well have punched him in the face. "What did I say?" Charles backs up out of office muttering "I'm really sorry, Doc. I was just worried about you."

"Don't worry about me, worry about you!" I shred the words. The other side of my face isn't pretty when confronted with matters that diminish my image, the one I put out there. *I'm such an asshole.* I chastise myself until Chiller, a heavyweight asshole, shows up and takes the pressure off me.

"Read this copy of The General Educational Development manual, it's fascinating."

I toss Chiller's trash aside.

"What in the hell are you doing, asshole? That program is read by hundreds of thousands of people each year who are better than you'll ever be ... blah, blah, blah..."

While Chiller blah, blah, blahs, I doodle as I change channels in my head. I pause on the idea of Art History taught with the emphasis on erotic art. Any Venus will do. Botticelli's *Venus,* winks at me, only this Venus is doncha. *She'll think this is brilliant. Literary titles like* Lady Chatterley's Lover, *Anais Nin's Erotica, and Henry Miller's sexually raw literature will be at the top of the reading list. doncha will have lots of good ideas...she's been encouraging me in this direction.*

Chiller kicks the desk. "You don't listen to a fucking word I say. You'll pay for this. Lerner!" He huffs out limping.

"The Chiller must be a closet queen. Nobody is that dramatic all the time without a baton up their ass." My approving audience, waiting in the wings, tends to agree. Scenes like this contribute immensely to my popularity. In a theatrical mood, I throw Chiller's manual in the wastebasket and light it on fire. "All systems devoid of life are better off dead and buried. That boring twaddle would never appeal to men like you; you need more stimulation, not less."

With the men following me in the tradition of residents, I select a book from the shelf, but I can't say I recognize any organization to its placement. "It would be better if the books were arranged more traditionally, alphabetically by authors, within categories. You know what I mean, Charles. Fiction should be on one shelf, nonfiction on another; separate biography from science and so on."

He blushes. "I was experimenting with a new approach. I thought it would be challenging and draw in the non-readers."

I recheck the shelf. "Clever, Charles, placing *To Kill a Mockingbird, Flicka* and *Of Mice and Men* with books about animals like *Training your Dog* and *The Sexual Habits of Mammals*." I return the book titled *Anxious Pleasures: The Sexual Lives of an Amazonian People* to the shelf. "I'm amazed that one wasn't checked out."

Gaffer rushes over and grabs it. "But then, you have your own peccadilloes, don't you? Take Charles' system a step further." Gaffer leads us back to my office. "For instance, your headquarters, Doctor, could very well be considered a federal offense; you could, for instance, put law books in your office. No, wait; most noticeable right of the bat is the scent of stale tobacco and food inside cups of coffee in various stages of decomposition. I suspect an ongoing science project is in the making. This, my friends, is a truly male cave. I would say it's the burial place of human remains but I know Chiller has not yet departed."

Charles eyes open wide. "Is someone *really* going to kill Mr. Chiller?"

"Yeah, Mrs. Chiller."

"I try to keep Doc organized, but Doc's office has what he calls organic properties."

"I immediately noticed that it stinks worse than any of my farts and I've been perfecting them since I was a kid doing my own science projects." Gaffer closes the door. "Let's blow, Daddy-O."

Gaffer asks the conjuring question on our way out of the building, "Did Chiller read your manifesto on educating the geniuses?"

"Never mention the devil's name for fear of summonsing him." Too late. Chiller's head pops out from behind his office door. "Doesn't the Chiller look remarkably similar to Bettlejuice when, with that long snake neck, he turned reptilian and his eyes gyrated out of his head?"

"I'm warning you Lerner, you asshole…"

I grab Chiller's pointer away from him, (or whatever it is that he carries around) and swashbuckler that I am, I roar, "Away, you black-hearted blood-thirsty villain."

Chiller retreats.

I advance. "If I don't succeed with these noble scholars, do with me what you will. I'll walk the plank."

"Are you crazy talking to me like that?"

"Your authority means nothing to me, barnacle boy. Your mind is a locked down detention center of impaired neurons. And I am a free buccaneer." I twirl the baton/pointer, toss it in the air, catch it, and toss it back to him. Before slamming the office door, Chiller threatens, "You'll pay for this." I hope he can hear me through the cheers promise, "Yes, I know, and you're going to be the currency, Herr Chiller."

"Doc's got style." A hard case straggling in the hallway confides in his friend. "I'm gonna check out what he's up to. He's way cool." Another straggler won over exclaims, "The man's not bad if he can stand up to the camp asshole. He's got balls." After seeing me in action for the first time, campers on the way back to the dorm for count spread the word that I'm not so bad. Gaffer leads the pack in congratulations. Walking arm and arm, he discusses the finer points of this latest sabotage.

"But weren't you the teensiest bit nervous about where that baton thing he carries around with him might have been last?"

Cringing, I thrust my hand into a frozen puddle of ice water.

Gaffer's conversation changes direction as we *pass* the post office. "I must tell you, my friend, being the apple of so many eyes is a huge responsibility. Don't be jealous now, but the truth is, I receive more letters from chicks than I can possibly read, and I'm sure you will, too." Gaffer pinches my cheek. "As devilish cute as you are. Most of the guys get pornographic letters. Lucky assholes. My letters are from chicks with good taste but no imagination…."

My head aches thinking about doncha not writing to me, seeing me, or ever speaking to me again, which brings me back to my underlying desperation caused by not knowing what she's up to.

A voice from the speakers on the trees interrupts my dark spell, broadcasting: *The snow evacuation team is to report to the motor pool one hour before it begins to snow…whatever that means. Happy upcoming holidays, campers. This is your host. Don't look around. Look up. Look down. Most of all look for a good time and sign up for a tournament, and, by all means, bring a date to watch you kick ass. It's going to be a blast up here in the honeymoon suites, with our heart shaped tubs and our bubbling Jacuzzi blizzards. You don't want to freeze your petunias off, or your other precious parts. Protect your jewels. The two you have are irreplaceable. Dress up pretty in your winter uniforms and pack away your summer skivvies for that Caribbean cruise.*

A sense of humor, good friends, and work go a long way to cheer me up. If I don't end up in a nut house for revamping the education department and educating these men, I'll be okay.

Chapter Twenty-Two
Dorm Mates

With an hour to spare, I head over to the honor dorm to checkout my new digs. A ghastly apparition lying on the floor next to the bed I have yet to sleep in startles me. "You scared the breeze out of me, Einstein. You're in desperate need of a healthy dose of vitamin C, fresh air and sunshine. You've been inside way too long. I thought you were a corpse."

"We thought that you look a little peaked yourself."

I stretch out on the bed. "I'm beat."

"Usually the patient lies down where you're at presently." He eyes my bed covetously.

"You need to consider how unusual the circumstances are." To make him feel better, I share my cookies and gummy bears with him.

"We must say it is a tremendous relief to have a real, not to mention outstanding, Doctor available, even if it is for your expert opinion alone. These are delicious cookies, have one," he tells his other self, using his other hand. "We heard about the two house calls you made last night…that must be where you got these treats. Have you noted, in our brief acquaintance, that a bipolar personality disorder is doing a tricky little duet in my head? Fortunately, we have mainly manic episodes. There were a few depressive incidents… *those* left me nearly suicidal."

"Do you have a family?"

"I have two children and they definitely do not adore me."

"Tell me about it."

"It all began with a businessman building a low-priced tractor for a third-world country. That sociopath was my partner. He's a resident here. Without my knowing it, he received five million dollars for an entire fleet, but he never manufactured more than the one tractor. During my trial, I was depressed and delusional. Twisted, I became a humiliated angle worm."

"What happened after they gave you electro shock therapy?"

"With my ass hanging out of those stupid gowns I ran out of the hospital and somehow ended up on my front lawn mooning a dozen squad cars parked in my driveway."

I feel Einstein's pulse.

"I *was* an angleworm."

"No kidding, you *really* thought you were an angleworm?"

"Who knows."

Making general observations, I listen to the rest of his story.

"I spent six months in a psych ward before I came here. That was two years ago. I didn't dare have my Lithium adjusted. I may be a nut but I *most emphatically* do not approve of nut houses."

"Sit on this chair." I help him up off the floor to examine him. "Once your blood levels are evaluated we can determine the necessary pharmacologic agents available."

A good doctor makes an appropriate diagnosis by knowing all there is to know about a patient. It's all there in the details. The one detail I forgot is place. Realizing I no longer have an office, I feel like *I've* been given a few volts. "In the meantime, I think you should use the gym to improve your metabolism and mood, and get outdoors more often. You look like you've spent your life in the stacks at the National Archives."

"Fine, yes, anything you say, Doc. We think you're new office is nicely situated."

"I thank the both of you."

My new office is a spacious corner room with good light and a Paul Bunyanish view of the great outdoors. The honor dorm originally served as Bachelors Officers' Quarters (BOQ). Walking around, I think of the time I spent as a Light Colonel in the Medical Corps. After meeting the characters in this place, my stint here could end up resonating with my MASH unit days. I wouldn't mind that at all.

For a man recently wearing designer clothes and driving fast cars, I step easily into this sparse, but potentially rich life style. I have *almost* everything I need - an office and a medical practice. Gratified, I'm more content today than I was yesterday.

Circling back to my room, I notice that the bed, perfectly made, before I got into it, is messed up *a little*. Nice sheets, two four-ply army blankets, and two soft feather pillows are a definite bonus. *I bet Whacky made those hospital corners. I've heard a thing or two about Whacky, but he obviously hasn't heard all he needs to know about me or we wouldn't be roommates, or so I've been told. Rumor has it that we have the absolute propensity to be the odd couple. Cleanliness is next to Godliness is gospel with him. I advocate perfection, too. There won't be any difficulties on that score.*

When the gods spoke, he who tumbled from lofty heights landed his ass in the joint, without the usual crew to sort him out. That's a far way to fall.

Whacky and Gaffer enter. My eyes follow their poignant glance to the ash falling from my cigarette. Gaffer breaks the silence. "Doc, let me fix you another cup of? Was it coffee?" He gathers the empty cups Einstein and I used as ashtrays.

To give Whacky credit I can barely hear him say, "How can such a smart guy like the Doc, who operates on brains, be such a slob? It don't seem right. Scheisse!"

I have the same *I don't get it* thought about some of the men I meet. I don't understand that part of them which led to their ruin.

Whacky refolds and rearranges my clothes, putting my belongings into perfect order. He doesn't utter a harsh word *too loudly* while sweeping up the floor or dusting away cookie crumbs. Under his breath is where he registers his complaints. "His highness is use to butlers kissin' his royal ass. High muckamuck's not gonna think much of me. I'm not gonna kiss his royal rear day and night." While Whacky works himself over, with no visible means of release, a hack enters the room to take count. Whacky pushes him out. "Don't be steppin' in my way, putz. Can't ya see I'm busy in here?"

Aggravating this six foot three pillar of lean massive musculature when he looks out-and-out mean and determined to put his foot down could be dangerous to one's health.

"My job description before coming here was Collector for The Boys. I've always been a hard worker. There's not a lazy bone in my body. See what I'm talkin' about?" Whacky admires the perfect order he's reestablished in the room.

I lift my head and acknowledge that tidiness has indeed been reinstated. "Neat, like the brain. A brain is very clean. Nicely done."

"I like that. Nobody ever called me a brain before."

Gaffer joins us with fresh coffee. "Thanks, pal." Whacky and I say at the same time and laugh.

"Hey Gaffer, you hear that? Doc thinks I'm a real brain. He ain't a brain surgeon for nothin'. I admit I screw up sometimes. But I ain't no dummy; that's for sure. You're okay in my book, Doc."

Putting on my glasses, Gaffer assumes a professorial attitude. "I often wonder…"

"I won a scholarship to Oklahoma to play defensive end… before I never finished high school." An admission Whacky speaks quietly.

"That's too bad." I say knowingly.

"I know. Then I got sorta screwed up when the Fed's busted a house where I was collectin' a gamblin' debt from some asshole drug dealer in Vegas. They got me with trumped-upped possession charges. Now my job is Head Chef at Club Fed. Nobody goes hungry with the Whacker around."

"You're food is delicious."

"It's tough stayin' on top of the purveyors. They're always tryin' to pawn off inferior stuff. I warn 'em not to do it cause

I have eight hundred men to feed and I ain't givin' 'em nothin' that ain't wholesome."

"It's admirable that you care so much."

Unable to keep my eyes open, I fall sound asleep.

I'm awakened by Captain John Flagg, affectionately known as Mon Capitan, standing next to my bed. He's a legend around here. His twelve o'clock shadow warms his southern accent, spreading wide as the masts on a galleon ship.

"Well, good mornin', sunshine. Nice to meet you at last, after all the monstrous good things I heard about you. With the strength of his firm grip he pulls me to my feet. "Have dinner on me tonight. I'll tell you the short version of how I came here."

"Is it *really* time for dinner? I feel like I just fell asleep."

"From what I've heard you did."

I expect a band to march across the parade ground we pass through on way to the mess hall. The leafless birch trees in the distance mock my desire. With volumes of silent sky overhead, I covet the horizon. "If I had a horse, I'd ride out of here so fast it would make everyone's head spin." Facing restrictions, I comfort myself singing, "Give me room, lots of room, don't fence me in…"

"The word is you have enough work around here to put you back in the saddle again. You're pissin' Dr. D off takin' over his turf. There ain't any secrets around here, cowboy."

"One of my patients, a local farm boy, told me he always needed a brain doctor but he never could afford mental health. He actually tried to pay me in quarters."

"I guess you'll make up for it chargin' me double."

"Only if you bore me."

"That's unlikely." His playful bad boy blue eyes turn chain gang hard. "Once upon a time, I had a very profitable business arrangement with my dearly departed brothers. They were pilots but they never made another drug run with me, not from Belize or anywhere else on this planet. I caught those sons-of-bitches leakin' information to the DEA, sellin' me down alligator alley. Nearly broke my heart. Bet your boots *that* shipment never happened. The day we were supposed to fly out, the brothers, God rest their wretched souls, got run off the road.... looked like road kill is what I thought."

I glance at him out of the corner of my eye but I wouldn't dare say a word.

"Asshole cops picked me up at the funeral, but I was acquitted. Several years later, the coast guard pricks in Miami caught up with me. To circumvent spendin' my life behind bars I sacrificed my cargo to the deep blue sea. Crawlin' out of that swamp on my belly, I didn't get but fifty feet. It's funny how a man gets religion when there are twelve shotguns pointin' at his head. Don't do any drug traffickin' in Miami. This place is like heaven compared to that scurvy dump."

"All I want do is make myself useful to the men I live among. I pray I will never again become addicted to any drug for as long as I live."

"You better not, or you ain't the Doc we all count on. I don't like bein' disappointed."

"I'm always grateful for the opportunity to be of service."

Chapter Twenty-Three
Nachos in the Night

I wake up with the blues. They come and go of their own accord. Fortunately, I'm never alone long enough to get really maudlin. Mon Capitan catches up with me on my way to breakfast. Lonely for doncha, I'm grateful for his company. "Tell me, how do you spend your extra time?"

"Makin' outstandin' moonshine. The brew's so good it makes you wanna slap yaw Mama."

I laugh at the rank southernism.

"Taking a cargo of moon on my beautiful ninety foot ocean goin' Catamaran - *The Bonnes Riches* - and navigate the seven seas is my one ambition."

"The prospect of magical Caribbean islands in the land of legends, with a stash of hooch to boot, is right out of the swashbuckling pirate escapades I lose myself in when I have time to read George MacDonald Frasier's *Flashman*." I feel a bond of shared dreams is in the making, a confederacy for those who dream, to dream on. This traveler, and his vast adventures on land, sea and air, intrigues me. Although the skipper's carburetor zonked out, he manages to keep his motor running. A whiskey still in the joint is no small undertaking.

When Mon Capitan's young roommate joins us, my new friend is all smiles.

"Doc, I'd like to introduce you to my darlin' roommate Shakey. Shakey say hello to the Doc."

"How did a solid kid like you end up with a name like Shakey?" Nearly everyone takes off; they already know Shakey's story; it's not dissimilar from their own.

"Smuggling coke and using more than I sold gave me the shakes, until I made heroin my best friend…a wicked habit for anyone, anywhere, anytime."

Listening to Mon Capitan tell how he took care of Shakey, while he was *jonesing* during diesel therapy, I have to trust that before the brothers betrayed the Capitan, he was loyal to them. In that instant, Mon Capitan knows my mind wandered and he knows where it went. He simply recapitulates, "All addicts need to fill voids or are filled with voids. For you guys, exercise does that job perfectly."

"Now that I have free time, I'll workout my imperfections in the gym. A sweaty gym where men look like Greek gods appeals to my vanity and my sanity."

"Let's workout."

I like Shakey's suggestion, but my mood changes and my heart aches as we pass by the one room that has connections with the outside world. I avoid the pay phones, unless I'm phoning out between eight-thirty and nine-forty-five in the evening, when campers are allowed five precious minutes. The process is usually orderly if there aren't any Dear John I'm not takin' your call calls.

My palms are sweaty and my heart is pounding imagining what doncha might be up to. Mon Capitan takes my mind off the haunting possibilities, pointing out the camper responsible for lending out paraphernalia in the Rec room. "Irish dots his i's and crosses his t's. He's wound so tight, the man crosses his legs. I'd lay a wager he'd hunt someone down to the end of their time to have a game he lent out back in circulation. Can't help himself, he's compulsive like all bankers."

Irish, the definitive Brooks Brothers type, joins us. "Everyone in this place has a story and I heard you're listening to all of them. I've seen you around, Doc, but someone else was always bending your ear. I'll tell you my tale of woe, if you want to hear it as a professional, of course."

Not as guarded as I expected him to be...but then, if he were, he wouldn't be here. "I'd love to hear your story, Irish."

Mon Capitan and Shakey take their leave and Irish and I get comfortable in the worn to comfort circa Fifties vintage lounge area. Reminds me of a huge version of my father's waiting room where I often got cozy with my books, waiting for my father to end a long day.

My parents conditioned me for my life as a doctor. They told me the stories patients tell might take hours but if I listened closely it would facilitate my ability to hand over a confident diagnosis on a silver platter at the end of the consultation. Knowing the importance of this trait, I became a good listener. My willingness to pay close attention to what others have to say supports the need others have to express themselves.

Irish gets right to the point. "My life of crime was born when I made my first loan to a dead person. I filed and filled fake loan petitions materializing a vast number of deeds on properties that were nonexistent."

"That sounds strangely familiar."

"I didn't know you were involved in embezzlement, Doc. I thought you were dealing drugs."

"Please, continue your story."

"I was in possession of half a million dollars, until a bank examiner became suspicious when one too many of the loans I made defaulted for coincidental death. Did you return the money, Doc, or did you hide it?"

"There never was a question of money. It was a question of medication, not money. Medication returned to me from prescriptions I wrote to my patients. I also wrote some of them to dead people or fictitious people. That's all I meant. It just slipped out."

"What did you do with all that medication?"

"I took it for pain. Getting hit hard playing football all those years destroyed my hips. I never had the hip replacements I should have had."

"You took that much medication for pain? Incredible."

"I took what I needed to lessen the pain." *I understand that Irish is confused; I'm confused about losing my freedom for that very reason.*

119

"I'm a member of this Club, aren't I?" *What did I do that was so fucking criminal that I'm in jail? Doing time. Unbelievable. Doctors kill patients and hospitals hide the deed. And, I know for a fact that doctors get medication without seeing other doctors; it's absurd that they sent me away for it.*

"My punishment was much too grave. I'm a banker who made a mistake, I'm not a criminal."

"I'm not a drug dealer. I'm an smart ass who made mistakes. I thought the truth would straighten everything out."

"You're not a smart ass. Smart asses get off easy. There was a former bank president in the habit of borrowing from the vault on Fridays to finance weekend trips to Vegas. They sentenced him to six months. I think about that everyday. My sentence is four years." Irish's hand goes to his gut.

"Take into account that when we break the law the odds are stacked against everything coming out equal. Cicero was correct. Remember *Nulla avaritia sine poena est.*"

Irish sighs. "Greed is not without punishment."

"What's up with your gut?"

"Nothing much. Would you like to sign up for a holiday tournament event? Gaffer wants to play handball against you."

"I'm game."

"Beware, he hates like the dickens to lose."

"I'll kick his ass. He doesn't know what competitive means."

A gruesome trio of law reckless attorneys, willing to share their over-the-top lunacy, ex-large drinks, and lion-sized stinking cigars, join us. Before leaving me to the loquacious threesome, Irish quotes the Bard. "And the first thing we do is kill all the lawyers."

Rocky's tenacious sneer nearly covers his head and eats his implants. He spits out the hatred he cannot repress. "Doc, you and I both had the tragic misfortune to get stuck with that muckrake schmuck judge, Assbern. Listen to me. On a dark night, I'd like to sneak up behind him and ram an ice pick through his ear and scramble it in the place his brains are supposed to be. Twist it, like this. Then, I'd bash the son-of-a-bitch's head in with a ball peen-hammer until I couldn't lift my arm anymore." Exhausted from the exertion, Rocky hurls himself into a chair. "When I finish him off I'll throw his remains to the hogs. Hogs eat anything, even clothes."

"Take it easy. Have a couple of cigarettes on me."

Froth, puffing his cigar, goes native. "Rocky's pandering is small stuff. I got nine years for jury tampering. A client's guilt or innocence is immaterial. Who really gives a shit?" He speaks his lawyer's creed. "You ought to come to the gym with us, Doc. I'm the steward. It really isn't bad here. You'll get used to it."

The last of the gruesome threesome calls after me "Hey, where ya goin', I wanted to talk to you."

"I'm taking Froth's advice. I'm going to workout." I don't look back. I want to get away from the courtroom stench they carry with them.

Tom the Arm, the FPC Quarter Back, puts up three hundred pounds, grunting, "Doc, we need you to be my back-up in the championship game." He brings the weights down. "I promise we won't humiliate you. Our fullback played for the NFL. The rest of the team is working out... they're all colossal mothers."

"You guys are going to see what *I'm* made of; I'll gladly play. I'll be back in fighting form in no time."

On my way out of the gym, I shake hands all over the place. I felt like Rocky, from the movie *Rocky I,* when those endorphins kicked-in.

As much as I need a shower, curiosity arouses the beast in me to check out what's happening on the dorm fire escape. A figure in the distance, hauling a huge sac over his shoulder, is encouraged to hurry by a bunch of my dorm mates. "Looks like Christian from *Pilgrim's Progress.*"

Zee nods, "Good analogy but off the mark."

"Our good Christian is more like Santa Claus. Einstein giggles. "Twice a week Psycho crosses over the field, goes through the woods, and walks along the creek to the swing-by and drop-in liquor store to load up on rotgut booze for us; quite a haul, but no toys. He's never asked why he's dressed the way he is or why he pays in quarters. With a liquor store every fifty yards, the money transaction is all that matters to the proprietors. On Psycho's last outing, he drank so much he lost his boot. Damn lucky he didn't lose his foot from frostbite."

As Einstein examines Psycho to make sure he's all together, Psycho gives me a once over. "Who's he, a Hack?" The obvious question arises from someone named Psycho when he hears the answer. "You gonna fix me, Doc?"

I could have helped you. "Not tonight, guy."

Psycho baas.

Einstein encourages him to settle down. "Psycho spends most of his time in solitary. He has a nasty habit of walking behind Buckaroo making sheep sounds."

"Stick it in. Baaaa."

Psycho's demonstration ends when Mon Capitan shows up waving two *very* long prongs. Gaffer stumbles in right behind him; producing a huge pot, from under the oversized coat he's wearing, clarifies why he looked pregnant. I want to ask what's going on when Psycho baaas. "Are we cookin' up some Buckaroo tonight, boys?"

Mon Capitan comes too near my head with his makeshift electrodes, causing me to snap out of my loony bin flashback. I watch him electrocute the three bricks of cheese, thrown into the pot Gaffer brought, instead of me. He grins deviously. "Handy little gadgets these; they melt cheese nicely."

Whacky stomps in with a tray balanced on his shoulder. "Tonight we have salsa, peppers, onions, mushrooms, cooked sausage, and whatever else I made part of this heist. Add this mother load to the fromage."

I'm cackling and salivating with the rest of them as they slide the concoction into two industrial garbage bags. Stuffed into the clothes dryer, set on a hot gentle cycle, to spin for fifteen minutes exactly gets it all toasty and gooey.

Mon Capitan ribs me. "No one is going to eat anyone and I wouldn't lose any sleep over it if I was you 'cause you ain't that sweet."

Did he really hone in on my one dark thought about my lobotomy nightmare? Sorrowful association. This is sweet. Gorging on Jailhouse Pizza (aka Nachos in the Night), slamming back rot gut booze, I'm back in college. After too much of a good thing, we're all slurring and tooting from our rear ends. On that note, well-sated friends propelled to their rooms sleep like infants, while hydrogen sulfide bouquets blossom in the air.

Hey, what did you expect? We're just guys.

Chapter Twenty-Four
On the Road

Dreams dreamt the hour before waking are the most vivid. When dreaming about love, it's painful to begin the day with Rocky's hair implants seeding in my face. Wishing for a warm good morning, Rocky's nerve-racking routine is what I get. "You like it here, don't you Doc? I stopped smoking again, but I had a strong desire to have one this morning. Did you know that most accidents aren't accidents at all?"

"Shut up, Rocky, and let me return to my beautiful dream."

Gaffer and the Whacker are of the same opinion, only more so. "Can't you see we're sleepin', asshole?"

"The dictionary defines an accident as an unexpected and undesirable event, without apparent cause."

I open one eye. "Are you saying that I belong here, Rocky?"

He shrugs. "Most accidents aren't accidents at all. They're collisions that could have been avoided with a little insight."

"Asshole Dago, we don't need no driver's ed class." Even though Whacky's pissed-off and I'd kill to finish my dream, I light a cigarette and sit up. "What can I do for you, Rocky?"

"I know you feel my sense of injustice. You're good hearted; there's a difference in you, Doc. Forget that you could be a party animal, you were a hard working son-of-a-bitch."

Whacky exerts himself and Rocky is halfway down the hall when a brainstorm's electrical currents stimulates his implants. With his first new thought, from the day the pizza pie caper went wrong, he scurries back. "Think of all the money I, I mean we, could make in a medical malpractice business. With a class act like you, Doc, there would be no soft tissue ambulance chasing. A brainy up-right person doesn't need that kind of business. We could revolutionize the industry." Rocky's thoughts continue to be those of a full-blown opportunist, not a rank criminal.

On the way to breakfast, Whacky comes to the point of his not entirely pleasant demeanor. "Like why don't you make an appointment with the Dago and shrink him? Yeah, yeah. I know your screwball philosophy but he ain't the only one who got gipped around here. They got me on drug charges and I ain't got nothin' to do with no drugs. I was tryin' to make a livin' and I got busted, no different than him; so what's his beef?"

"Moral anguish is the province of the innocent."

"Jesus, Doc, what's that supposed to mean?"

"Because Rocky never engaged in criminal activity he suffers...."

"That Dago won't need elevator shoes with you around. Check out my playbook. It has eight plays in it. Not a lot but they work. Make 'em suffer on the field. Don't be such a softie."

I sit down at the table with my tray. I don't eat. I'm hypnotized. "If you continue to eat like you have two assholes, Gaffer, you'll need a crane to lift your fat ass off that chair. Don't you ever give your jaws a break?"

Whacky disapproves of my interference. "Let him eat. He'll get plenty of exercise today. Go on eat; you need to eat, too, Doc. Doc ain't even listenin' to me. Wait. See, he's smilin' cause he started readin' the playbook I gave him. He likes the Whacker's plays. I knew he would. Doc's smart like that."

Imagining I'm releasing a football into the air, I let it go like a javelin. I can already hear the receiver call out, *hey, Doc, that ball had a lot of shit on it*. Chiller approaching me with an insinuating cheesy grin that most anyone would like to scrape off doesn't throw me. Whining, "You think you're a super star. Well, fuck you *and* your favorite fan. He wants to see you." His chalk-scrapping-the-blackboard-voice doesn't spoil my mood. I simply say, "Go away. I don't know any Stan." But that doesn't work with Chiller, he persists.

"Don't be an asshole, I mean the Warden, or Bill. That's how he signed this stupid note."

"Back off, Chiller, I don't want to kiss you and don't breathe on me, you probably have the pox."

"Go ahead, kiss the Warden's ass. I don't give a damn what you do; he likes me better. I'm related to him."

The expression on the Warden's face is not one of a fan. "Your plan for the GED program is *exceedingly* optimistic. This is not medical school." Shaking his head, the light in my halo dims; apparently, I have one of those auras that easily change colors. "These fellows have been away from books for years. Tutor them... call on your educated friends to help out."

"Good idea, Warden. It would be unacceptable to let students fall behind. I promise you this project will not fail."

"Your program is too advanced. I heard you discuss neurophysiology in a lecture I attended."

"I didn't see you."

"I was in the back; it was crowded."

"Ohhh, well, that happens. Did you ever see the movie *The Bird Man of Alcatraz?*"

"Good movie."

"Robert Stroud, the character played by Burt Lancaster, had a third grade education and he became the world's authority on bird diseases while in the joint. His discoveries were very beneficial, especially in the poultry business."

"What can I do to help?"

"Einstein needs medical attention."

"Chiller tells me Einstein is certifiable..."

"Many illustrious minds suffered bipolar personality disorders. Virginia Woolf, Abraham Lincoln, Tennessee Williams, Isaac Newton and Keith Newman, the other Einstein, Michelangelo, Leonardo Di Vinci…"

"I get the picture."

"Fortunately, I know a talented neurosurgeon in town. Here's his number. If you contact him, he'll see to it that Einstein is put in the right hands. We need Einstein."

"If you were on one of your missions, you've succeeded. Before you go, tell me you're not filling-in as backup quarterback in today's game."

"But I am."

"Because Chiller is referee, the game will be a free for all; angry cops, no holds barred, are bound to worsen your old hip injuries."

"If that's it, I'll get back to work…but before I go I want to say I'd bet on us, if I were you."

"I don't think you're going anywhere fun." Chiller flicks a wad of paper in Einstein's face. "Special delivery, misfit. Bill Warden finally came to his senses and graduated you to a locked down psych ward. So long, sucker."

Einstein is green and speechless.

"Einie, listen to me. If there was a BOP memorandum for your transfer you would have intercepted it." Einstein looks to the guys with eyes that beg agreement. "You'll be feeling a lot better in no time. Get back on your feet; you're not an earthworm. You're our pal and you're going to have your lithium levels managed just like we discussed."

On our way over to the mess hall, the camp driver passes by with Einie hanging out the window blowing kisses at us.

"Wow! You unquestionably know how to get things done around here." My buddies pat me on the back.

"What did you expect when your quarterback's in play?"

"Hey, Daddy-O, our quarterback is always in play. What a relief. We don't have to lose any sweat over the dastardly Dr. D. killing Einstein." Picasso gives me a thumbs-up. "You're a regular irregular kind of guy, and visa versa."

Chapter Twenty-Five
Football

Waiting for Whacky to come out of the kitchen to introduce me to the players on the team - consuming mass quantities of high carbs and protein driven food at the training table - I approach with reverence and listen in as Tom Right finishes going over a well organized play with the team. I'm looking forward to playing with these football apostles.

"This game is a religion with us, Doc. We worship at the altar of the holy game of football. Cops versus robbers has us saying our prayers; we'll take absolution *after* we murder the pigs."

"Who did you play for in college, Tom?"

"Nebraska State. I would have gone pro, if I didn't screw up."

Whacky gives him a friendly cuff. "We all make mistakes, Tommy. Sellin' coke to Feds is kind of a theme around here. Plenty of guys wind up in the joint for doin' it."

"Sure, I know."

"The giant sittin' next to Tommy is Shorty. He's our wide receiver."

Shorty nods. "I'm six feet six and I'm faster than the speed of light and just as wide."

"Come and sit over here next to me, Doc. I'm Tiny." Tiny never toked coke, not seriously. Pot would have to have been his drug of choice.

"What do you tip the scales at?" I ask squeezing into the seat next to him.

"Three fifty…now that I'm dieting but I'm six foot five…. look at me, *I'm* really built."

Swallowing an entire hero sandwich, he chases it with three diet cokes.

"You'd be difficult to move."

Alternately smiling and frowning, Tiny scoops the food squishing from his mouth back in with his tongue. "I'm the middle linebacker that plugs holes. I used to be a fullback and a blocking back when I played pro but I got too slow munchin' out."

"What talent, ain't it somethin'?" Whacky radiates from his sunnier side. You're going to play backup to Tom the Arm, Doc, and backup at free safety on defense. You can fly and you're tough." Whacky crows, "Let's do it! Let's murder them coppers!"

"AMEN!" Slapping their hands together, they slap mine. I'm on the team.

"I'm tellin' ya, Doc, flags ain't nothin' more than strips of material hanging from a belt. The object is to pull the strips from the belt around the pigs' waist; that puts the oinkers out of play."

"I've played this game before." I remind Tiny, as we walk over to the field.

"You have to be on your guard with pigs."

"I'm aware of that."

"It's true 'cause being gang tackled to get the flag out… don't perturb yourself, Doc. Tiny will lookout for you."

Gaffer sits next to me on what little space is left, after Tiny attached himself to me.

"Whacky said I have to play if somebody gets hurt."

"You don't look happy. It isn't about playing, is it?"

"I want to ask you, on behalf of Whacky and myself, not to bring another lost soul to our room." Gaffer indicates Tiny with his head. "We don't approve of your visitors, or shall I say your patient's office hours; and we don't like our privacy disturbed. The people that fascinate you drive us crazy."

"Have a look in the mirror; this place is filled with people who have unresolved issues, or they wouldn't be here."

"Can you choose your patients more discriminately?"

"I don't always choose them, *sometimes* they chose me. I've taken a life long oath to be there for *anyone* who needs me. Remember that, because I'm never going to forget it."

I trot out to the field to warm up and throw some passes. The campers, already in attendance, cheer me. My present life and my past life are not in conflict. It's awesome to be in love and play football. I feel lucky!

Rainbow and two other pom-pom girlie-men skip past me. "Hammer and tong, hammer and tong, you take the hammer we'll take the tong." Stretching out limp wrists, they push their crotches forward. "Go, FPC! Go, Doc!"

The police force has a history of embarrassment; not winning a game in five years makes for meaner than usual moods. That's not attractive in a cop. However, their traditional diet of coffee and donuts, beer and fast greasy food keeps them mostly on the apathetic side - not to mention obese. Their jiggling bellies are the last thing to stop moving doing jumping jacks and their push-ups are a joke.

"Hope the cops murder you, Lerner."

"You're too kind, Chiller. I must say your referee jersey looks stunning."

Smoothing out the wrinkles in his shirt, Chiller saunters out to the field for the coin toss, disappearing into the mass of hulking players, grinning like Beelzebub. FPC wins the coin toss and elects to receive. Chief, a full-blooded Sioux, receives the kickoff at FPC's thirty. Moving like a young stag, he takes it to mid-field where his flag is pulled, compliments of the sadists in blue. My teammates retaliate and they keep the shots coming.

Obscenities, vicious as the snow is razor-sharp, stimulate a fightin' mood. Constantly defogging his glasses, you would think Mother Nature hit Chiller, the wimp, harder than the rest of us; she's playing too rough for a clumsy oaf like him. When they drag a bloodied cop off the field, he jumps on me. "If there's anymore violence, Lerner, you stupid prick, I'll call the game."

"Why tell me? The captain is on the field. I can tell you those plays were legal. Don't blow another gasket. You're already light headed. Put some weights in your shoes. Your traction will be a hell of a lot better."

He spits in my face, yelling, "Holdback your team or I'll personally see to it that those cops give *you* what for. And why the fuck would I put weights in my shoes, you dumb ass."

Whipping around, he lands on his.

Tom the Arm intercepting a pass at the forty-yard line ends up buried under a pile of badass cops out for blood. The fat asses around them high five each other. Bouncing off each other's bellies they grunt and squeal, "More revenge. More revenge."

Dropping straight back, not able to see an inch in front of me, miraculously the ball finds my receiver. The linemen on defense are seething. "He's cupping. Goddamn asshole is cupping. We'll break your legs, you fucking cheat."

The stands erupt on our side. "Go FPC. The Doctor is in... the Doctor is in...."

We score on a pass play. Tiny crushes the cop that downed me. "Low-down cops are good for nothin' bastards." My protector is bouncing on a boy in blue, raising a ruckus. "I take it back, copper, you're a damn good trampoline."

The Warden, *barely* understood over the microphone, sounds like he said the game is officially over.

From this point on it's all last shots. We're cheered on. "Hammer and tong, hammer and tong, this time we're right and the cops are wrong." The loudspeakers join in. *Congratulations FPC on a magnificently played game. An additional foot and a half of snow fell in the last hour. Visibility doesn't exist. Go for broke.*

We heard break some bones.

On our way to the mess hall, Gaffer grabs me and holds on tight. "Don't lose sight of me, Doc. I don't have any bread crumbs. A guy can get lost in the woods."

"We're at the Gingerbread House, Hansel. You can let go of my arm any time now."

Ice-covered, satisfying enormous appetites we defrost ourselves with Whacker's, good mother that he is, celebration dinner that sticks to the ribs. Nothing But Trouble, our in-house bookie, stuffs his face to match the winnings in his pockets, laughing, "I pity the dummies who bet against us. Doc, we can always count on you for anything. How about it, Tommy boy? You were magnificent…always on the money. I can't stop eating. This food is fucking awesome. Whacky, I don't know what you do better, hit or cook. Jesus, this is an agreeable life style. Pass me more bread. I love bread!"

Filing out of the mess hall bragging about what each of us did to which cop and how many times, we take the designated rope path, reliving sweet revenge in vivid details. Best of all, we find Einstein in the gym; safely returned from the hospital. Practicing basketball, wearing his parka, he looks like an injured penguin attempting flight with no water in sight.

"I feel like a million bucks. Watch this!" A set shot made from half the customary distance misses the backboard. Dribbling ferociously, he ends up on the floor. "I'm not normal, but I'm happy and that's plenty good enough for me. After we shoot some hoops with him, he's satisfied he's made his point. "Now," he giggles, "I want to prove to you how appreciative I *really* am. Mon Capitan has looked after a little entertainment for me."

We help him to his feet and leave the Rec Center with great expectations.

Snowdrifts lean against the buildings in waves like rippled sheets. The crews have been solidly at work fighting nature's crazy scheme for hours. We make it back to the dorm, with the protection of each other's bodies, exhausted and almost late for curfew.

"This will warm your innards and your gizzards, compliments of Einstein." Mon Capitan hands out paper cups, like it's Holy Communion. I pull a face and gulp down a spot of moonshine. After a little festivity, we're beyond bushed.

"A pleasant evening ends a not too terrible day. Now, my friends, it's time for sweet dreams to top-off the perfect day."

"About football?" I send Tiny back to his room to figure it out, hopefully, while he's asleep.

"Sweet dreams, lads." I turn out the lights.

"What a good idea. If you guys tell me yours..."

"I ain't tellin' nobody nothin'," Whacky protests before snoring so loudly he drowns out Gaffer's monologue, which is probably very inventive.

Chapter Twenty-Six
Coming on Christmas

Holiday mornings are meant to be intimate. Drinking long cups of coffee, half-reading the newspaper, listening to the woman you love recite excerpts from the literature she consumes with a passion is my ideal. Not that us guys don't love each other, we do. It's just the all too apparent absence of feminine vitality makes us melancholy. Reminds us of who we are and where we're at, in case we forgot.

For Whacky, good Catholic that he is, coming on Christmas, he contemplates redemption and Christ. Bringing his hand, but not his head, out from under the blankets, our friend shoos us away. "I want to be alone." His tone is predictably introspective. Gaffer tries to persuade him to have breakfast with us but Whacky is adamant. "I'm not eatin'. I need to pray. For the first time in my life, I want to be alone. I can feel pain. It won't kill me."

"Fine Greta, be like that."

However sudden the Whacker's conversion may seem, we're all traveling the spiritual road lightly, but not without baggage. At this particular juncture, our souls do not concern us much. We three wise men are *presently* more interested in our stomachs. It's not surprising that human appetites, diverse in variety and degree, are the foremost cause of trials and tribulations.

It's better not to eat heavy. I warn myself off the temptations on the buffet. *Maintain discipline. I need every advantage playing against Gaffer in today's handball tournament and I don't feel too terrific. Please let me kick his ass; I couldn't stand being humiliated by that competitive cutthroat, no matter how much I like him* is a silent prayer of sorts.

Mon Capitan entertains us with monologues about various insane escape attempts that earned the camp the celebrated title

Camp Walkaway. Knowing the present group makes the past heroes creditable. The least plausible thing going is what and how much Gaffer is eating. "That smells disgusting; why would you eat that?"

"Because," he shovels in more, "I need energy, high protein, carbs and all the power it provides to kick your ass."

"Seems to me you'll be sluggish."

"Leave me alone. I'm concentrating."

"That only means your head's in the trough."

I leave the table and make tracks to get outside. *It's too damn close inside, always inside. That's why people go to Florida, or the Bahamas, or Mexico. Am I crazy? I can't go past the gate.*

Trapped in cruel stark whiteness, I resemble the dull trees, burdened with the dearth brought on by winter. The difference is they have it in them to plead to the sun, lost in the barren sky. Never again will I reflect dazzling light. There is no relief from that miserable truth. My gaze returns to earth where hundreds of boots, treading this way, have pounded out the crystal life of fallen snowflakes. When brilliance is destroyed, all that's left is mud.

I raise my head and cry out to the icy void, "This is enslavement!" An involuntary reflection of a concentration camp and the isolation and desperation of every man, woman, and child denied their rights scar my soul. The idea of life sickens me when each step I take brings me no closer to home.

At the post office, I reach for doncha's fragrant letter, not believing it's really there. I hesitate, aching with desire powerful enough to destroy me. *This letter is her messenger,* my mind encourages, *go on take it. Nothing from doncha can hurt you. Yes, I know. But it's not the type of nearness I want. I need her. I need her. I need her.* Sobbing, I crush her scent to my chest. Backing into a dark corner, I devour her words, until my sense of living returns.

Bernard, my love, I am waiting. I will never leave you. You made me angry, leaving me; you shouldn't be away from me. If you feel you've committed a crime that necessitates imprisonment, you're entirely wrong.

Think of all the great and amazing things you've done. If you need to be hard on yourself, be harder on yourself for the ways that you have gone wrong and that you are able to change. Still, try not to do yourself in over it. Consider, for instance, not smoking. Once you've conquered that monumental feat, take on another ....even if it is a few lifetimes from now.

Laughing, I begin to relax - not an easy task for me to master straight - and without doncha. I never suspected I could be so fragile. My sanity and peace of mind restored, I finish the tender portion of the letter. Returning to the dorm, I am peaceful knowing that I'm loved, unconditionally.

Whacky, busy ironing and humming, is in a peaceful frame of mind, too. Burning incense reminds him of Church and keeps him close to his Savior. I get an unexpected, "Sorry about throwing that shoe last night....that wasn't nice of me. I'm beggin' you, Doc, sleep on your side or somethin'. You and the Gaffer raise the roof snorin'. That and the thunderin' farts comin' down on me makes my brain hurt."

"It just so happens that when I sleep on my back my airways get physiologically and partially obstructed. In the future, I promise to try to sleep on my side. If I slip up, throw socks, not shoes. I, too, am delicate."

"Can you go through that again? Never mind, you know what you mean and I'll catch on to the rest in class. You'll excuse me for sayin' it, but I'm not gettin' mad about your other drawback anymore."

The truth is, Lerner, you rarely own your faults...what do you mean? I'm my most stringent critic. Other people seeing that major addiction issues ruined my life would be too much to bear. Well, so what, some of my best buddies may say, who doesn't have heartbreaks over addiction? I can never say so what....when it comes to me.

"Doc, because I loves ya, the Whacker will keep you organized."

My new woman...I wouldn't dare say that one out loud. I couldn't relay so condescending a thought to doncha, either. Housework overwhelmed

139

her… and she sprayed my lit cigarettes with water from a spray bottle she used like ammunition. What a temper! With a good housekeeper we lived happily… I don't want to remember how my life was before. Every time I go there, my Jewish guilt gets me in a suspiciously Catholic way. I'll have to drag around a cross to remind myself that for a Jew I can beat anyone at the mea culpa game. I miss my life with her. The bad times only seem good. Everything was wonderful, even when it wasn't perfect. Passion smoothed the rough spots. I always knew in my heart that she would never leave me.

To be helpful, I attempt to put the ironed clothes away. Whacky insists on doing it himself. "You're a good friend, Whacky. I'm going to lie down and take a load off."

"I'm gonna relax, too. Then, I'm gonna watch the playoffs… and then I gotta check up on tomorrow's Christmas dinner. My turkeys better do me proud and all the rest of the stuff or I'll have to kick some ass in the kitchen…and I haven't studied yet." Whacky's yawns are cavernous. "That's why I need my beauty sleep. I also got sucked in by Irish to show tonight's movie. *It's A Wonderful Life* makes me cry like a sissy girl every time I see it. You guys think 'cause I'm big, I ain't sensitive like. Don't be mentionin' that to anyone."

"I'm as silent as the grave…your secrets are safe with me." I fall into a weightless sleep until Whacky shakes me. "Lazy bones, get up; you don't wanna miss your game with Gaffer."

Chapter Twenty-Seven
Tournaments

"What the fuck do you think you're doin'? Get lost! You're in *my* chair!"

"*You* get lost," the camper engrossed in the NFL game throws back. Nobody owns chairs in the Rec Room." Whacky yanks the trespasser eye level and uses a somewhat parental tone. "Don't be speakin' to me that way or you won't be havin' my good dinner tonight." He swipes the card from the seat. *Whacky sits here...beware where you put your stupid ass*. He shoves the card in the trespasser's face. "Can't you read English good?"

The camper scrambles from sight.

"When I don't sleep proper I'm such a grouch. Want a comfortable chair, Doc? These guys don't know how to read; they need to be schooled."

"No thanks. I'll walk around for awhile and see what everyone else is up to."

Two attempts to beat Picasso by chess opponents have failed. Pulling his goatee keeps Picasso alert. "Hang Daddy-O. John's up next. He's an all right straight-up kinda guy for a hack, but alas, it's dullsville playin' anyone so square. By the way, I saw Gaffer havin' a powwow with your man Charles. What's up with that?"

"Can't say I know."

"I'll make it like lickety-split with John. Your scene with the Gaffer should be very entertaining."

I write down a chess opening and hand it to John on the sly.

Opening Chess Gambit:

1) Queen's Pawn to d4
2) King's Pawn to e3
3) Queen's Bishop to c3
4) King's Bishop to d3

"Really?" John looks doubtful, "I can do that?"

"Go for it. Picasso loves a challenge."

On our way over to the handball court, I find-out Nothin
But Trouble and Seagull made Gaffer a favorite. Gaffer has been
bragging he's going to destroy me.

"You didn't bet against me, did you, Whacky?"

"That would be the worst day of my life. The trophy for the
holiday competition is gonna be an eye sore in our room, one way
or another. Tell me, Doc, what should a guy like me do when I live
with guys like youse two?"

"Be like the Swiss. Stay neutral. I know you really wanted to
bet on me."

"Gaffer said the same thing. See what I mean."

To ascertain the truth, I look in Whacky's eyes.

"I'm one hundred percent for you and I'm one hundred
percent for Gaffer."

"You should have been a diplomat."

Four regulation-sized handball courts, courtesy of the
previously occupying Air Force, are at our disposal. An observation
area sits over the top of the entrance to each court. You can feel the
excitement in the anticipated question - Doc or the Gaffer – which
competitive megalomaniac will win the tournament?

Gaffer struts onto the court like a matador, only he smells
like the bull. Charles follows behind retrieving the layers Gaffer
sheds. The revelation is Gaffer in a bright red nylon running
suit. Not having made enough of a scene, my opponent stretches
flamboyantly, reminding me of the hippo ballerinas in *Disney's
Fantasia*. I can't resist telling him what a clown he is. Suppressing
an urge to laugh, I also can't help liking him for his antics.
Nevertheless, I pull a straight face and buckle down to get in a
fighting mood.

It's true that Gaffer played hockey in college and I've been told he's ruthless on the ice. On the other hand, that was years ago before he hung up his skates for his adventures in South America. He's overweight, smokes, and he counts while the other person workouts....he's lazy and he eats like a pig. I should beat the pants off him, if he doesn't drive me crazy with his poorly executed dialects.

We volley for serve. I win.

"Good shot, hombre, you got me. You're versatile and you've got some stunning moves but you limp like an old geezer when you *think* no one is watching."

Backing me deep into the corner, Gaffer knocks me off my feet with a startling bout of flatulence.

"Foul!"

"No way, Jose. I was just getting in position for the next shot."

The referee calls back "No foul."

The bookie is the ref. This will be a long game.

I hit another one that Gaffer can't answer.

By the end of the first round, I'm ahead 20-18.

Gaffer begins the next round firing one to the other side of the court; a great opportunity to shuffle his heavy ham hocks into my path.

"Foul!"

"Bullshit! I was trying to get in position for the next shot."

"Ah so, Quack-o. Forgot to practice your backhand, loommate."

"I think you need to change clothes."

"I don't give a shit what you think! What did you mumble? Go on, I dare you, say it again."

I fire several perfectly placed shots to the opposite half of the court. Gaffer answers them, leaving a trail of gas behind.

"You're incomprehensible when you attempt to speak English; it's no wonder you mimic other languages, amigo. The reason you won the second game is because I couldn't breathe. The score, I might add, was 24 to 22. Even with all your cheating you barely won."

"Fuck you, you poor loser." He gestures pompously for Charles to bring him water. Meanwhile, I'm choking on unremitting stench.

The final match. I look up to the full observation area.

"Hey, amigo, everyone is here to see you lose. You jump around like a jumping bean, but alas, you do not hit the ball. Senor, I promise you will fall flat on your face like a tortilla."

"Hey, Nimrod, quit speaking like you fell head-first from the Tower of Babel."

"Better than falling on my ass."

"The place needs fumigating because of you. As nauseated as I am from your cesspool crap scent, I've managed to hold my own." No sooner said I drop my defense. Gaffer's purple face alarms me. I drop to the floor next to him. "Are you all right, Pal? You fucking lowlife! Stop farting before you kill us!" Charles runs over, with a towel tied around his nose and his mouth, and helps me to my feet.

The spectators are coughing and choking, sick with the stink. Gas in a container will burst forth if there's a hole in the container, changing potential energy into kinetic energy. Huevos Rancheros expansile gas fills every nook and cranny of the entire court.

"You see, man, you've met your match." Gaffer gloats.

"It's not you; it's what's in you that beat me."

Sickened from contaminated air, I run outside. Collapsing on the bench, I put my head between my legs to keep from vomiting. My friends, laughing like lunatics, are unconvincing in their efforts to console me. "Where's Gaffer?" I moan.

Mon Capitan stops laughing. "He's still inside. Damn, that's hard to believe. He's must be immune to his own pong. That stink bomb had better not give me back my runnin' suit. He best throw that tangy thing in the woods and let the bears eat it."

"Speaking of woods," I can't help but laugh, "I was riding in the woods behind a horse that prolapsed his rectum and dumped all over on my leg. I thought that was bad until I opened a gunshot wound through the colon. That made me sicker than almost anything I ever smelled, until today. My friends, Gaffer farts are the crown jewels of rancid, the Hope Diamond of gross. Gaffer could easily make the United States Olympic flatus crystallization team. We should change his name from Gaffer to Gasser."

Everything is funny…until it gets uproarious. Fully dressed in his original layers, Gaffer shuffles out the door, his thighs rubbing together, he takes mincing steps. Going nowhere fast, he stops and waves. Instinctively, his other hand goes for his butt. Holding onto the seat of his pants, he hobbles away.

"How full do you think the Gaffer's underwear is with fecal waste, allowing for the quantity and quality of methane gas preceding it?"

Whacky shivers. "That's a scary thought…I'm not goin' there."

Settling down in the Rec Center, Whacky returns to his lounge chair, Zee and Einstein are back at the bridge tournament beating all competitors, and Picasso retires a last attempt to displace him as chess champion. Charles, sad as the day is long, approaches me.

"The Gaffer did me a huge kindness and arranged things so I could live in the honor dorm with Little Lee and Irish. He didn't tell me he was playing against you in the handball tournament, Doc. I asked him if there was anything I could do for him in return…. and you know the rest."

The villainous Gasser, fresh as a daisy, enters to a loud volley of boos. "Thank you, thank you," he cries out to his adoring fans, bowing to the left, bowing to right. "I haven't had this much recognition since I was busted at the airport with the goods."

"Incidentally," Irish informs him, "we had to open the windows in the court to let out the appalling gas before the next match and now it's freezing in there. Please try to limit your bean intake for the remainder of the tournament."

"Of course, Irish, I wouldn't dream of misbehaving." The Gaffer puts his arm around my shoulder and leans on me. "I had to do it in my own special way. I couldn't pass up the opportunity. And you know, that I know, that I would have beaten you anyway."

"I accept your apology, and Gaffer, that was a very nice thing you did for Charles. Thanks."

A light Christmassy snow is falling. We sing carols on the way to dinner. To make it more festive twenty of us sit together enjoying dinner at a gentleman's Christmas banquet. Whacky and his kitchen magic crew conjured up another out-and-out feast. Gaffer, over-excited claims, "If they let me out for Saturday night I'd stay here for the rest of my life." We get a kick out of that having a fabulous time ourselves, especially with all the sports events.

On Christmas Eve and Christmas Day campers are allowed to make calls all day.

doncha volunteers to come up North after I tell her how dejected I feel without her. "I suggest you wait; it's below zero; that's an eighty degree difference between here and Miami." I say no, but I don't mean it. There is a monster called jealousy in me. I take advantage of the fact that doncha always means yes. She doesn't relate to the concept of *no*. She'll ask *what exactly do you mean when you say no?* It's not part of her mind set. Being partial to the affirmative, she is easy on me. Phone conversations in the joint aren't always a kiss in the dark.

Singing carols, we head over to watch *It's a Wonderful Life*. Four hundred campers happily relax in vintage chairs, munching popcorn. The campers' argument over butter or canola became so intense that the Warden left the decision to us. We now pay ten cents with canola oil and twelve cents with butter. We'd argue over anything…keeps us on our toes.

When a familiar voice in the dark, pants, "You're going to do what with that big hard hammer?" Whacker stops the film. "Does anyone want to shanghai their girly asses out of here before I get annoyed mad? I ain't no party poop or nothin' but what the fuck do you wanna go and ruin my best movie for? Datin'…. what kind of hullabaloo is that in the joint?"

Even though it's not a chick flick, all the softies cry as the story ends. It tempers places in our tough guy hearts that are receptive. Where there is receptivity, redemption is always a possibility.

Chapter Twenty-Eight
The Demise of Doctor Death

"Rocky, is that you? I barely recognize you." With the early light streaming through the window framing Rocky's gothic head, he looks like a reverend monk straight out of a stained glass window from a medieval cathedral.

"It's Christmas, Jew boy. I went to mass early......and alone." Rocky looks down at his hands folded in his lap and shakes his head. "Christmas without my family...what's Christmas without family?" He wipes away a solitary tear. "I prayed Judge Assbern would choke to death on his Christmas pudding or on his Chanukah latkes. I really don't give a damn which one he chokes on, as long as he croaks. But that wouldn't be painful enough."

As the prophet of doom continues mentally murdering Assbern, I envision an alternate icon – a godfather is the exchange. Rocky wears gangster pinstripes and a fedora. Substantial diamonds pay homage to his sausage fingers soliciting benediction. Communion transubstantiated into pizza with fifty-dollar bill toppings makes the godfather of pies-in-the-sky, raking in the dough, ecstatic.

"What are you thinkin' about, Doc? You look strange."

My vision evaporates. "You should talk. Actually, I was thinking of you."

"Me?" He touches my forehead. "Are *you* okay, Doc?"

"I was thinking you need to make a few changes. It would be good for your head." My eyes unintentionally glance in the literal direction.

"I like my head the way it is, thank you."

"What are you checking for, nothing is growing. Your head is still full of holes."

"Speaking of holes, I would like to have taken a ball-peen hammer to Assbern, before he was a judge, when he was an attorney."

"Take it easy, pal. Judges are nothing more than Klannish attorneys dressed up in black robes and silk stockings…"

"I can see his blood all over the concrete running into his fancy swimming pool. I get a rush when I envision that… yeah, a huge gush of happiness."

I offer him a cigarette. "Put the ice pick away. You need to change…"

"I'll change my name, after I kill Assbern."

Whacky points to the door. "Do some judges for me while you're at it."

"See you later, Doc, and Happy Chanukah, and a Merry Christmas to you, Whacky and Gaffer." Rocky shuffles out the door and Whacky sighs. "That guy is depressin' comin' in here talkin' creepy like that when we're tryin' to sleep."

"Whacky, it's Christmas."

"So what are you lookin' at me like that for, Doc? What are you tellin' me… you tellin' me to be like Christ?"

"I didn't say a word."

"You're right. I should be good and stuff. I got good friends. I'm lucky, right?"

"Virtue is its own reward."

"Give me a for example."

"If you're willing, you'll have plenty of occasions to be…"
"What? Christian?"

Whacky is ready to hear profound words of wisdom. I don't want to recite the gospel in bite-sized clichés from my missing in action past, trapped inside me in explicit scar tissue. "You will have plenty of opportunities to be a hero." An epiphany; these words are as true in the present as they were when I said them to the residents before any number of surgeries.

"I know it's painful. It's painful for me too. I'm different lately. It's kind of weird. I'm all sensitive like."

Gaffer sits up and lights a cigarette. "What are you turning into? Rainbow will love this."

"Scram, Gaffer. It's not that. It's somethin' stupid."

"Like having dainty tea sandwiches with the girls in the music room. How do you take your tea with sour puss lemon or titty milk instead of cream?"

Whacker moans. "Shut up with that. It's worse."

Gaffer stops laughing.

"I don't think about seriously fuckin' guys up anymore. Not really, even when I talk the talk."

"Don't tell anyone that. You'll ruin your reputation. I'm outta here... see you homos later." Gaffer kisses us on the cheek. "Tootaloo, Sweeties."

After Whacky and I have breakfast and a long conversation, we're not as tender and we're not as tough. I spoke of the Hospital. Whacky revealed suppressed grief about his lost scholarship and disappointing his parents, taking the wrong road. Transformation is gruesome business but the options are undesirable.

"That wasn't easy puttin' it out there like that, layin' it on the line. Maybe I am turnin' into a fag." Whacky drums his fingers on the table.

"Gays are fantastic."

"Come on, Doc, you know I ain't a gay blade."

"You're impeccable in everything you do. So are gay men. I respect gay men. They seem to have the best of both worlds... well almost. They've got a lot of class, you have to admit that."

"They fuck up, too."

"Who doesn't?"

The fire of purification, without consent, but not without assistance, is efficient. It takes awareness and diligence to eliminate the unwanted side of ourselves. We have to be on it all the time. Memories don't necessarily imprison us. If we are willing, our histories can set us free.

"Because we aren't the men we use to be, we have to reinvent ourselves. We have to create new lives from the remains of what is praiseworthy from our pasts."

"Doc, tell me the truth, you really think I have the kind of values we talked about…that I could be a hero?"

"Absolutely!"

"I'm a long way from perfect."

"You'll have plenty of opportunities to do the right thing."

"I like to do the right thing."

"I've noticed that."

"Have a beer and like chill out." Picasso hands Whacky and I extra cold ones, the way we like them. We join the party going on behind the scenes at the Rec Center. Taking a long slug from our beers, Whacky and I burp at the same time, confirming we speak the same language, on many levels.

"Doc, ain't this a nice joint, after all." Whacky leans on my shoulder. "Hey Irish, what's up? You don't look so good."

"If I don't stay on top of this stuff the men won't have any games or equipment left. There are men here who would walk off with the whole kit and caboodle."

"No kidding! Have a beer on me. Relax. It's Christmas."

"Irish, have a beer with us and stop obsessing."

"Thanks for the offer but I'm afraid to drink; I started belching after breakfast and I haven't stopped."

After examining Irish, I ask him "How long have you had gallbladder disease?"

Lifting himself onto his elbows, he chokes back tears. "I won't go to Dr. D. He'll kill me."

Shakey whispers in my ear. "He's scared."

"I admit it, Doc, I'm scared. We watched from this window the day they put our dead friend Rabbit in the back of the FPC pickup truck. Shakey, tell the Doc what that murderer did to poor Rabbit."

"Rabbit had his middle finger extended in a farewell gesture, meant for Dr. D. That asshole withheld Rabbit's insulin when Rabbit had his tooth pulled. That did it...that killed him. It was the scariest thing we ever saw, Rabbit carted off like that."

"I'm sure it was."

After listening to them reminisce about their lost friend I give Irish advice that he agrees to follow. However, sentimental Irish decides his medical problem is not going to interfere with his Christmas.

"A true Christmas is never just somewhere else." I speak into the microphone placed in my hand. "Let's raise our glasses to the Whacker, our Jesus Christ Superstar of the kitchen. Whacky, we thank you most graciously for this fabulous feast. We know you put your heart into it; that's where your inspiration comes from and that's why you feed us so well. Here's to our good friend and great chef, Whacker!"

"I'm just trying to be a good Christian." Whacky blushes as he takes his bows.

I was in the audience when Baryshnikov, after performing *The Prodigal Son,* received the same intense admiration Whacker receives today, applauded in the same way.

"Thanks that was nice." Whacky glows with pride, overwhelmed when they don't stop, he cries out, "Irish is gonna present the champions with tournament awards. Don't applaud to the end. This way youse don't have to put your forks down while eatin' your dessert. Irish, my man, take over. Thanks, gentleman... you must have liked your dinner, a lot."

Before Irish speaks, I whisper in his ear. "You should have stayed in bed."

"I'm fine." He wipes sweat from his brow.

"I'm right behind you, if you need me."

Irish has a hard time keeping a straight face. "Handball has been the most contested sport in the tournament. Doc says, as far as he's concerned, it stinks. Through all the games one man, and one man only, stands out like horse manure in a perfume store. His wild style, his use of foul and foreign languages, on top of his not too terribly amicable professional style has made Gaffer the new FPC handball champion."

By the time Gaffer, lit up like a Christmas tree with bright smiles, runs up to the podium to accept his trophy, Irish is in a cold sweat throwing up bile. Without a stethoscope, I listen for high-pitched bowel sounds. "I feel tenderness in his right upper quadrant. His pulse is faint." Whacky picks Irish up and carries him out of the room and Gaffer yells "What are you going to do, Doc!"

"If anyone happens to have a shank on him, I could take out Irish's gallbladder right now."

Time passes slowly waiting to hear news from the infirmary. Having dismissed Irish, mostly as too serious, is demoralizing for the men, now that he might be lost to them. What is shoddier is the possibility that a man who lived among them could die without the recognition he deserved.

Whacky barrels in. "What are you all lookin' like that for? I took care of it. It was just like the Doc was talkin' through me. I was brain surgeon confident like, smart as a whip. Everything Doc told me to say, I said like Doc would say it. Dr. D showed up with the Chaplain in a piece of shit car. You can always tell them alcoholic's cars; they're filthy and fucked up. Then, the damn asshole fell off the moat. You should have heard him cryin', "Oh my hip. I think I broke my fuckin' hip." Whacky makes us laugh, sounding just like the good doctor. "Oh my poor dainty hip, ouch, that hurts, you mother fuckers."

John injects. "It wasn't easy getting Dr. D inside the infirmary; that's what took so long. Then, the Chaplain had to be hauled out of the backseat of the car so he wouldn't freeze to death. Whacky carried him in over his shoulder like a sack of potatoes."

"More like a sack of shit."

Arriving at the infirmary, the Warden's special request, I find Irish and Dr. Death exactly as Whacky and John described to me on our way over. When I inform the Warden I have a license to practice in Minnesota, he gives me permission to pick up where I left off somewhere else in time.

"Irish needs fluid. The NG tube is drawing bilious peat green sewage moss. Give me two eighteen-gauge CVP lines. I need another eighteen-gauge IV for his peripheral vein and a bottle of Ringer's lactate." I draw a CBC, electrolytes, liver enzymes, and a coagulation profile, cross-matched and typed, in case Irish needs a transfusion. "Monitor his blood pressure and pulse every ten minutes." I direct a nurse's aide not accustomed to taking orders from a prisoner, even one who knows what he's doing.

"Now that Irish is stable, let's take a look at Dr. D. I can tell you right off the bat, his left leg is at least two inches shorter than his right leg. He has a left transverse trochanteric fracture. We need an x-ray. Dr. D is combative. Will someone please restrain him." Whacky slams Dr. D down on the gurney. "Now we're going to place a *very* large catheter in your penis, Dr. D," gets a round of applause.

By the time the ambulance team arrives both patients are stable.

"Don't stand there, John. Get the car. Doc's going into surgery."

"Don't mind if I do, Warden."

Recovery is similar to lead transformed into gold. Is it alchemy? Magic? Science? All of the above? I couldn't say, but when it happens, I love it!

The men drift off to their rooms confident that Irish is safe and Dr. D is not on campus. They feel better for having people that they can count on around them. I turn out the lights thinking how profoundly altered we all have become in a short time.

"Good job, Whacky. Good night and thank you."

"Call me Doctor Whacky, Doc. I want to hear how it sounds and feel how it feels to have that much respect."

"Good night, Doctor Whacky."

"Good night, Doc. That felt good, but I bet it feels better for you, being the real thing and all."

"Good night, Gaffer, and congratulations on kicking my ass in the tournament. You definitely know how to get things done. Charles is grateful to you for getting him bunked in the honor dorm and so am I."

"Good night, Doctors." Gaffer sighs. "I believe what you said, Doc, about a true Christmas...that it's never just somewhere else."

"You've taken well directed evolutionary steps, Gasser of the Pen. Rest assured that you won't be a stinker forever. Even in that, you're not alone. Remember, some of the best saints ever were sinners."

"Very comforting, Doc. I'll sleep better knowing my halo is glowing in the dark."

Chapter Twenty-Nine
The Day after the Night Before

Not only have Christmas Eve and Christmas day passed, the same is true of the medical assault that followed. Never knowing when the next person will need me, or when the next crisis will happen, I indulge myself and take the opportunity to sleep in.

Rainbow, feather duster in hand, waltzes in singing jazzy lines in a confidant soprano. "Oh!" She acts coy, knowing perfectly well she was going to find me in bed.

"Baby, you've had a long night and I didn't even get a piece of it. Heard you didn't come home until after three. Bad boy. Bet you weren't at the hospital all that time. Where did you go after? Tell me the truth. I'll know if you're lying."

"You could be somebody's wife." I interrupt her third degree. When I focus on her costume, I change my mind. Pelvic gyrations jingle bells on Rainbow's rendition of a French Maid/Santa Claus costume.

"No way. Not me; I'm not the wifely type. Charles is the wifely type. He brought you this breakfast. Doc, honey, stop inhaling your food. You'll make yourself ill. Now that you brought first class health care to FPC, you may think it doesn't matter. Do you know what this means after all everyone's been through?"

"I do know, Rainbow. You have no idea." I chug two large glasses of freshly squeezed orange juice. "Bad medicine turns my stomach sour."

"Could have something to do with how fast you eat, honey."

Pulling dirty clothes out from under the bed, she blows off some steam. "Peeuee! What are you doing with your shorts?!"

"I wear them inside out to save you work."

"Don't be doing me any favors. I need to soak these in extra hot sudsy water…twice. Men are so nasty….pissin' on toilet seats, makin' messes all over the place.."

I'm happy to see her smiling on her return.

"I saw Charles in the laundry room. You should have seen the way he looked so sweet when he told me that Irish would be back in a few days. I'm thinking he and Irish might just be an item."

I shake my head no.

"That's too bad." The jingle bells jangle. "If you don't mind me saying so, I want to be there when *you* come out of the closet, honey. I'll settle for your fine ass coming out of the shower. Ooops!" She clasps her hand over her mouth. "You know what?" She frowns.

"What?"

"I shouldn't speak to you that way. Because of my absolute respect for you, I'm going to modify my behavior. I've been very naughty." She hangs her head. "And look at this costume I'm wearing. It's so…" She looks up and giggles. "It's sooo cute."

"Just be yourself, Rainbow."

After breakfast and a decent amount of sleep, I feel like a champion. Everywhere I go I'm met with a barrage of praise. At the Rec center, I'm patted on the back. I'm hugged. Everyone shakes my hand. Whacky comes in and receives a lion's portion of praise as well. The Gaffer, not to be outdone, jumps up the table. "Hmm. Hmm. Hmm. You guys are gonna be blown away by this and it just happened. A low life redneck yelled at Willie, 'Willie *boy, when you're done washin' my dishes, I want you to be like a good nigger and come over to my dorm and blow me.'*

"What?"

"No shit, what a pig."

"Two humongous black arms came through the hole in the wall and the bastard bigot disappeared. Just like that." Gaffer snaps his fingers. "Just like that the redneck was a goner.... disappeared into the car wash head first."

"Wow!"

"What happened next?"

"It was a no-nothin' struggle." Whacky's stance is contemptuous. "By the time we got back there the asshole was already bleedin' buckets and cryin' like a sissy. I said listen up you ugly piece of southern fried chicken shit; you slipped in the water and fell and cut your ugly puss up and that's what happened, unless you wanna become a *real* accident prone son-of-a-bitch."

Gaffer reminds us "If Willie got into a fight, for whatever reason, he would be sent back behind the wall for his last three years. We saved his ass. Willie was about to kill that hillbilly harlot pimp."

"You guys are the best. If I'm ever in the trenches, I'd want you two right there with me."

Gaffer and Whacker halos grow bright bowing to a round of applause. Gaffer gets what we all want – approval.

Picasso, the only one to speak to me when I come in for the staff meeting, doesn't even say hello and no one pays attention when I try to tell them the story about Willie.

"You know, Daddy-O, you're like insane. How do you expect me to teach English with Zee the zombie sleepwalker? I'm ready to storm the Bastille and look at him; he needs crazy glue to keep his eyes open."

doncha told me about some astrological configuration, possibly a full moon, or maybe Mercury is retro something. I marvel over everyone's unpredictable behavior and go to work on sleeping beauty. "Zee, from now on you need to sleep during the night, never during the day. Sleep is more beneficial that way."

Einstein irrupts. "I have come up with a plan to take our school, which we'll call the *School of Survivability with Hard Knocks,* on the road and disseminate our upbeat philosophy across the country, traveling exclusively by train."

"Good title. Let's talk about that later." I pull out a chair for him to sit in. "We need to remain in the present and work on the GED program and…."

Einstein ignores me. He's on a roll. "We'll call our foundation the Church of Higher Education. I bet there's a lot of money available to support foundations. Ha, ha. We could set up tents in each town. You remember the movie *Elmer Gantry;* that's how he did it. I would love to come out in front of *my people* and write tasty morsels of delicious wisdom on a blackboard as I speak them out - it's more dramatic that way. We'll teach only what is heartfelt. I can see myself standing there in a glorious white robe with tiny gold stars appliquéd on it. As my robe flows in the breeze, I'll embrace my people with my arms wide open, I'll cry out to them…oh my people. All of them," he giggles, "will be cheering, cheering for the SSWHK." Einstein falls back into his seat, breathless.

"Crazy, man, I'm diggin' your scene." Picasso easily vibrates on Einstein's frequency. "We can teach Kerouac and Hunter Thompson and Ferlinghetti and other genuine stuff."

I cut them off. "I'll let you guys know when you know what's realistic, at least for the program we should be working on now. Take one S out of the SS acronym for School of Survivability with Hard Knocks so you don't sound like Nazis."

Picasso sneers. "We can't do anything unless it's Doc's way. It's Doc's way or the highway. Doc's philosophy is like win or let none of us come back alive. We play according to Doc's rules or…" Picasso scratches his head. "We can dig that, too. I'm thinkin' right after we blow this pop stand we'll do Einstein's gig. We'll do Doc's gig now and Einstein's gig later. Fair enough?"

"Now you've got the right idea. Remain focused and everything will be groovy."

"I've got copies of the first *Joint IQ* for you to look at." Charles passes out copies of his creation like new papas hand out cigars. "The *IQ* includes all the pertinent camp news and gossip."

"Congratulations." We shake his hand.

While the staff and students read Charlie's creation, I head over to the Warden's office to give him a hot off the press copy of the *Joint IQ* and to discover what he wants to see me about *this time*.

"What's this?" the Warden glances at our rag. "I'll check this out later. He hands me a folder. I want you to interview new applicants for the position of camp doctor. Dr. D is no longer an employee of this institution. That's all I have to say on that subject or any other work related issues. The rest of the day is a holiday. Relax and take it easy. Thanks for a job well done, Doc."

Relax and take it easy. What a joke. This place gets as much action as Cook County Hospital.

On my return to the library, I find the men huddled together, groaning. Einstein informs me "We just found out that Whitey took off. He was about to be schlepped around for diesel therapy because he wouldn't rat on the other guys busted in his case. I hate the unpredictably and total irrationality of the system. It turns my stomach earthbound, as in earthworm. Whitey would have *legally* been out of here next week. Pulling this on him kills me."

Gaffer, the eyes and ears of the camp, adds, "I happen to know Whitey owns some *real* real estate in Central America. His wife divorced him and his children have turned against him…essentially a no lose situation to get out of town, and Chief helped him."

Chief corrects him. "The Nation helped him. Whitey took off from the Nation's secret passage from the back road, after we spray-painted the FPC pickup truck white. We looked out for him all night."

The atmosphere is paranoiac. The dorm is eerily calm right up to four in the morning when the fire alarm goes off. *Get your asses outside for line up! Get the fuck outside!* The loudspeakers blast until we're all freezing outdoors.

Chiller runs up the stairs onto the makeshift podium with a bullhorn in hand. "I want to know where Bob White is!"

"He's not your type Chiller."

"Go back to bed and take Buttfuckaroo with you."

"Watch it smart asses!"

Laughter, lewd gestures, and hundreds of flipped fingers rejoin.

"If anybody sees, or has seen Bob White, *please* contact administration. There could be a reward in it for you."

"Get on your knees for someone else."

"Stick your money where the sun don't shine."

Chiller runs inside. Eight hundred shivering campers do the same.

The getaway truck turned up in Éclair, Wisconsin. Picasso receives a coded postcard from Whitey inferring he and his stash are living on top of the world.

On my afternoon rounds, I make the art studio my last stop. Looking over Picasso's shoulder, at his latest masterpiece, I ask him, "Do you know anything about the production of fake passports?"

"You know, Doc, I was hip to Whitey's situation. He had a ruthless prosecutor who was into nothin' better than his own ambition. When men take that attitude, we have to protect our own. Otherwise, the world we live in will eat us alive. Besides all anyone really needs to be cool on the outside are a passport, a credit card, and a little W.A.M. You dig?"

"Wam?"

"Walking around money. I whip the stuff together in no time. Let's leave it at that… unless you're in need, my man."

I leave it at that.

Chapter Thirty
New Arrivals and Rocky's Revival

From Christmas Eve through New Year's Day, skeleton crews of hacks occasionally mope around campus. It doesn't matter that the camp is understaffed; the initial talk about heading south that Whitey's success stimulated didn't really motivate anyone else to take off. Even a reprieve from camp labor doesn't mean a thing. The entire Department of Education, to include the students, driven like Furies, challenged beyond the expected in preparation for the GED and other studies, have had a paradigm shift.

Since I laid down the no-bullshit law, after several bouts of arm wrestling, everything is straightforward. The once upon a time *I'm going for a cigarette* and not coming back is past tense. In my subtle way, I made troublemakers feel like shit-heels, if they behaved like shit-heads.

Einstein slips out of our meeting of the minds to retrieve news hot off the computer. Huffing and puffing from running up the stairs, he's in a hurry to catch his breath. He can barely wait to say, "Jaime Escobar of the Escobar South American drug cartel family will be a guest here, any minute. The G got *him*...they never get the big-timers; they're in South America. Tommy Latoya, a member of the infamous Latoya family, is on the bus with him. Tommy's family runs bordellos. I'm going to pick his brain. I bet that lucky so-and-so has seen a thing or two."

After two thousand miles of diesel therapy, the prisoners are dumped out of the bus like garbage and released from their cuffs and leg irons by an asshole spitting tobacco. Jaime Escobar and Tommy Latoya rise to our welcoming cheers. Standing tall, they wave iron stressed arms. "Delighted to be here. Thank you for having us." After the ordeal of crushing chains, putrid body odor, and incredible urges to piss and shit, that were rarely satisfied, Buckaroo hissing obscenities at them doesn't faze them. Charismatic, they emanate gentility and warmth like the sunshine of their native countries; although they're so parched from dehydration they can barely speak.

The evening becomes cozier. Irish has returned from the hospital, purring like a kitten. "I'm still living! I'm actually glad to be back here. It's almost like coming home!" Meeting the Duke, as Tommy Latoya has already been dubbed, and Jaime, Irish in a fit of emotion exclaims, "You wouldn't have known me if Doc hadn't saved my life. I'm indebted to him forever." Irish drops to his knees before me. When his hands come together in a prayer motif the action is translated by our new arrivals into "Doc is a Godfather?"

Pulling Irish to his feet, I whisper, "Walk back to the dorm with me. You need to rest. You're extremely animated tonight and *you're* not accustomed to that." Because I'm physician of record, Irish heeds my advice.

A godfather/neurosurgeon/educator would be a peculiarly oxymoronic combination. Holding court is not my thing. With me, it's less pomp and more circumstance, reminiscent of office visits where the physician was father confessor, counselor, and seer into the soul type of healer all rolled into one, and then looked down your throat.

Enroute to the dorm, Irish pleads, "Doc, if there is anything I can do for you, any way at all I can pay you back, it's yours. I owe you my life."

"Then save my ass and tutor the guys that are having trouble grasping math concepts" is all I need to say. Irish is off and running. "We could use finance as a medium. The guys will pay attention to anything that has to do with money."

Rocky takes a seat, lights a cigarette, and curls into a seated fetal position. "Doc, you like it here, don't you?" Rocky speaks from his inverted posture. "You don't fool me. I happen to know you're a really sensitive guy. I can't even imagine what could get so fucked up to make a talent like you end up in a place like this... other than we live in a drop a dime society. You don't belong here any more than I do. Damn, you were an amazing neurosurgeon!"

"I am a neurosurgeon; they didn't take away my medical degree."

"It would be a miracle if they didn't make it useless. I know that you and doncha could party; everyone in the city knew that. They were at the same parties. That's nothing. There's not a corrupt bone in your body. In fact, you have the reputation of being a soft touch. The good news is you're tough, and you're a bossy deep fucker, like a Dago."

"I recognize the value in that. Would you mind telling me what you've been up to in the library?"

"Schlmo and Jake, the whiny pharmacists that you bunked with when you first got here, had Charles write their sentencing judge a plea for rockmunis. You know that term don't you, Jew boy. Have some rockmunis means have some pity."

"If judges had rockmunis most of the guys in this place wouldn't be here."

"Good point. Whatever happens, those cry babies are short timers. They'll be out of here in six months, tops, and one in a halfway house. Boom, that's it. It's a done deal for them. The tiny one said that it would be incredibly difficult on his mother and dog to be without him. The tall one suffers from separation anxiety..."

"He's terrified that his wife will leave him."

"That's not unreasonable, but this one really kills me. They can't imagine how the members of their temple will be able to qualify for a minion on Friday nights and holidays without their holy tushes. This is what those two wrote to the judge. The joke is they're guilty. Charles put all this snivel in legal terms for them to file. After reading Charles' brief I asked him what the fuck he wanted to waste his time for."

"Don't be hard on Charles, Rocky. He's only trying to help."

"Those two whiners are going to do hard time waiting for a positive reply from the court. That's what happens around here and in all the joints all over the country. Poor dumb schmucks schlep their fed-up asses around because some Shylock attorney conned them out of their last dime promising them a shot at parole. You know, Doc, you're the one who told me to live here and now and not make myself crazy putting my life on hold until I'm on the outside, right?"

"If we don't dedicate ourselves to doing something constructive, the mess we're in will poison us."

"Bear with me; I'm just learning. I gave those guys the same advice you gave me. Be useful. Think of someone other than yourselves for a change and you won't be so fucking pitiful. Can you imagine *me* telling them that?"

"Good for you. You've turned your head around."

"To tell you the truth, you saved my soul. I was going straight to hell the way I was carrying on. Headed for no good every day of my life from the first day all my troubles began. All I had to do was leave the pity pot behind. I'm not God so I don't know, maybe He listens to assholes. He didn't listen to me, but then, nobody likes a whiner."

Several men have gathered to listen to the defrocked attorney take on his natural role - giver of good advice.

"Some of you are aware that a post conviction attorney does nothing more than what Charles does, if they even do that much. Only, attorneys don't think about anything when their dicks are in someone's mouth. What's in place is a system designed to suck you dry *while* they're getting blown. So forget about early retirement. Make good use of your time, my friends, or time will make bad use of you."

There's an attentive silence before Mon Capitan pipes-in, "Let me tell ya all, I'm tired of foolish dreams. I've survived enough of them to know they're nothin' but an appallin' waste of time, energy, and money that I might as well have flushed down the toilet instead of wastin' it on bullshitin' lawyers. Bring on the truth. What can't destroy me, Nietzsche said, will make me stronger. Look at me I'm in great shape."

Rainbow comes in in her kimono. "Darlings, did you see the new guys? I'm stating for the record that my new main squeeze is going to be the Duke. What a dreamboat. I'm going to be dedicated to him, at least, for the rest of our time together here. Do you think he'll want me to look after him right away or should I give him a little time to settle-in and notice me on his own?"

"There is one little hitch."

"What Gaffer? What?"

"The Duke's family runs a bunch of whorehouses. It's unlikely he'll bite when he's use to a harem of *women* to choose from."

"Yo, Rainbow, use your time more constructive like." Whacker turns his face to the wall. Rainbow continues prattling until Whacky yells, "Jesus, bitch, don't ya' take a hint when I'm bein' nice and patient. Now get outta here."

"Good night and have delicious dreams, my sweeties. As for you, Whacky McDougal, you must learn to treat a lady like a lady and stop being so brutish. Brute! At least you finally got my sexual category correct, even if you were being rude."

"You shouldn't wear women's clothes and perfume. It drives me crazy until I see your face." Whacky puts his pillow over his head.

"We'll there's definite possibilities in that confession. Goodnight, my darlings." Rainbow tiptoes away.

I spend most of the night tossing and turning, dreaming of Rocky's head. Instead of implants there are tiny keys emerging from his head. *What does any of this stuff mean? I don't want to be tormented when I'm asleep.* I have to hold back or dive into the darkest night of my soul and I fear the descent would be endless.

Where is my justice? Rocky should help me. If anyone can, it's Rocky. I want to know what these dreams mean...or do I? I'll have to go along with Gaffer's interest in dream symbolism to figure it all out, before I drive myself crazy obsessing.

Chapter Thirty-One
New Year's Eve

"I'm bummed out! This sucks! I want the kicks I had in past New Years when we partied hearty. I'm sick of everything existing only inside my head. I want it real!" Shakey puts an end to private reveries and listening to the snow crunch. "Enduring arctic freeze was not part of my holidays spent in Jamaica smoking foot long dubbies all day and all night long. Those were *the* days, my friends. If only we could go back in time and hang out in Negril together. What a blast from the past that would be. Scoring the best weed. Making love all day. Lying about in hammocks. Fishing... swimming....fucking..."

"You lose your grip and then you slip, no different than you did before." Mon Capitan catches Shakey as he's about to fall. "You've got to quit thinkin' like that boy. We just had a hell of a good time with all the tournament events."

Gaffer sighs. "Smoking dope on a beach... I would gladly die and be acquainted with heaven, if only I could smoke dope and fuck my brains out for the rest of my days. Back to reality. I can't wait to see what the Whacker has up his sleeve. He's been bragging that he can get us high, without dope. Talking about addicts, Whacky's big-time. He's a food show junkie. Illustrates how susceptible we *all* are. Did you ever see him imitate Julia Child? That's his idea of funny. His idea of *getting clean* is trading in a history with the mob for a future with a kitchen. Diving into an expandable culinary budget is all the rush he needs. If he goes to work in a posh hotel in Jamaica when his contract here is up, I'll be right behind him. I swear to God."

To sidestep irritating Mon Capitan, again, Shakey whispers, "Do you think it's possible that the Whacker made Alice B. Toklas brownies?"

Picasso can't stop licking his fingers. "Take it from an old pot head, these brownies are a confectioner-junkie's dream. Whacky, my friend, you're fabulous; and I'm tellin' ya, your Beef Wellington would have made the Duke of Wellington proud. Happy and Merry New Year, bro!"

"Your welcome, Mr. P, that makes me feel good. My Beef Wellington would have made Winston Churchill proud, too. Even if it is an imitation, it's a damn good one. Beef Wellington was his favorite dish."

Picasso raises his glass. "You're all cool cats and none of you are pussies. Stuffing another brownie is his face, the crumbs lodge in his goatee but he doesn't notice....he's mesmerized. We all are.

"Killer food and gorgeous guys and music...yes, yes, yes, I smuggled in music." Rainbow mambos in shaking her maracas, dressed like Carmen Miranda, the Chiquita Banana Girl from a late 1940's movie. *"I'm Chiquita Banana and come to say we're going to have a party and I'm here to stay. So get off your asses and play, play, play."* A few minutes watching Rainbow is all that it takes for Jaime and the Duke to kick things up a notch. "Do you wanna dance" can be heard all over the room, from the gays and the straight guys. Gaffer, not to be outdone, comes in with a rag mop on his head. Lipstick nearly covers his face and he has grapefruits as breasts. "Come on, Doc, dance with me."

"Ask Picasso to dance, gorgeous. My dance card is filled."

"He stopped dancing when they quit doing the fish."

"Just don't kiss me goodnight."

"Picasso, this type of dancing should be up your alley. It's as dirty as beatnik slinky."

"Maybe, but it's not as cool." He protests as we drag him up to dance with us. We're having a fabulous time, why shouldn't he.

Shakey's finally happy, dancing for all he's worth. Where are we? Jamaica? Brazil? Columbia? We can't help but to have fun, we're wild and crazy guys. Can't take that away from us; we'll always have a good time, it's a character thing....we want to be happy!

Chapter Thirty-Two
Doc Takes a Stand

"The purpose of this conference is to discuss the new students enrolled for the new semester. The files, like other government documents, *meant* to be impressive, are at least out of the ordinary. Rather than judging the information as negative, let's say it's encouraging."

"You're giving us the heebeegeebees, Doc." Picasso winces. "Give it to us straight."

"A total of forty-two of the applicants for the GED program never came close to finishing high school. Broadly speaking, most of them were on the street committing crimes for at least eight years before incarceration. Their records communicate strange tales of descent. Limited reading skills but broadminded financial schemes..."

"You expect us do deal with dummies and sleaze balls?" Zee voices his one eye open point of view. "They'll never read what I like to read. I'm not into this."

Picasso pounds the table. "These men are criminals."

"Be grateful you have something in common because you'll have to work from there. How do they look?" I ask Einstein on his return from the auditorium. Friend or foe?"

"Whacky is out there, so I wouldn't agonize over them kicking our arrogant asses. Chiller is out there, too."

I face a crowd of perspective students to tell them about the proposed curriculum. "At least a high school diploma and the opportunity to attend a university will now be a matter of choice."

The smart alecks *ooo* and *aaah*.

Easily enraged, Chiller's tarnished battle cry precedes him as he charges the stage. "They're morons and they're ingrates and you and the Warden are bleeding heart fucking liberals."

"The part of *your* anatomy that bleeds is your hemorrhoids, and they're not limited to your frontal lobe. Take it easy with that baton."

"What? What are you saying?" Chiller sputters.

Returning my attention to the audience I notice they're smiling, or smirking. "Let me define my terms, my friends. The expectation that you will study and do well is taken for granted. It is in the realm of possibility to become reasonably well educated, which is no small accomplishment. This is a rare opportunity. If you take us up on it, you will become acquainted with *how* to think. Thinking is different than that noise you hear between your ears."

"I thought that was the ocean."

When the more rowdy campers settle down I let them know I'm serious. "Lose the cynicism and gain an education. It doesn't matter if you want to call our team of scholars Professor or not…."

"That's what we call a piano-player in a Naw Orleans flophouse."

"They probably earned the title. I'm the Professor in this house, where, if we don't get our shit together, we'll be flops. We're offering you a first class education served on a silver platter. The only expense you incur is hard work. You have to earn your way, but you'll do it with an impressive collection of PhD's and other brainiacs. Quite a team. Play ball with us and you'll be champions. Every one of you has what it takes. I've done my research."

"What the fuck does that mean?" The voice of a questioning mind inquires.

"It means you guys have a second chance, but you have to apply yourselves….we can't polish turds."

"I'm signing up for this team. I'm ready to earn my PhD degree right after I get the GED thing done. I'll show you guys the Whacker ain't just another pretty face. I'm smart enough to know we have a whole university thing goin' on here. No way am I missin' out on another opportunity."

"Whacky, we've been waiting for you. Your place is right up front." I point to an open chair.

Chiller hisses, "There'll be tests. You'll have to pass!"

Whacky snorts. "You're a real genius to have figured that one out. Not coming prepared for class, you fail."

The new school is not without trials and tribulations.

Greco, a diehard individualist, storms into my office. "This Einstein character tells me," he indicates Einstein coming in behind him with a jerk of his head, "that it was the Egyptians or Babylonians that had somethin' to do with inventin' numbers as we know them. Maybe they did, maybe they didn't, so what. I've been doin' numbers for most of my life and I'm tellin' ya it don't matter who invented them, it's how they add up that counts. You got me? That fraction diddlyshit makes no sense at all. A buck twenty-five is still one buck and twenty-five cents exactly and not one hundred and twenty-five percent of one hundred and twenty-five, or somethin' like that. Sayin' it like that sounds dumb to me. Nobody talks like that."

Not the best man to discuss money in fractions or any other form, I pat him on the back. "You do the books for Unicore and I heard you're damn good at it. You should have little difficulty catching on to mathematical concepts. Don't let this glitch throw you."

"Doc, I'm a man two times over; do I *really* gotta relive this stuff? Am I a punk kid?"

"You've got to play by the rules set for the game. I know you like Irish. Both of you worked with numbers, that's part of the reason you're here. I'll see if I can get him on board to tutor you. I would like for you to have your own personal tutor every inch of the way."

"A personal tutor… that sounds classy."

"You always say you're a dinosaur. The way I look at it, you're a smart dinosaur, like the Troodon. Although we can't really measure a dinosaur's intelligence, a large brain in a compact body build for speed is how I see you … and that's how the Troodon functioned, or so they say."

"Chiller will have my ass kicked outta here if I don't pass the GED again. A Troodon is smart and fast. Sounds like a bigshot dinosaur, like a Godfather. You got to be smart and fast to be a Godfather."

"You also need a bullet proof vest."

"It's impossible to educate a Brontosaurus Rex" is Irish's reaction to my scheme.

"How about the promise you made me when your ass was on the line? I don't like to bring it up…"

"I humbly submit. My apologies, Doc."

"You and Greco are equally compulsive personalities…this could be a psychological breakthrough of immense portions for both of you."

"Don't pat yourself on the back too soon, Doc."

Irish, in time, states emphatically, "I'm impressed with Greco's philosophies; they're predicated on loyalty."

Greco, for his part, has taken Irish on as a role model. "I want to be a gentleman, like Irish. He's got class."

"I thought you wanted to be a Godfather, Greco.."

"Doc, what's the matter with you. That was before I found out how smart I am."

Picasso is back to being breezy. "We're puttin' out truly commendable mind expanding trippy shit. I'm diggin' it. You're not pissed are you, Doc, that I gave you a hard time about teachin' anything other than my art gig. I'm not half as flexible as Whacky." Picasso tilts back in my office chair and drops a handful of my gummy bears in his mouth, one by one.

Whacky takes the bag away from him. "You better quit eatin' between meals or you'll get as fat as John the Hack. I know a lot more than any of youse realize. Readin' the newspaper every day keeps me on my toes. Besides, I'm good at whatever I do."

I reclaim my gummy bears. "No argument there. The thing that made you sluggish was your previous life style. Without that interference the possibilities are endless."

Jaime, finished teaching his first class, joins us in library. Not a minute later Chiller is tirading, "I'm going to put an end to this conspiracy if it's the last thing I do at FPC. Jaime," he spits out Jaime's name, "isn't even a real American. He can't even pronounce his name like an American. I'm not standing by while *he* infiltrates *my* department. I'm reporting this to my people in Washington, immediately."

"What's buggin' him? Man he's uptight!" Picasso strokes his goatee.

"He's nuts." Whacky loops his finger around his ear. "He's fuckin' coo-coo."

The grapevine needs a few short hours before the Warden muzzles his son-in-law. Merely a shadow of his former self, the mad dog has sworn vows of silence to avoid an offensive transfer. The Warden does not want *anyone* interfering with his pet project, and Jaime with his impressive education, is a major contributor.

Greco is all smiles. "Now that the shoe is the other foot, let that creep Chiller see how he likes being threatened. He'll be out of here before me, I'll bet my credentials on it. This would be quite the place without him spoilin' everything you people are doin' to improve it."

"Personally, I can't resist tempting the jerk to break his word. Here he comes…my big chance." Everyone stops talking. Chiller stands there, glaring at us, beggin' for it. "It's a new year, Chiller, so make a resolution never to speak again and stick to it or tell us what you're up to."

He flips me the bird and takes off again, but he'll be back. He always comes back. I must do something about that.

"See that," Picasso nudges me, "he wants to continue communicating with you. I think that's sweet."

"I'm not going to allow him to setback or spoil my course of action."

"You talk like this GED project is as weighty as brain surgery."

"I've undertaken to graduate these men. They're my responsibility. I've seen their faces."

"Doc, whatever Chiller is up to, he hasn't got a chance against you."

"That's right."

"Good. I like to see that twinkle in your eye, Docster."

Chapter Thirty-Three
News about doncha

Today's preoccupation is The Super Bowl. Kick back and relax. No sweat. Not exactly. On the edge of their seats, male banshees wail at the losing team, "You guys play like pussies." "That guy runs like he has a load of spunk in his pants." "Fucker's you stink."

This is the public side of male passion. Private unexpressed thoughts concern love, sex, and the loss of feminine charisma in our daily lives. In the world of macho, pain and hurt are words associated with sports. A contained deeply interior emotion is not as readily expressed as get the lead out of your pants or go fuck yourself, asshole.

My roommates and I are interrupted in the middle of a post *I'm the authority on football debate*. Rainbow, emoting like a drag queen, barges in with Charles in tow. "Sweethearts, I was with my most recent adorable conquests, Jaime and Duke the Dream. They tell me absolutely everything. And I do mean everything." Whacky points to the door with his middle finger. Unfazed, Rainbow leans against the door on the hallway side and continues, "Jaime, my sweetest boy, confided in *me* that *his* wife moved up here."

I wish it were doncha. No, she couldn't bear the cold. It's just that I know she's left me. The noose around the neck that erases tomorrow and obliterates my peace of mind just got tighter.

Charles whispers "Get to the point."

Rainbow stops twisting her scarf and she stops cooing. "I heard because there's a marathon in town, a very pretty redhead couldn't find a decent place to stay. The one single place with a room, and this is *not* a room with a view, was the YWCA. You *know that* was a last resort.

"So what?" Whacky looks to the Gaffer and me and pleads, "I don't get it."

"Rumor has it this particular female turned a sparsely furnished cell at the Y into a little Zen-like sanctuary and pronounced unequivocally that she's here to *stay*. John the Hack's friend Carol works at the Y and she told John all about the *little* room."

I light a cigarette and pace.

"This *strawberry blonde*..." Charles glances at me before he continues. "Well, the people over at the Y say she is very unusual. When she arrived she asked the desk attendant to have the porter send up her luggage... and tea... to her suite."

"Charles, what the fuck are you wastin' our time for?"

"Hey, Whacker, speak for yourself. Let Charlie finish. This chick sounds cute and classy. Don't you agree, Doc?"

Not wanting to exasperate Gaffer or annoy Whacky, Charles turns to me. "May I continue?" I nod my head, not completely trusting the stability of my voice. Charles watches me closely. "This lady told Carol, the manager, that a mistake was made because the room didn't have a private bathroom and the linens aren't too good and it wasn't a suite... you know what I mean. She's not the type that stays at the Y. But then she said she has one reason to be here and the rest doesn't matter because she's staying."

Rainbow sighs. "To be close to her love, that's all that she cares about. She put her luggage down in a Y for the man she loves. Love is the only explanation because she has nothing to look forward to five days a week other than freezing and sleeping in a cold lonely bed, sleepless, night and night. I sincerely hope you are worth it. Doc, tell me the truth, are you a good man where women are concerned? Not good the way men are good, but good the way women are good. Would you do this for her; would you give up your life and relocate for her?"

"How the fuck do you know it's her? You never, not even once, seen her and they didn't tell Charles it was...you know."

"Women's intuition, silly." She rolls up her eyes and shakes her head as though Whacky should have known. "She made them promise not to tell. She wants to surprise Doc."

"Yeah, right. Looks like your next letter is gonna be a Dear John, Doc dear. "What can I say, guy."

Rainbow's hands rest on her hips. "Tell the truth, Doc, doncha's unpredictable, isn't she?"

"I can never be certain what she'll do."

"See! That's what I mean."

When everyone else hits the sack, snoring, I would like to do the same. Instead, I spend most of the night escaping possibilities that terrify me. When I finally fall asleep, I dream of doncha in a convent. I follow her through the cloisters to her cell. She opens her brown sackcloth robe at the throat, exposing her neck. Tilting her head and shoulders back, she brings her heart forward like a divine offering. Naked beneath silk, not sackcloth, she turns from me to put on her ballet shoes, hanging from the back of a cloister chair. The heat from her breath, warm and sweet, is in my ear murmuring, "I just wanted to keep you on your toes, Bobby." I am mesmerized. Her voice has the sound of tinkling water in a fountain rippling from its source.

Feeling as though I'm drowning, I wake up in a cold sweat gasping *she's here*.

Not necessarily in touch with dreams or intuition, nor do I adhere to the cult of courtly romance, or understand the mystery of the tarot, or the rewards of astrology, or any of the other arts doncha follows; regardless of my disbelief, I will not deny that I know the dream portends her presence.

Chapter Thirty-Four
Sprucing-Up

Speculation is not my thing but sometimes my mind lives a life of its own. *Wild and free doncha up here; that's unlikely. Wearing a coat makes her claustrophobic. She's better off reading on the beach, sipping iced teas. What would she want with a poor busted-up schmuck like me stuck in Siberia.*

Agony is par for the course. I need to take the edge off so badly I can feel my molecular structure vibrate. Add gossip to the equation and I'm ready for unruly. Everyone has heard 'Don't say I told you, but the Doc's girl may be in town, or she may have given him his walking papers.'

Chiller's cold-blooded line of attack is to corner his natural prey. I resemble the burrowing owl with my eyes, *seemingly,* wide open. As vulnerable as I am right now, Chiller rattles me. "I heard you and your lady love are going to have a nice machine lunch in the visitor's lounge. I bet you'll never see her again."

Pushing him, but not his words, away, I rush over to the post office praying I haven't received a Dear John. A letter with a local postmark is balm to my splintered spirit and my cranky bones. I could tap dance catching the scent of doncha's perfume in the air, remembering the way she looks when she looks at me. I can hear her say *Didn't you receive my message, Bobby? I was mentally communicating with you.* I answer *I did, sweetheart.* I'm ecstatic over my luck. *Deep down I trusted her love. I know that now. Through the intensity of my fear, I also know that if she left me I couldn't bear the pain. I'd spend my life grieving.*

Dearest Love,

I haven't been able to communicate with you for what seems an eternity. Paradise shall not be lost, we will be touching and close every Saturday and Sunday or... I'll drive the get away car and you can bail out. I hated that you left me. I didn't believe you could be so cruel. Alone, I smoke dope and laugh at all the crazy things we did. Alone, I cry, aching for the want of you. Life's a vicious circle that I can no longer tolerate with equanimity.

I'd prefer to live with you as an outlaw.... the punishment of separation is too brutal to endure. Being with you is the reality that moves me. Even if I do hate you for leaving me, it's agonizing living without you. Because I love you, I need to be with you always... wherever you are in time.

doncha

The first person I bump into is Rainbow. "I know, I know, I can tell she's here by looking at you. I think it's absolutely *too* marvelous for words. I can't wait to meet the divine doncha. First, go directly to Juan's and snatch up that coat he held for you, or I'll be grabbing it and having it redesigned for myself. Wait, wait, wait. On your way back, stop at the Barber of Seville's and have your beautiful hair cut...and you need a shave. You look like a bit messy, sexy. Never mind, I'll make an appointment for you. You have to look like the gorgeous neurosurgeon professor that you are for your honey. Women like that."

It's so exciting being bossed around, again. I never knew I liked it so much. It amazes me how anyone could say I'm chauvinistic. An inner voice sets me straight. *You are a chauvinist, you've always been, and you always will be. Leave me alone.* I turn off my liar of a conscience and enter Senor Juan's haberdashery.

Presently, the enigmatic tailor has a uncanny similarity to Salvador Dali, working on a set design. Juan, to give him credit, stops painting to mark up my new wardrobe for alteration. The importance of the event I am about to face is not lost on him or the new campers hanging around waiting for army, which is now camp issue. Assuming he assessed my situation, one of the freshmen sings:

If you want a lover
I'll do anything you ask me to
and if you want another kind of love
I'll wear a mask for you
If you want a partner
Take my hand
Or if you want to strike me down in anger
Here I stand
I'm you man.

Another wise guy cracks, "It amazes me how men forced to live without women will accommodate them in ways they would never have considered before."

"That's because we aren't too bright. My girlfriend told me that men have to lose what we want the most before we value what we have, or had and lost. You know what I mean. She says that's the reason I deteriorated."

"It's the music you listen to that messes you up." His friend tells him and I have to agree. "Leonard Cohen can't hold a candle to Frank Sinatra, but doncha thinks Leonard Cohen's a poet. If she was on a deserted island with anyone, besides me of course, she said it would be him."

I'm your man.
And if you want a boxer,
I'll step into the ring for you..."

"If you do everything a woman wants...what happens when the honeymoon is over."

"doncha believes in forever honeymoons." I can hear her sing and see the way she moves when she does it. *And if you want a doctor, I'll examine every inch of you.*

"Really? How long will that last?"

"Forever, according to her, if I play my cards right. If being in the joint and all that went with it wasn't a deal breaker, I don't what could be."

A beautiful tenor voice publicizes that I have reached The *Barber of Seville*. Rainbow is already in the chair bossing him. "Giovanni, she gives him that exasperated look of hers, one blonde streak is not enough and you know it. And..."

"Rainbow, I'a told you, I'm'a not gonna color your hair, it's nice the way it looks'a now. Now behave like'a nice lady that you are. I gotta do the Doc."

"Doc, do you think I'm lovely? Do I look a little like Farrah Fawcett?"

"More of a combination of her and Michael Jordan."

"I'm sure I like that."

"I'm'a sure too." Now that Rainbow is satisfied, Giovanni chastises me in a heavy Neapolitan accent. "Doc, what's a matter with you...you look like'a junk'a yard dog that got caught in'a rain storm. I'm'a gonna fix it just right and shave that face'a like your sweetheart will'a like'a. In Napoli everyone likes'a to sing'a opera, not like'a America. Why'a Doc, do you think'a all'a the singers come'a from'a my country?"

"Although Wagner and Nazi go hand and hand, Wagner's...."

"The only thing'a those people can'a do'a is'a make'a cars, tanks, and gun's. I'm'a gonna give'a you'a beautiful razor cut'a to be'a proud of like'a Doc should'a have and while'a I a do it'a I'm'a gonna sing'a an aria from'a Donizetti. I'm'a gonna sing'a the Daughter of the Regiment'a."

Reconditioned, relaxed, and remade under the heavenly influence of Giovanni's spellbinding voice, I do not speak or move a muscle until Giovanni breaks the spell to tell me that he has sung ten high C's.

"I feel fortunate to know you, Giovanni. Thank you." I look in the mirror. My haircut is perfect. Exactly what Rainbow in her infinite feminine wisdom ordered. I press a handful of quarters into Giovanni's hands. "That's all I have in my pocket. I'll bring more, later…although your priceless voice could never be compensated with money."

"Don't'a be silly, I'ma glad to do it after how'a you told'a me what'a my daughter should'a do for my grand'a baby. I got'a all your buddies, Whacky, the Gaffer, Charles, Jaime, all'a the guys I gotta do'a today. I'a guess'a all'a the women will'a be in'a the visiting room'a this weekend. So will I'a with'a my'a famila. You got'a somebody'a important comin'?"

"As important as breathing."

Everyone expecting a visitor tomorrow is so revved-up that collectively we could have a heart attack. Even Rocky can't help himself. Licking his lips lasciviously, he boasts, "I do magic with these." He's not the only one acting randy.

"Let's discuss the perfect day with your girlfriend's hand in your pants." Einstein calls the meeting to order. "That would be where the pocket was before making the necessary alterations." He shows as he tells. "This is the design I perfected and I'm passing on my trade secrets to you, my friends. When you're creative anything can happen… you can *get off* many times in one weekend if you cut open your pockets…and then sew them up after visiting is over."

"I take exception to inappropriate behavior." Herbie Applebaum snivels. "After all, my mother will be visiting me." Gaffer pulls Herbie's chair out from under him. "Let someone with meaningful visiting room know-how take your place. Scram! Or I'll inappropriate you with my scissors."

"With the devotion of Penelope, sewing will engage my mind and heart."

Rainbow is all ears. "What are you talking about, Zee? Have one of the girls converted you and not told me about it? Tell me, tell me, please, who is the cheeky wench? I really need to know."

"Take it easy, Rainbow. I was making a literary allusion to Penelope in Homer's *Odyssey*. Penelope sewed and undid her sewing just like Einstein suggested that we do. The difference is she performed the task for twenty years. She did it to keep her suitors at bay while waiting for Odysseus to return home from his travels. None of us are in for that long, thank God, or I'd turn into Sleeping Beauty, and Penelope can fuck whomever, whenever."

Gaffer lights up. "I like when Zee's awake; I get the literary perspective. I've often wondered how many Greeks Penelope was *really* doing while Odysseus was away. Penelope, the pussycat, was playing; don't believe everything you read."

"Let's finish talking about tomorrow, guys. Saturday will be the case out job and Sunday will be the heist. And I'm going to heist it up to the hilt." Einstein performs his idea of an erotic dance. I know a woman who could show him a thing or two.

"Einstein, we loves ya. Thanks for the tip and the show." Our other heads are all we can think about presently. After the rather inspiring meeting, we head back to our rooms to get ready for tomorrow.

"Open the pockets on every pair of pants we own." Whacker takes the iron away from me. "You couldn't press a good crease if your life depended on it, but you cut good, Doc, I'll give you that. I don't want to think about you not lookin' just right when I introduce you to my best girl and my folks."

"What about me?"

"Don't be like that, Gaffer. You already met 'em. Let's face it, you ain't no brain surgeon."

"I have plans. You'll see."

We spend the remainder of the evening anticipating tomorrow: Modeling our improved without pockets pants, flexing muscles, we enact primitive male rituals. "Yes, we're lookin' mighty fine and don't we know it." While Gaffer struts around the room, Whacky razzes me. "It's about time you're lookin' smart. This is the way you should look all the time, Doc." Whacky doesn't like to confront me with my foibles, like the fact that he doesn't regard my shabby as chic. Harping on my faults would imbalance a perfectly harmonious domestic arrangement.

"The last time I wore dress khaki's I was in the United States Army Medical Core. I swore I would never wear a uniform again. Look at me now; even without the silver what do you call em's on my collar we don't look bad. We've lost about ten pounds each in a short period...working out does the trick."

"Did I hear trick?" Rainbow strolls in wearing a shirt studded with orange rhinestones.

"You're blindin' me; you look like a Vegas neon sign."

"Why thank you, Whacky, darling."

Mon Capitan is right behind her, stifling an urge to laugh. His southern good manners *almost* prohibit him from saying, "Rainbow, aren't you a teensy bit worried that you'll be on the next bus out of here to a joint of the opposite persuasion."

"Being around female cats is not purr moi. They'd scratch my eyes out for my wardrobe." She follows us like a kid sister, with painted toenails, to the lounge.

"Einstein, we've come to shake you down for more advice."

"My brilliance and my brilliance's brilliance are at your disposal, gentlemen."

"It's about the visiting room gig; we need to know more, so get *down and dirty*."

Like dogs waiting for that delicious bone, panting with desire, we chew and gnaw every scandalous word. Leaving us breathless, he tells us the other straight up facts. "They call for you as early as nine a.m., *if* your visitor has arrived and checked in. Visitors can't bring anything other than quarters for the machines into the visiting room. Personal belongings are stowed in lockers. Because the women aren't searched, they bring all kinds of goodies and necessities in with them. The hacks would give up afternoon naps for a year to go over the women and do a cavity search. After their stupid hack speech, where they say no heing and sheing, or sheing and heing, or heing and heing - which no one listens to anyways - the game is afoot. I don't want you to be too disappointed so I'm telling you up front, the visiting room is institutional in the extreme. There are tables and chairs and vending machines and that's it, nothing more."

"I can't stand that there aren't any beds. I know someone in the joint in Central America and he said *they* have beds and they use them all the time."

"Sorry, Zee, no such arrangements have been made, at least not here. I, for one, wish they would get up to snuff. The patio, except for those making their own body heat, isn't heated. I guarantee you, it can get hot out there. The best news is most of the time the hacks don't go outside, with the exception of Buckaroo. That bastard would freeze his ass off before he would let us get any. By the way, the patio is the *one* place on the base that's fenced in."

Einstein seems to be reminiscing about the times he wanted to walk off base with his woman and shack up at the closest motel.

"At four o'clock the visiting room officially closes and the guests return to the world from whence they came. Our brothers are asked if they have received anything from the outside before they're let back in. Lie. If you received a new pair of sneakers, wear them in. You can get stuff in by wearing or inserting it inside your body. Buckaroo is the only one to have anyone drop their drawers and spread their cheeks. The creep has smelled fingers. He would do a cavity search in a heartbeat, but he knows ninety percent of the men would take a dump on his hand in a New York second. The good news is you can put your arm around your woman and kiss from time to time. When it's more than a smooch that you're wanting…"

"I want way more than a smooch," echoes around the room.

"The solution is hand signals. A man on duty at the door will give the guys ready for action, with holes in their pockets, the green light. A hand job is a cinch done like that. Well, good luck comrades and good hunting. Remember a bird in the bush is better than one in the hand, or visa versa. Never mind, you know what I mean. Are there any questions?"

Whacky raises his hand. "How do we get what we need, when we need more?"

"There are no official conjugal visits. There are, however, two places to get lucky - the bathroom and the patio."

"It will be difficult to sleep tonight." Zee surprises no one with the declaration, taking into account the amount of stimulating conversation engaged in before going to bed. We generally don't talk about our women; it's too depressing, and not everyone has someone visiting. We don't want to bum them out.

Chapter Thirty-Five
doncha's Debut

Snow blown drifts sloping into curves remind us of women and beds. Shifting clouds are Reubenesque bouncing beauties. That's on the way to breakfast. At breakfast, eggs devoured like breasts are snuggled with sausages dipped into yokes. What doesn't have a sexual connotation when you're obsessed. Kinsey said men think about sex constantly...other researchers say men think about sex once every seven seconds. We're proving Kinsey to be correct.

Waiting to enter the visiting room, Gaffer makes it worse; he hasn't stopped groaning. "This is harder than pulling out when I'm ready to cum. Every time I hear the static from that damn microphone, I get a rush and a hard let down follows. Listen to me, I'm panting like a dog in heat. Who needs *this?*" is dismally answered "We do."

"Although this joint doesn't have that cozy nineteenth century bring your family with you kind of thing going on, that I would like, admit it, if you had the option, any one of you would jump at the opportunity to have your women inside with you." Zee buries his head in his hands. "If I had the chance to be with her like that I swear I'd rarely sleep."

No sooner do I say "I agree" than my name and number are called.

"Come on, Doc, we'll walk you to the dividing line, the place where we can't put our big toe until they call *us,* if they ever do. This separation is one more reminder that we're dickheads."

"I didn't need to hear that; it's fully tattooed on my brain. Stark divisions have a built-in haunting feature."

Painfully aware of my inferior position, I walk over that line that is not just spatial. *Real people with real lives are in the visiting room. Events that everyone takes for granted, like being with your woman...don't go there, Lerner, knock it off; you're dressed up, cleaned up, pressed up, and you're perfectly presentable. Just get past Buckfuckaroo without losing it. Remember, you are impervious to amateur tormenters.* I repeat the words until they are firmly rooted in my mind. Stepping into a world of embraces, intimate conversations, and noisy children, I freeze.

I'm captivated. A mesh of veil, a black web, covers her face and traps sunlight in the waves of her glorious hair. I ache to tangle my hands beneath that web and set us free. A fierce tremble seizes my body. doncha's embrace will suck me bloodless and leave me to perish bone dry. She leads me to an out of the way corner. With volcanic emotion of the erotic type, doncha absorbs me in a voluptuous embrace before she becomes furtive. "Let me slide onto your lap, Bobby." The woman means it.

Sighing, I can say nothing more than "doncha."

Mouthwatering and smooth like golden syrup are the words, "I'm naked beneath this dress." I believe her.

I believe she has set up a decoy to keep everyone away; I trust my Mata Hari's powers. My hand seeks the small of her back. "I want to take you to bed." Whispering my desires, she calls me "My love." Every look tells me "You are perfect." Kissing my face, her hands travel and learn that I have no pockets. "Ooh la la. I do like that." The sound of her voice tickles my ears. Deliberating which way she wants to get at me first, my hand fills with her hair. Absorbed with the indentation at the back of her neck, long and slender, my fingers work her like a musical instrument. A *spy in the house of love,* with a cape covering her, relaxes into the chair.

"Show me how pleased you are that I'm here."

My voice saddens. "I'll be here for a long time."

"Then I'll be here a long time." She speaks softly. "There is a very good library in town."

She moans.

She fills me with pleasure.

I'm overcome.

Comforting each other, doncha's tears are mine.

The Gaffer comes in with a lip-smackin' grin pasted on his kisser. "My fiancée is a hypersexual nymphet. I'm such an inspiration to women. The hitch is how to get through copulatory withdrawal. Feel my head, Doc. I'm shivering from sudden and overwhelming deprivation of decreased body heat. "

Whacky interrupts Gaffer. "Hmmm. I'd like to introduce my parents and Kim."

A fine-looking blonde that Whacky boasted looks like Kim Basinger is not an exaggeration. Conceivably, she's the reason he's a study in contrast in the visiting room. Not aggressive or boisterous, I almost can't recognize Whacky as the Whacker.

At the first opportunity, his gentle father takes me aside. "I never knew my son could be serious about academic achievements. God bless you for helping him." Whacky's father sheds a few unconquered tears that inspire me even more to do all I can for my friend. Loving Whacky, we value his potential.

Not too much inhibits the campers' or the visitors' intimacy. Waiting in line to buy sodas, candy or pre-prepared sandwiches, everyone becomes acquainted, joking and laughing. Crying, too, sharing divided lives, the day is relaxed into until a sensation that resembles normalcy settles in. Zee's woman hasn't stop bossing him, in a caring way, and he hasn't stopped smiling. Rainbow swishes in with Jimmy, who woos her with fancy footwork that everyone applauds. His dance, as limber and as graceful as his conversation, wins her heart, which I don't believe he ever lost.

Looks of longing and the question "When and where" travels around the room. The word gets back. We will meet tonight to determine a solution to a pressing problem.

As families, lovers, and friends ready to leave the men they love and care about promises are made for tomorrow. Staying behind, I help with the garbage to gain ten extra minutes. Having doncha close does not erase my fears. I'd be astonished if she'd come back after seeing me diminished in this way.

A hack calls my name.

"I love you, Bernard." She kisses me. The tenderness of it makes me suspicious that that kiss may be the last kiss I ever receive from her; it causes me to panic. *If she turns around it will be an omen that she'll return tomorrow. Please turn around, doncha. Please.*

The hack keeps calling my name.

doncha, please turn around. I need to know now if you're leaving me; it will be easier knowing the truth now, rather than fooling myself.

She *actually* comes back. "See you tomorrow, my love. I can't wait for tomorrow! I love you more than I could ever express and I want you to know I'm happy to be here."

What a woman! I wipe the tears from my face.

Einstein calls rabidly excited men to order. "We are going to review hand signals, the key to getting as much as you can, undisturbed."

We're riveted.

"If you're on patrol at the door leading out to the patio, scratch your ear lobe to indicate the coast is clear. If a hack or the Warden comes near the windows or walks toward the patio door rub your forehead, like this." He demonstrates and we monkeys imitate him. "This signal is important. Stop whatever you are doing, no matter how difficult it may be, and behave like nice little chimps."

"How long do we have to…you know?"

"Four participating couples at a time are covered for sport for one half hour. A list of names and a schedule will be printed and handed out to players. Let's have a little drinky-poo and some nachos and practice."

No one slips up. We practice up to the time we fall asleep, and then who knows. Every gesture counts as though our lives depended upon it. To ward off spontaneous combustion, nothing can go wrong.

Chapter Thirty-Six
Sunday is no Day to Rest

Sunday is sunny and warm. Mother Nature did us an Amazonian favor and forgot she lost her way in the North Pole. Stimulated by compromising weather, Einstein, chomping at the bit, nearly whinnies. "Female visitors of the romantic persuasion are merely a stride away. While waiting at the gate, let's take our heads out of our pants before we go crazy."

Gaffer grabs fistfuls of his hair. "I can't take this!"

"First of all, check to see if you're wearing the pants that have a hole in one or both of your pockets."

"My beau is ambidextrous; naturally I need both my pockets free of material encumbrance."

"If it ain't about women, Rainbow, it ain't worth sayin'." Whacky is so nervous he hasn't stopped cracking his knuckles.

Einstein giggles. "Thank you for sharing with us Rainbow, but I have to agree with Whacky. We'd be more likely to listen to what you have to say if the thing between your legs was what you think it is. In conclusion, check to see if you have cleanup materials in your back pocket. That's it for now. They called our names. Good luck. You studs really want them fillies. Giddy-up. Giddy-up. Go!"

Walking along the corridor, Rainbow belts out, *"You can't always get what you what, but if you try so hard, you just might get what you need…"*

"I'm blind to misdemeanors," John the Hack reports as we come to the point of no return, singing. We're hoping he's blind to sexual felonies.

doncha is dressed for long strides. Her body-fitting black skirt zips to close. It's not zipped, at least not all the way, or she wouldn't walk the way she does. Moreover, she wouldn't look like Sweet Charity, fresh from the streets of Paris, in that beret. A cigarette holder extended from peachy lips is all she needs to complete the image. *I love that woman.*

Pressing her close, I breathe in the fragrance of Calyx. I'm ready to erupt. Molten lava, not contained, is immensely potent. "My gorgeous love…my darling." Desire fills me with rhapsodies. Lusting for assurance, I beg she'll never disentangle.

Our wise and compassionate Warden, aware that the majority of us are built for passion, *appears* oblivious as couples get cozy. To sanctify the Warden's position, Picasso and his beat generation girlfriend distract him with a game of chess. Zee and his mail order bride willingly detain John from his rounds by feeding him tasty but healthy treats, knowing that they will soon have their turn to warm up. As fat as John is, the heat surrounding him, if he took his head out of the feed-bag and noticed, could be hazardous to his health.

The team waiting to play is edgy. Einstein, over-extending his position as umpire, is signaling *full steam ahead* to the guys already in action. I nudge him. "Get a grip on yourself and stop being such a voyeur."

"Passion is contagious, Doctor. That sweet mama sitting on the Gaffer's lap has infected me. The damn sun has been in my eyes; I'm waiting for it to go down. Not Gaffer's dick, the sun."

"Behave yourself. Your woman is pissed off. You're not paying any attention to her. C'mon, it's past time to change shifts and you know it. Signal a whistle stop."

Satisfied couples light cigarettes, suggestive of movies from the Fifties when smoking *symbolized* a complete sexual encounter. In the Sixties, a love-in and dope crowned the day, but that was another place and time. doncha knows more about that than I do.

"Do you want to hear a soft porn story about an ex-camper? Of course you do." I'm listening to Action Jackson, even as doncha leads me away. "Buckaroo caught Jimmy with his hand in Arlene's panties and no one was going to stop them. Buckaroo warning Gennaro to stop only encouraged faster and better friction..." A startling crash brings indoor activities to a standstill.

As inconspicuously as possible under the circumstances, Kim slips out from behind the door of the men's toilet. Whether Whacky was on fire or just blushing the shade of cherries, he comes out behind her stammering, "The damn sink was loose. When I leaned against the dumb thing, it fell off the wall. Now, it's like Niagara Falls. I'm fine," he tells the Warden, racing over to see what happened, "but you should have the water main turned off. Someone might drown."

"I bet they were using the sink as a launching pad." Einstein giggles.

"Whacky's the man." He's called "Upstanding" and "Hard to beat" and not least of all "Hero."

Having an extraordinary day, parting is never sweet. Couples, desperate to remain curled-up in imaginary beds, separate. Watching the woman you love walk out the door would shred inconsolable souls if there weren't so many softening tears.

The blues internalize. Upbeat external rhythms take over around dinner time when anyone that hasn't heard hears the story about Whacky. Presented the Finger Bowl trophy, a donut floating in a bowl of water, he's kidded. "Come on, Whacky, tell us the truth; is it true big guys have small dicks?"

Retorting, "I should have gotten an inner tube and a swimming pool," many plumbing jokes follow.

Chapter Thirty-Seven
Wolfman Takes a Hike

Even though Whacky got the trophy, we all got first prize. Weekends with women have their rewards. The best part of yesterday is with us as we go about today's business. Memory is a convenient tool when you want an instant replay from every vantage point.

Einstein, more frenetic than usual, interrupts a delicious daydream, giggling his nervous giggle. "A new camper coming in on a drug conspiracy rap got eight months. I've checked the local newspapers for jury verdict reporting and plea bargains... I even went back six months and looked in all the informative publications...couldn't locate an article anywhere. Wolfman, ha ha, I should say Narc Man is a mole on a job for the Feds. A full-fledged informant will be living among us."

Mon Capitan bites. "Let's fuck him up."

I stare out of the window contemplating the satisfaction of revenge on a real live G-man. I blow a perfect smoke ring and put my finger through it. *Gotcha*. I open the window and yell out to Chief. "Be a pal and go over to the mess hall and tell Gaffer we need him."

"Something's up?"

"Not if we can help it."

Gaffer comes in winded. His eyes, wide with questions, narrow into mean slits with the answer.

"Government assholes are sleazier than the C."

"C?"

"Criminals, Doc. You don't know squat for being one." Mon Capitan looks mystified. "I don't know how *you* became a member

199

of this exclusive club. I have to say, for our sake, we're glad to have you. Anyways, when I was in that stinking dump in stinking Miami, a mole was on me like white on rice. Pumpin' me about my connections in South America, he tried sucker baitin' me with pretty post prison plans. Who the fuck did he think he was foolin', I can smell G stink a hundred miles away. I fed the degenerate bullshit. Told him the head of the Miami DEA was on the take. Broke me up when he hung himself in his cell. In the end I suppose there were no other options."

"Why not?"

"Guys like that belong on the end of a rope they strung up for someone else doin' a line."

I grasp this type of revenge, in theory.

After some discussion about who would draw in a mole, it's unanimous that Jaime, because of his cartel family, has the only profile that would draw in informants.

Wolfman is a hot topic all week long. "His demeanor is suspiciously ambiguous. Forget the unshaven face and mass quantities of shoulder length hair…"

"Shoulder length is Jacky O, Doc. His do is white boy Rasta."

"Thank you, Rainbow; I stand corrected. Scruffy doesn't work….the manicure is recent. We're going to nail the bastard."

"Drug conspiracy, my ass," Gaffer sputters. "I know the type and he ain't it."

I can't put my finger on what it is about Wolfman that rings a bell. In addition to everything else that doesn't ring true, his striking a familiar chord bothers me.

Jaime joins us and confirms our suspicions. "Wolfman is all over me asking questions about my families operation. He ignores everyone, even when guys are friendly; he's not going to be a happy camper until he has me as his special friend. Must have heard what a great dancer I am. "

The wooly one shows up in my office, smirking. "I thought Chiller was the head of this place. Never mind, it don't matter to me. I want to get my GED thing done while I'm inside."

"It's too late for you to catch-up, Wolfman."

"Why are you doin' me this way? Dumping' on me and castrating my attempts to succeed."

"Give it up."

Five minutes later Chiller kicks up a storm. "Who in the hell do you think you are denying our new student an education? You're an idiot. This is the Department of Education, or am I stupid?"

"Are you also Wolfman's patron saint or do you just like that imbecile."

"That's enough. I know all kinds of things that you don't, Mr. Smarty-pants."

"You're a sly one, Chiller. And your protégé's sly, too."

"Ha. Ha. He's in the program. I personally enrolled him."

"Two rodents with attitude around here are too much for me. Get lost."

The weekend means women in general and doncha in particular sneaks in lox and bagels, which disappear immediately, if not sooner. Our minds are temporally off Wolfman.

Personally, I'm oblivious to everything but doncha's fishnet stockings with the garters peeking out on top.

Everyone is fully concentrated his or her own thing, except Wolfman. The mole rat has no visiting cousin. You can tell he's in disguise because mole rats have very little, if any, hair. All their relations, of the pig variety, spend their lives in darkness, precisely where Wolfman will remain. Narc boy's persistent attempts to corner Jaime are annoying and his investigative efforts may break up a love-fest, but Wolfman uncovers absolutely nothing about

Jaime's family's operation. Wolfman's visiting room encounters are not satisfying.

The following week, in the classroom, Professor Zee increases his testiness. "Mr. Wolfman, referring to the novel *Dr. Jekyll and Mr. Hyde,* would you please tell us why Dr. Jekyll turns into a G-man. I mean a beast man?" Gaffer follows him around for days asking. "Do you dream like a man or a mole?" Picasso hands the Wolfman a canvas when he shows up in the art studio. "I would like you to paint your worst bad trip and then imagine while you sleep that it gets trippier… like an entrapment."

Wolfman receives instructive lessons epitomizing how ineffectual a G-man he truly is. He's an inside joke, but he's not laughing when he storms into my office. "We need to settle something, man to man."

"You mean man to mole, don't you? Actually, I can't figure out if you're going for Neanderthal, wooly beast, or rat man….but I understand the body language."

"Look asshole, you better stay out of my way with your condescending bullshit and that goes for your prick friends, too."

Whacky walks in on the scene. "Mangy mutt, if you don't give me one good excuse why you're givin' the Doc and his friends shit…naw, never mind, they're aren't any good excuses so I'm gonna toilet train you."

"Hockstrap! I see you behind that muff." In that instant that I recognize him, the crazed idiot goes for my throat. On the mark, Whacker goes for the fink, scarcely making it out the door when I yell, "Stop, Whacky! You don't need the aggravation!" Whacky, left with a fistful of hair, is appalled.

"You know that bum?"

"That creep was the federal agent on *my* case. When the judge changed his mind or had it changed for him and sentenced me here instead of a mental hospital, he obviously didn't notify the alphabet boys."

"Shit, Doc, you're full of surprises. How come he didn't know it was you?"

"I guess I don't look the same when I'm not wearing Armani and driving a Maserati, or maybe he forgot all about me after he ruined my life. He's stupid like most of his breed."

"I've got to clean my hands. I touched that mongrel."

Campers are buzzing with the news *Wolfman is missing*. Quizzed to see if any of us know his whereabouts, it turns out that nobody knows *nothin'*. That doesn't stop two predominate theories from circulating. The least intriguing theory is that after I blew Wolfman's cover, he took off with his federal tail between his skinny legs. The favored scenario involves the drug cartel picking up the rat for diving lessons. In diving lesson number one, agent Hockstrap takes a dive from ten thousand feet into shark-infested waters. Lesson number two immediately became redundant. Whacky likes the second version because sharks leave no mess behind. The rest of us just like it.

Life has a way of working out for the best, in the *best of all possible worlds,* when you work at it. Having had that first-class experience, bursting with gratitude...we party.

Chapter Thirty-Eight
The Warden's Brilliant Idea

Lately, the Warden's complaint is the same "Conversations *should* be about intramural softball by now. These heart-numbing ice storms have turned the men into bears. You never know what a bunch of pent-up men, as mean as hungry bears after hibernating, are capable of doing."

"Just seasonal affective disorder," I comment off handedly. The Warden takes off for his constitutional around the camp to stimulate his little grey cells, not getting any assistance from me.

When he comes across Picasso, doing a headstand, Picasso returns to his feet, not happy to have his bliss interrupted. "Spare time is scarce, Warden. I hang in the Rec center to refresh my aching brain cells. Honestly, I needed a breather. You dig what I'm sayin'? Workin' with Doc is mind blowin' exhaustin'. I'm not jivin' around."

"Yes, I know." He answers preoccupied. "Bring this note to Doc, but first tell me what you were doing."

"Stimulating my exhausted mental powers; we're all beat with the exception of Doc. Driven like a battery-operated so-and-so, that man's relentless."

"Exactly."

"Hey, Doctor Frankenstein the Warden sent you a love letter. Each of us with a dilemma places you right smack dab in the middle. Livin' under your rule is too damn bourgeois for me. You're turnin' out to be the straightest cat on the planet. What kind of joint is this, anyways? The whole thing is kooky, if you ask me." Picasso kicks into a mellower tone, a benefit of his yoga practice. "I can't deny I'm diggin' it, too. It makes time fly. Still, Einie's right about you, Doc, you're not one of us. You vibrate on a weird, but not unwelcome frequency. We just can't figure you out sometimes."

"Don't worry about it."

Stomping the remaining snow from his boots, Picasso swats the remaining chill from his bones with his beret. "I can't wait for the day I'm cruisin in the sun, livin' in Miami where there's only one word for snow…like snowbirds that come south for the winter. What miracle of magic is your man Oz cookin' up now that he's groovin' on our department bein' the cat's meow?"

"The Warden's not unreasonable."

"He doesn't have to be with you around. What's reasonable to you is hard labor to most of the dudes around here. We're supposed to be on holiday. Remember, man, this is a Club Fed, as in Club Med. I dig my down time. Standing on my head is fantastic for my complexion. Why don't we teach groovy stuff? Be cool. Contribute to quantum leaps in human intelligence."

"We'll see."

"Don't pacify me.

"I want to know what the Warden wants to see me about. I can't find a clue in this summons."

"Have you been diggin' how he tapped into our exceptional gene pool? The inside people, we campers, we few will be talked about, remembered as the Warden's successful experiment on Doc's Ward. We should, at least, do far-out theater productions."

"I suppose you want to start with *Henry V.*"

"Your drive and the Warden's ambition, what a combination; the possibilities are endless. What bums me is never having time to work on the life I'm going to have after I bug out from this dugout."

Picasso looks out the window. I'm sure he's practicing visualization techniques. "Counterfeiting is bad for your health." I give him a sideways glance, but I don't push advice. Let's continue the work at hand, smarts."

I take my own advice until my stomach demands attention. Charles, always in sync, points to his watch. "Lunch?"

About to face the elements, I bolster myself. "A good hot meal is what I need. I've been working all morning getting poor readers up to task. It takes a lot out of me. The air will be refreshing." Not believing it myself, I suck it up. To keep my mind off my aching body, I telepathically communicate with doncha. "Good God I'm a lucky man." I speak my thoughts as I enter the mess hall, without realizing I spoke at all.

"Shut the fuck up! You're in here like the rest of us assholes." Volleys of insults follow. Charles keeps his head down; with his eyes on me, we finish our meal in silence and headout, not a minute too soon.

"No need to walk." Dark Cloud flags us down from his vehicle. Come aboard." Dark Cloud amazes me; he doesn't wear a coat or hat or gloves. His high cheekbones are bright and polished from the freeze and his sleek black ponytail is shinier than usual from the ice in the air. A beautiful sad specimen of his race. Besides being able to brave the petrifying cold, he's also an able philosopher.

"Is it true," Charles asks through chattering teeth, "that we risk entrapment in a mental Siberia every time we step outdoors? Did you guys ever hear that?"

"Don't lose sleep over it, Charles; there are other things to be concerned about." I answer from behind the scarf covering my face.

"Good advice from one compulsive to another. On our pickup last night, in the north woods field, there was a sweater with your name on it, from doncha. One thing among others left like offerings, along with a pair of ladies panties."

"I happen to know Rainbow made that particular requisition. Any other news?"

"Ashamed to say it, I returned to camp because I got caught smoking dope in the reservation halfway house. The saddest thing is not what happened to me, or to any of us in here for doing dope. The saddest thing is that white race never redeems itself. The character of this country has been cashed-in in unbelievably mercenary ways. I'm thankful for the good people, because negative materialistic values produce more than a fair share of dead souls. Too many selfish jerks are in business making bad laws and living the lives of hypocrites."

"Sorry to interrupt you, but do you think I'm a dead soul, Dark Cloud?"

"Not you, Charlie. You vibrate on a damn good frequency. Every dumb thing done on a low frequency comes to haunt *all* of us eventually, not just its perpetrators. We are never freed from the spirits and we need our medicine men to heal us because we're all suffering from our wounded souls." He pats me on the back. "Well, here we are. Send up a smoke signal when you finish. Doc, you smoke too much. You probably got that from the old black and white movies. Bet you thought it was sexy the way they blew smoke in each other's faces. Did you ever notice how much the smoke blinded them? So awkward and stupid but that didn't prohibit the sharks from selling cigarettes....it's all about sex. Those old movies are great. Let's face it, nothing's perfect; we always have to put up with something. If those movies had all the cigarette smoking edited out, they'd be perfect. Then those sexy scenes would be cool and hot."

"I could give you a platform for your ideas if you have the time to teach philosophy or political science, or film; I'm always looking for inspired educators."

"I need to be outside with the Spirits. Ask doncha what I'm talking about. We've had many conversations in the visiting room. Your woman is an old soul, a free spirit. I do my part in my spare time working with slow readers. It helps me to become more patient. When you finish up with the Warden, have him page me. I'll come back for you. We've got to lookout for you, Doc, and you, too, Charles."

"Doc, Charles, a cup of coffee? Have a sit down. Nice to see you." The Warden circles before he finds direction. "You've done a fantastic job in the Education Department. The morale around you is downright infectious. Ha, ha. You know what I mean. I mean tremendous, and in so many ways. In addition, I have you to thank, Doc, for getting Doc Frank to take over. I can tell you that a man who does his job perfectly in this system and isn't a bully or incompetent is of great value to me."

"I've had very few house calls in the middle of night since Doc Frank came on board." *This is going to be an ordeal when The Warden can't come to the point.*

"Now, *that* pleases me, Doc. However, we have yet another stumbling block. The other day, the social worker/psychologist, who taught the drug education classes, stepped-out in the middle of a class and never came back. "

"I killed a few minutes in what had to be one of Siggy's most uninspired monotonous as rote lectures. Besides having a formidable German lisp, he's an obese grass hut of a man with staggering body odor. He actually drew a picture of a fried egg on the blackboard and stated this is a brain on drugs. The initiated call him the Egg…I don't know if it was because he smelled sulfuric like rotten eggs, or if it was his limited perspective on the subject matter, but I never went back for a second dose. I don't think his leaving is much of a loss. What's on your agenda, Warden?"

"There are at least two months before we'll see a real spring around here. Half the campers are already a *little* restless with eight hours of free time on their hands. Because most of these men are prisoners of the war on drugs, your ability to educate them, in this case about the negative effect chemicals have on the body, would channel their curiosity and keep them from old habits…taught your incomparable way."

"You want me to teach *another* class?"

"You got me thinking about it the other day when you said President Reagan's war on drugs is a war declared on his own country. Let's kick ass one more once, as you would say, with a new program."

Charles and I exchange a disenchanted glance.

"Most of the men used drugs, despite the fact that they are smart. Let's have a drug education and awareness program for men that take the right road when they're straight. Only when they were doing drugs were their lives unnecessarily complicated. You know what to do. What do you say?"

"We're swamped right now." Struck with a flash of brilliance, I complete the thought. "However, if you would approve an Easter and Passover Holiday dinner with our families and significant others, we may well manage to do what you want, too, Warden, dear."

"Well, why not!"

"Not that that's settled, would you mind paging Dark Cloud? We need to return to work and accomplish a few more miracles."

Chapter Thirty-Nine
Conning Gaffer

"Gaffer, you've been reading that page for the past half hour. Has dyslexia permeated your fingers?"

"Is that a trick medical question? For your information, I read for the beauty of the language. Reading literature is different than reading comic books, in case you didn't know."

"In my professional opinion, you might have better results turning the book right side up."

"I discuss literature with doncha, not you. We discuss the gestalt: where the ideas come from and how they evolve within the book and society. For example, take *Don Quixote,*"Professor Gaffer pats the book he's reading, "if you want to start with one of the first modern novels in Western literature..."

"You're not reading Cervantes, you phony. You're reading *Story of O*, glorified pornography and what else, *Hustler?*"

"What's your point?"

"There is a subject on my mind that involves reading, learning and teaching - all three at which you excel."

"Let me guess. Would this have to do with the new drug education classes I heard you got sucker baited into teaching."

"Having ingested and injected every chemical known to man and then some, your vast research on the subject is a valuable resource."

"You're no novice yourself, sweetheart."

"My experience is mainly with opiates... although I have dabbled occasionally in cannabis, cocaine, and popped a Quaalude here and there when the need pressed."

"You mean when your dick pressed against your pants."

"Because I haven't been as far down the rabbit hole as you, my knowledge is not as comprehensive as yours. I thought you might admirably employ your charismatic redeemed junkie self in the service of others."

"I could do that if you are the one that prepares the lessons that will guide me. Doc, are you listening. You need to do the science part."

"Campers will attend classes out of curiosity… and to hear you speak pearls of wisdom, of course. After they're addicted to your charming affability, they're ours forever. If you would allow me, I would help introduce the chemistry and patho-physiology… you just mentioned that didn't you? I wouldn't want to intrude. It's undeniable that *you* have the personality and proclivity to become a world-class addictionologist."

"And a psychiatrist; I'd like to have the best credentials."

"When psychiatrists have office visits, the patient does all the talking. Every now and then the shrink might ask the patient 'How do you feel about that.' Now, I'm asking you, Gaffer, how do you feel about this?"

"Most excellent…*although, quite honestly* I've been contemplating teaching literature in an all women's college. Oh what the heck, I'll do this in the meantime….with a few perks thrown in to keep me happy. However, I'm stating for the record that in my practice I do the talking. The patient listens. I talk. I'm avant-garde. Get it?"

"Got it."

"Good."

Whacky yawns. "You forgot good night." Trying to reconstruct the negotiations that transpired, Whacky is not able to determine if one or both of us were conned. "Turn out the lights, gentlemen." You two tire me out, and I'm in the dark anyways."

In the next few days, Gaffer and I outline a syllabus and teaching plan. Classes are to cover cocaine, amphetamines and methamphetamines, opiates, alcohol, cannabis, short-acting hypnotics, and Valium. We limit the drug selections to those close to home.

The focus will be on: (1) <u>MODE</u> of <u>ACTION</u> (2) <u>SIDE AFFECTS</u> and (3) <u>COMING DOWN</u>.

To complete the task Gaffer is educated in physiological and psychological aspects of drug ingestion. He's a quick study - hot to make his mark and debut as a budding rock star and resident psychiatrist.

Drug Education classes are promoted with a no frills straight-up approach in the Joint IQ. *Living in a drug infested, pharmaceutically habituated society is dangerous. Temptation, for those of us who can resist anything but temptation, is never ending. We pop pills for this, that, and the next thing - mother's little helpers hook you up - diet pills, uppers, downers - black, green, yellow, sky blue pink - whatever, you'll take it. Invented to make you feel better — inventive being the operative word - you take more. Crashing, you go for broke and wonder why, after crashing hundreds of times, your body aches permanently.*

Drugs wreck havoc on all your systems — physical, spiritual, mental and emotional. Someone, somewhere, profits, but that someone is not you. You lose and you lose big time.

Pharmaceutical companies are the financial beneficiaries. We humans are the guinea pigs. Falling for the trap, disguised as a quick fix, adds sizable profits to companies' financial bottom line and ruins us in the bargain, with or without our permission. Ignorance isn't bliss and it's no talisman against incarceration, either. Don't play with meds, unless you want to pay.

I know most of us were busy, before we joined Club Fed, doing chemical research. Thing is, we forgot to take a detached evaluation of what we were doing. We never knew scientifically how the goods work. We just closed our eyes and took our medicine. Now that you have the time, catch up. Do research, even if it is postgraduate research. Be wise; know all that you should know.

We aren't here to evangelize. We would like to fill you in on what chemicals do to you. Eventually you will be able to make a well-informed decision on your own. Knowledge is power. During the course of the new drug education classes you will see a lot of yourself in the activities that various chemicals cause you to exhibit when you abuse them, or should we say yourself, using them. For instance: irresponsible behavior, side effects, and what to look for, if you're foolish enough to fall into the habit again and jones. Once we're out of here, we don't want you to return for a refresher course. Let's get together and learn by talking about it. When you leave FPC, leave with the ability to make an informed decision and do the right thing for yourself. That, at least, should be your goal; or has your taxing research ended without the facts? Think about how good you feel now that you're straight. Evaluate that against how you felt on dope.

Classes begin Tuesday at seven o'clock in the large chapel. Graduate students are welcome. If you have any questions stop by the Department of Education or look up the Gaffer, Doc or Charles in the honor dorm. There is a sign-up sheet in the Education Department, or just show-up! P.S. Bumper stickers are not yet available.

Gaffer bursts into my office, nearly purple (not his best color). "Why the fuck did you let Charles publish an invitation to come and see us in our room. Are you out of your mind? We'll be listening to every druggie in the joint. Just tell me why you added that comment about coming to our room? OUR ROOM!"

"I can't always fit in everyone that needs to see me during the day. Besides, think of the practice *you'll* build overnight."

"Have it your way; you will anyways. My personal reading time is over. I'm going to end up hating living with you. If you weren't pathologically unselfish, you'd really be a selfish asshole. Fuck you, you selfish asshole; you don't give two shits about me or the Whacker."

"Take it easy, Gaffer. You know I love you and the Whacker best. We're like three little peas in a pod."

Chapter Forty
Drug Education

"Today, fellow campers, the new and improved Drug Education class will cover cocaine and amphetamines." Gaffer's voice shakes and his bowels rumble. He didn't expect such an immense turnout and he definitely didn't anticipate being nervous. Someone from the audience calls out, "Every time I thought about coke I had to shit, too. We can smell you down here, Gasser."

In the professional mode, Gaffer responds, "Hebb, a famous neuroscientist, said that neurons that fire together wire together. One of the moving properties of cocaine is that it makes you run for the toilet. There was also, if I remember correctly, the frustration of being hornier-than-hell and unable to do the deed; I hated that. A wallop of paranoia was no fun, either, fixating on cops busting-in, because guess what? My procurement wasn't legal. I didn't pick it up at the neighborhood pharmacy. Although, I bet a lot of you do recall pharmaceutical blow.

Most of us, if you were like me, stayed in the game, totally freaked out and fucked up. So what if we had a leaking nose that drained our sinus cavity out of our head. Do you remember how those rock hard boggers could only be blown out only after warm water softened them up for an hour? Breathing was another big problem, even when my cats weren't sitting on my head…good thing because *that* would have done me in.

Then there were the midget bass drummers that played scars and stripes forever inside my chest on so many occasions I can't believe I'm still on planet Earth. Although, let's face it, we're in a camp. Still, didn't you congratulate yourselves as you out-clawed the bottom dwellers on your inner-Galactic explorations, doing another line? Bleeding knuckles was nothing for us in those days; we were tough; we hung on for another round.

Following one too many gargantuan tokes or hits off a pipe, sounds startle the shit out of you, if there's any left. Your damn TV somehow turned up the volume on its own. What's spookier is that the people inside the box sent out coded messages while stranger characters scared the beejeezus out of us party animals from the other side of the window, and sometimes it was in a high-rise building on the seventeenth floor. Must have been supermen or noisy neighbors with suction cups on their bare feet, because when I finally got the nerve to investigate they weren't wearing shoes or clothes; they were naked.

Any self-regulating person would have reevaluated the situation and asked what the fuck am I doing? Doubting our actions never occurred to us. For us, more was unquestionably better. The gods of coke, take another toke, didn't open our minds enough to take a measured look at reality; we had our heads too far up our asses for that. But, we could eyeball an eightball like nobody's business.

You've been there too? I didn't think I was talking *just* about myself. How about this one? I've known people who sucked-up coke like anteaters and then shot-up the walls inside their own homes to protect native habitat, where a stash was hidden in eighteen different places. Apparently, it seemed a reasonable thing to do at the time. Others I've known grind their teeth until they crack, or pick their skin until a running abscess is explained away as a surgical intervention - a bug needed evacuation. Withdraw your head from your ass before you dig your grave is what I would say today; but that's today.

After doing so much damage, if no one got arrested or beaten up, shuteye or work was still impossible. It was usually five am before anyone knew it was tomorrow, which might have been yesterday, or three days ago.

Your next bright idea, if you were anything like me, was alcohol. To take the edge off I'd drink: bourbon, whiskey, vodka, brandy, beer, wine, perfume; whatever, the flavor didn't matter.

216

In a moment of shear brilliance, a handful of sleeping pills was the chaser to beat all chasers. If not sleeping pills: pain pills, aspirin, Motrin, birth control pills, anything! Only thing missing was a reality suppository.

Even though I didn't show up for work on so many occasions I got canned and forgot my best friend's wedding, I survived being an asshole. Being what I was, or I should say what we all were at that time, making a mess of our lives didn't stop us from our next party. Partying was what is was all about. And, weren't we more desirable for having lost all that disturbing baby fat, despite the hole in our noses and pockets. Hey, coke was more effective than any diet we ever tried and didn't stick to. Thin was in, but Biafra wasn't anywhere near the best look."

The entire room shutters.

"When you use drugs: you lessen your humanity, jeopardize your life, and sometimes as it happens, you lose your liberty. But what difference does that make when you're making new friends? The realization that cocaine pals are not to be trusted follows the natural course and history of the disease. You can stick to the principle that they don't trust you either. Why would they? You diminished your mind, life, and soul, thereby altering your history as a good man. The realization that it doesn't have to be that way brings us to the present and the neuroscientific consequences of drug abuse. Doc will take over now; when he finishes speaking, questions or comments are welcome."

"For those of you that don't know me I'm Bernard Lerner. Mostly, I'm known as Doc. In this lecture series, I'm going to introduce you to *my version* of what Timothy Leary, in the Sixties, called *Every Citizen a Scientist*. In the process, you'll find out all you need to know about neurophysiology. This is an introduction to neurophysiology or Neurophysiology 101.

Let's begin with what I call The Target Syndrome. Starting out from the furthest point of the target's center, repositioning ourselves, we come closer and closer to the bull's-eye, which essentially means we're sliding down the proverbial rabbit hole. In so doing, we become a shell of our former selves. Jobs, family, appreciating sports, reading a great novel or your favorite comic books, the desire to eat a good meal, taking in a movie, things that were once appreciated no longer interest you. As we degenerate, we ultimately wind up alone and desperate. Bull's-eye! You've scored!"

Some say addiction is genetic. Others say it's chemical. My opinion is it really doesn't make a difference when you spend most of your day, seven days a week, procuring drugs. It's difficult to get real and stop romancing the stone if the only one knocking at your door is your dealer, or your pals with habits of their own.

I had my first interaction with the wicked lady during my residency in neurosurgery. Any time seven to ten grams of powdered coke were brought up from the hospital pharmacy, J.H., a colleague of mine, scrubbed. X-rays and heavy lead aprons didn't inhibit him. Cutting is where he drew the line. Running around like a mad hatter and jabbering like a jabberwocky, his explanation for this strange behavior was an over active thyroid. It was frosting his face that was actually responsible. I found him up to his eyeballs in a mountain of pharmaceutical coke. In the split second it took me to indulge, I changed the natural course and history of my life forever.

When you snort, inject, or smoke coke (similar to amphetamine or crystal meth) the Grim Reaper hangs out while you drag race your heart, going from 75 beats per minute up to 160 in 0-3 seconds, tops. You're the culprit who drove over the edge and starved your internal organs of indispensable oxygen. But what did *you* know? That was the *in the dark* you.

If the abnormal rhythm of your heart muscle turned into an arrhythmia, you wouldn't be around to clean up your act. Corpses don't turn around.

Adrenaline causes blood vessels to constrict, reducing blood flow. The brain is the organ moderately protected from this deprivation. The heart, kidneys, liver and intestines, for example, have the deck stacked against them. Constriction causes blood pressure to rise from 120/80, which is normal, to 180/110, dangerously high, high enough to cause muscle cell death, aka a heart attack.

Blood flow to the brain is self-regulating. Something we should all try to achieve. When blood pressure rises, brain flow remains constant, unless the pressure passes the borderline. When the bottom falls out you are set-up for a stroke. Stroke - you know what I mean – you become paralyzed, speaking is complicated, and it's feasible to die of a brain hemorrhage.

Signs and symptoms of a seizure sneak up on you, and not in the same way as that person with the suction cups on their bare feet. This time it's more than paranoia. More like border patrol coming down on you. Dangerously increased blood pressure, abnormal heartbeat, heart attacks, strokes, and seizures are deadly risks when you continually indulge in behavior that takes you to the edge.

Cocaine causes an increased production of adrenaline, exciting billions of nerve fibers to fire in a system of nerves in your brain stem. All sensory fibers to include: taste, smell, hearing, sight, touch and activities such as wakefulness, sex, and eating reside here. When vibe after vibe of impulses hit this amazing system, the works light up like a towering Christmas tree.... but without the proper wiring, watch out! With all that going on you can't help being crazed; acting, more or less, like the rats in the laboratory you still want more. You've lost control. Depending on what you wanted more of affects withdrawal. For instance, cocaine is metabolized faster than opiates; it takes longer to rid the body of smack and it's a lot harder to suffer through a jones.

The good new is that endorphins, a natural substance in brain cells that attaches to the same cell receptors as morphine, produce pleasureful chemicals without our assistance. A natural high is elicited *only* when we don't bombard cells with foreign substances. It takes endorphins time to recover, but they do. When you workout, endorphins kick in. People get addicted to working-out for that very reason. We're all addicted. It's a matter of what we're addicted to: gratification that's good for you, or poison that destroys you.

Let me remind you. Withdrawal symptoms include but are not limited to:

1. Nausea and vomiting: In this type of vomiting you feel as though your esophagus is about to telescope from your mouth.
2. Profuse sweating that has a distinct stench.
3. Diarrhea and Vomiting, often at the same time.
4. Anorexia. Not eating.
5. Shakes and chills are mandatory.
6. Seizures are a possibility.
7. Inability to sleep regardless of how much booze you consume to knock yourself out.
8. Restless twisting and turning.
9. Dangerously elevated blood pressure.
10. Tachycardia or accelerated heart rate.
11. Significant joint pain. Opiates form a salt that precipitates in your tendons and muscles.
12. Air hunger: An overdose of opiates or smack directly affects the respiratory centers in the brain stem, which could result in respiratory arrest. This is not an uncommon way to die from an overdose of opiates. An example is China Cat, or substituting fentanyl for heroin, which has equally devastating consequence, reducing respiration and suppressing the brain stem centers.

If you've had a combination of these symptoms, my friends, you experienced a true jones. No doubt you were attached to the receptacle you barfed in…if you didn't end up in an emergency room. Most people start using again to relieve symptoms. Starting over again is the biggest mistake you'll ever make. Ask Shakey, if you don't believe me. Better still, look in the mirror."

Shakey stands up and gives an affirmative nod. Others stand with him.

"Many of us are thankful to be alive, and rightfully so. The Gaffer will finish the lecture with news on drug testing."

Gaffer stands to a round of applause. "This time I'll talk about pissing, instead of shitting. When you are released from here and go to the halfway house, if that's where you're going, you will be doing a lot of peeing in a bottle - sometimes twice a week but at least twice a month. If they call you in for a random drop, you *must* provide urine, in most cases, within six hours.

The official in charge, watching your back as you urinate, has you initial the label they attach to the bottle, indicating date and time. The sample goes through a chain of custody. They discard most of the samples because testing costs. That's not to suggest you gamble; the odds are against you...and it costs big to lose.

They test urine for cocaine, metabolites, alcohol, opiates, amphetamines, and diazepam, among a number of other drugs available on the street. A specific gravity is done to ensure you're not diluting. They test for the various contaminates used to mix or dilute drugs, like quinine to cut opiates.

No show for a random and they call it positive. Unable to pee, you'll drink water until you can. In general, that means no drugs for at least seventy-two hours and no alcohol for twenty-four hours. Marijuana can stay in your system for months. For those who drink gallons of tea or buy those clean urine kits before you test, your deed is undetected, but you pay the price going to the bathroom every half hour and the tea tastes gross. Soap on your fingertips is promptly detected if they do a specific gravity. The three-day rule prevails with most drugs, other than marijuana. On the other hand, if the Feds test your hair, you're a goner. Hair reflects drugs long after you stop using.

Dirty urine breaks your probation. One of our campers wants to share a story with us. Today is Mon Cher's second day out of solitary. He finally agreed to take a job so they let him out. Mon Cher, please stand up."

Mon Cher is skinny. He's slithery. He's ungrounded and he whines like a tired two-year-old. His nickname is The Taster. His uncle is a federal judge or he wouldn't be in a Club Fed. He told me that when he was in a halfway house he wanted a taste, just a little candy to quiet his sweet tooth… so he lowered a pail with money in it down to his dealer on the street and then he reeled in a taste.

Called in for a random drop, Mon Cher rigged up a primitive Whizzinator, complete with his girlfriend's pee. With his back to the Marshall, he pulled out the tubing, instead of his dick. Trying to compress the Foley catheter drainage bag, located under his armpit, to release the pee, nothing happened. Aggravated, pumping for all he's worth, he breaks the connection and the urine in the Whizzinator bag ruined his new silk shirt. Fucked up as he was, Mon Cher forgot to loosen the device that released the pee into the tubing. That was the glitch. If he was thinking, he would have bought the original Whizzinator, complete with clean pee, a penis, the works."

Everyone in the place cracks up. Mon Cher cranks his arm, demonstrating his technique. He waves all around, sure of his importance.

"He is unable to reconcile to this day why the urine in his Whizzinator was positive, even though his girlfriend, the specimen donor, shared needles with him. I can't stress what a hassle it is if you don't keep clean. Memorize these times (if you're still shuffling the cards and rolling the dice with your life): seventy-two hours, twenty-four hours, and one month for drugs, alcohol, and marijuana, respectively. I see the Warden is among us today and I know he doesn't want any more graduate students working their way through the system. Doc will now answer your questions."

Psycho stands up and points to his head. "Doc, did that bad shit put a Christmas tree in my head?"

"I don't think Psycho's question is funny. I understand him perfectly. He's asking if his brain was irreversibly damaged from drugs and alcohol. The answer is not complicated. In Psycho's case, his neurological status, his nervous system, was impaired before he used drugs. Psycho understands everything that is said but he can't articulate what he wants to say. His condition is not psychological. People with severe verbal apraxias say yep when they want to say more; at the same time, they clearly understand everything said to them. Can a brain freeze in an apraxic form after partying? I don't think so. The brain can degenerate but not in a specific focal area. Psycho happens to be a genius among apraxics. Psycho does not have a Christmas tree in his brain."

Psycho gives the crowd the finger. After they applaud him he smiles and sits down, satisfied. Next up is Fuse. His roommate and constant companion is The Mad Bomber. The Mad Bomber is petite with the face and wit of a troubled child, one that likes to play with fire. Having gone beyond that, he's serving five years on a plea bargain. Fuse is a tall, bearded, under-educated Yankee, who fizzled out of small time drug sales. The Mad Bomber and Fuse have plans to go to Hooters in New York the minute they're free. That's three years away, but they think it's important to have a goal.

"Gaffer talked about guns and knives...stuff cocaine users like to have around when they get high. The Mad Bomber and I were like that. We free-based *a little* more than we sold. One night, shooting off automatic weapons, we decided it was time to get rid of our competition living out in the jungle, too. After we buried a potent explosive in his front yard, we waited in the bushes for him to come home. Smoking one too many batches of coke, we saw those strange men you were talking about watching us. I told the Bomber to lose the stuff. I never told him to detonate the bomb. We woke up in the County Hospital after putting a twenty-foot hole in the guy's front yard, and I lost two fingers."

He waves his hand for all of us to see.

"It took the Bomber several days to wake up and he's never been the same. My question is, if that's what cocaine does to you, why did *we* get arrested and why were we charged with possession and attempted distribution, *plus* handling of explosives?"

Blurting, "You guys must be nuts. That's like saying the devil made me do it." I give Gaffer a knock-it-off look and tell Fuse, "We can discuss that later. The Warden would like to say a few words, now." Gaffer whispers in my ear. "You're an asshole. What's this later?" As we leave the stage, I whisper, "Act professional." Out of ear reach from the Warden, I run my idea by Gaffer. "I think they should design t-shirts with one silver lightening bolt across a black background. They'll have a good logo and it might be an incentive for them to start a demolition business. It would be good for them to have plans for their future, besides going to Hooters. At the very least, they can design t-shirts. They need to sink their teeth into a project."

"Does the Mad Bomber have any teeth?"

"He has a few. In the meantime, you can shrink them; get them on the right track."

The lectures continue on a weekly basis. Before the semester is half over, the auditorium isn't large enough to hold everyone that wants to attend *Alcohol and all its classic symptomatology and central nervous system pathology*.

The Gaffer's description of the Mad Hatter Syndrome of the alcoholic infuriates the Chaplain. Storming out of the lecture, the Chaplain lets his rage loose in the Warden's office. "Doc and Gaffer have too much influence over the prisoners. We're in jeopardy of a prison uprising...predominantly with that subversive lingo-jingo about taking the body but not the soul. You know damn well they have too many people in the large chapel. I'm going to file a formal complaint with the Bureau of Prisons. Mr. Chiller, your own son-in-law, is behind me on this. These men are anarchists."

"And I'm suggesting this lapse in your judgment is an upshot of alcohol." The Warden puts his foot down and shows the Chaplain the door.

Learning has become the newest trip, the highest high. The men have improved their relationships inside and outside by widening their horizons. Discussing drug metabolism, central nervous system transmitters, and disease processes like Wernicke's encephalitis and Korsakoff's syndrome in alcoholics, campers stand in line at the microwave waiting for popcorn to pop and continue while waiting in line for beverages. The subject most often selected, when playing doctor, is degeneration in the hypothalamus leading to memory loss, a shot to equilibrium causing confabulating, essentially lying and thinking that it's true because of a gap in memory.

Having recognized the classic symptoms in the Chaplain, Gaffer plays the role of doctor, while the other campers assume the role of residents and interns, making an on the dot diagnosis. Walking with their heads together, congratulating each other on their skill, the men resemble doctors on staff at a military base, or a mental institution. They scrutinize everyone, and I get all the referrals.

Chapter Forty-One
The Italian Hour

Lamenting winds plague the building as Rocky broods in the doorway. Resembling Frankenstein's friendless monster, he listens to the happy chatter of others cozy in bed for the evening. Gaffer and I haven't stop congratulating each other on our fine performance in today's drug rehab class. Whacky, too, feels ostracized. He finds the drug culture strange, even stranger than the cards he's been around who bet and booze, rob and steal, and then beat the living daylights out of some poor shmuck for exercise.

Rocky's looming shadow lurches forward, startling us. "I didn't know I was scary." An incompetent grin appears on his unhappy face. "On behalf of my associates, I wish to extend an invitation for tomorrow night's Italian Hour, in honor of your contributions to our community."

"Stop with the Godfather routine, we're working on important business."

"Maybe if you shake your family tree hard enough, Gaffer, a Dago might fall to the ground."

"If Italian hour means you're doin' opera, cause I heard you guys do that, how do you get the fat lady with the boomin' voice through camp without anyone noticin'? Houdini's the only Dago who had any real talent, and he's dead. Anyhow, I hate opera. That son of a bitch Mussolini Linguini liked it. So why should I?"

Rainbow stands in the doorway shaking her head and rolling her eyes. "Whacky, dear, Houdini was of Jewish Hungarian-American descent. Have you actually heard any opera in your entire but not altogether *cute* Neanderthal life? Accept the invitation, graciously. I'm Giovanni's piano accompaniment. It will be the first time you and I will be in the music room together."

She ducks out the door. "It's about time you develop a taste for culture....and for me."

"The only Italian hour I attended I kicked the daylights out of a Dago deadbeat for the boys in Vegas. Now, Rainbow, I'm gonna beat the fuck out of you for nothin'." Rainbow runs down the hall, shrieking, "Do anything; just spare my hands. I know I'll love it."

"She'll love it...that's the only reason I ain't doin' it. Now tell me why I should come to the Italians."

"For two excellent reasons: tomorrow night's event cost bucks to cater and we need you to sit-in as sergeant-at-arms. Because you live around here the hacks don't like to mess with you for fear of retribution when you're released."

"I'll do it long as youse keep that female impersonator away from me. What's the other good reason?"

"You're a good guy, Whacky."

Chef Whacky prepared pâté for our pre-opera dinner. It looks like chopped liver to me. Gaffer is of the opinion that it stinks, no matter what it's called. Stuffing his face, he's mumbling, "Pass your liver paste over here, conservative diners." Whacky blocks his reach. "No way. You're not gonna stink up the Music Room fartin'. It ain't right with opera." "C'mon," Gaffer whines. "How often do we get chopped liver?" Whacky walks away grumbling, "I'm goin' alone. Make a pig of yourself...see if I care. I'm not sittin' *anywhere* near you."

Impressed with the presentation of the Italian Hour buffet, Whacky has an even greater respect for his invitation. Every care was taken to make the evening one of refinement, to include fine linens and crystal wine glasses.

Seeing us, Whacky frowns. "The Dagos are puttin' on the Ritz and look at youse two." We try to amuse him singing, *Puttin' on* *the Ritz. If you're blue and you don't know where to go to, why don't you go where fashion sits? Putting on the Ritz...*Gaffer stops performing. The high profile patricians flock-in. "If *they're* the audience the G intended to attract to their hoity-toity Club Feds why didn't the G let us plebs do community service instead?"

"Gaffer, my friend, did you ever know of a government agency that was run intelligently, besides the post office...and they nearly give it away. Look at our Whacker, the sweet little prohibiting Goliath is all content and comfortable now, sipping his wine. With that *I'm going to love opera* grin on his pretty boy face no one would suspect he's playing bouncer. Juan's here and he's not Italian."

After praising Rainbow's couturier, Juan joins us. "I'm surprised to see you gentlemen here."

"Aren't you of Puerto Rican descent, or are you commenting on our not being spit-shined?

"I'm an honoree member. Italian men respect their tailors."

Gaffer graciously offers Juan his coveted cigar. "We're just being honored."

Giovanni tinkles a crystal glass with a fork to get everyone's attention. "I wanna thanka alla my cumpas for makin' such'a bella affair. It warms us'a to feel so much at'a home'a in this'a place. We would'a, with special pleasure, like to thank'a the Doc, and the Gaffer and the Whacker for helpin' him, savin' us'a many'a time when we were'a sicker than dogs. Saluda."

Giovanni's tribute is an aria from *The Daughter of the Regiment.* Excerpts from Puccini, Iliacus, Campobello, and the final piece from Mascagni's *Cavalleria Rusticana* are powerful. Spellbound, without awareness of place, forgetting time, we're transported to a dimension where the soul is tended to and the spirit stretches far and wide.

In the middle of the Mascagni, Buckaroo attempts to enter our sanctuary but he doesn't have a chance. Whacky backs him up. "Look, asshole, we're all bein' cultured in there. Somethin' you'll never understand. Go away, unless you want to know what a mosquito sees when it hits a windshield."

"Are you threatening me?"

"You're not the brightest crayon in the box, are you? Beat it before I get scientific!"

Returning to the dorm at the end of the evening, the Whacker mutters, "I *think* I like opera. That ain't, isn't how it is. I really like opera. Does that mean I'm, you know, cultured?"

"In this life or your next, I would guess that you are destined to become a philanthropist and a patron of the arts, albeit on your own scale, which is no small thing."

"That means I got culture if I'm one of them fillythrops and the Gaffer don't know shit from shinola. Quit laughin' at me, Gasser."

"You're generous to a fault, Whacky. You're loyal, brave, and you cry at opera."

"*Very* true." Gaffer concedes.

"Don't go tellin' anyone about that. Dagos, I mean Italians, think it's okay to… you know…cry… because of the music and all."

Gaffer looks pathetic. After holding it in all night, he nearly explodes, but he doesn't do it in front of us. "Now, all of a sudden, he's got too much culture to fart in front of us."

Whacky's responsiveness to the evening bowls me over. Whacky, too, mulls over how far he has come in a short time. As for the Gaffer, he's chewing over how he can get his hands on the leftover chopped liver for a midnight snack.

Chapter Forty-Two
Ribbi's Arrival and Religious Survival

On Sunday in the visitor's lounge, telling doncha about the Italian Hour, she replies, "Because God or gods and goddesses love art, we mortals have the gift. The fact that incarcerated men...."

"I wish you wouldn't use the word *incarcerated* around here, doncha, say *joint* or *campers*."

"If I say joint, Bobby, I'll want one."

"What's up with the holy roller talk?"

Picasso, more in tune with discussions of this tenor, steps in. "It's like the dude Marx said, religion is opium for the masses. Now, how's about that opium?"

"Haven't had any since India," doncha answers nonchalantly, before returning to her train of thought. "Music, art, and literature are a medium to develop a closer relationship with the spiritual. Attempts to find meaning..."

"In our splintered lives." Picasso yawns. "Take us off the cross."

She narrows her eyes. "When you stood bare and alone, Picasso, didn't you, in your own inimitable way, question *why is this happening to me?*"

Other nearby atheists take a stand. "If there was a God there wouldn't have been an Inquisition, or a Holocaust, or slavery, or wars to mention a few incidents off the top off my head."

"Why do the sons of Adam attribute the sins of man to God?" Now that she's stirred things up she's on a roll. "Developing a higher awareness, questions come from deeper places and answers, if you find them, will be more honest. Hopefully the need to disparage others will disappear, even when you *are* on the rag."

"That's a woman's burden."

"That sounds awfully biblical to me." Encouraged when she stupefies, she goes for broke. "Can you image what it was like for men in primitive societies, when women were menstruating? Naturally, it would have been on a full moon… like tonight. Think about it; a whole tribe of menstruating women bleeding in full view, on a full moon. Primitives didn't relate a woman's cycle to child birth; to them it was powerful, like magic."

"doncha, please lighten up. You're too serious one minute and too weird the next." Slouching in my seat, I cross my arms over my chest and my feet at the ankles. She turns for support to those around her. "Was that complicated or convoluted? Was I annoying anyone?"

Einstein barges in on this scene. "It's the coming of…" Everyone is waiting for him to herald the second coming. He catches his breath. "A Ribbi is coming. I just got the news fresh off the BOP computer."

"What's a Ribbi?" Picasso is not the only one who wants to know.

"He's like a Jewish bishop…with sons."

"Einstein's probably gone off his meds again." Picasso grabs a cigarette from him and pulls on it as though it were a joint.

"That's it! Picasso. They made over a million dollars cultivating pot in a kibbutz-like set-up. Now what do you say? I think they're amazing! Maybe we could get something going here."

Firm in his conviction, I stand firm in mine. "It's time for me to spend time alone with doncha. We can discuss other point of views later, no matter how twisted."

Turning east to pray, the soon to be deloused holy family, standing downwind, reek atrociously from last night's supper.

Not an hour after their matriculation, Abba and Eba, his holiness's sons, quash their elevated status. A pair of rednecks disrespecting '*the kikes*' get their asses kicked, encouraging them to change their minds about Israeli soldiers not being all that tough.

Word travels fast. "Fightin' is an immediate trip behind the wall. No questions asked. So don't be so fuckin' obnoxious." No sooner does Whacky straighten out the sons than he catches the patriarch snooping around his kitchen. Chest to chest with Whacker, the Ribbi wants to clear up a few things. "*I* know about kosher. What can a *goy* know about kosher? Fighting, yes. Kosher, no." Whacky shows Ribbi his highly polished cleaver. "I'll finish koshering you, if you don't get out of *my* kitchen" changes the Ribbi's mind.

Being a practical man, Ribbi re-invests his energy racking up quarters teaching Jewish campers how to put on holy objects most of them never knew existed.

"There's an additional charge to learn the compulsory prayers. You do not want to antagonize God anymore than you already have, Doctor Lerner. *You* need special tutoring."

"You say that to all the guys, Ribbi."

"Strange that Doc can do brains but he has to have ten more lessons to wrap tefilin around his head." My dorm mates gather around to discuss my case. Gaffer is convinced that I finally met the king of weirdoes in the con department. Mon Capitan shivers. "You look like you've joined a cult man. Lighten up. You're starting to scare us." Whacker crosses himself and confesses, "I'm worried about ya, Doc."

Einstein has a different take on the subject. "Although Jesus would probably have seen the Ribbi as the same kind of phony as the money lenders in the temples, I plead guilty to admiring his capitalistic knowhow."

Picasso, leaning against the wall, lifts the beret covering his face. "What about spiritual well being?"

"The Ribbi is still my man. What do you say about that?"

"Nothing much, Einie; but Kerouac said '*Walking on water wasn't built in a day.*' Be smart. Become a Buddhist. Ribbi and the Chaplain aren't the best material for the God gig."

"Who better to negotiate with the numinous world than people so messed up it renders them vulnerable?"

Continuing on this subject, The *Joint IQ* publishes an article.

All dickheads turn to religion once they hit rock bottom. No one knows better than we do that confidence in the spiritual (not necessarily religion) helps elevate a failing human race. Spirituality is comforting; it's engaging; it can be educational; and, for those of you so inclined, it is a thriving business. Learn to count your blessings as you profit in our quirky Theology Department. There are religious and spiritual leaders waiting to be unearthed or smoked out in our own back yard.

Plans are also underway to build the first Sioux Sweat Lodge at FPC. Native Americans attending Catholic, Protestant, Muslim, and Jewish services, will now be practicing the religion of their choice in a space of their own. The members of Club Fed will no longer tolerate assimilation of the Native American race without regard for their traditions. We have honor. We play fair....is our slogan. Other slogans are in the making!

"Doctor Lerner, don't you think you might have spoken to me about building a Sweat Lodge, *before* your decision was put into print?"

"I'm delighted to see you too, Warden. It's always gratifying when you put-in a guest appearance on this side of town."

"Well?"

"If you recall, when we had our pre-publication discussion, I did mention the Lost Tribe of Israel. At least sixty full-blooded Sioux are full time residents. Most of them, if they weren't living on a reservation under federal tyranny, wouldn't be in the joint. When white men showed up, it was a dark day that never ended in the tragic history of Native Americans. We ruined this great country for them. The guys refuse to be part of that American travesty. It isn't fair that we don't recognize the spiritual identity of one group when we make so much of everyone else's. Was I wrong? A bunch of stones, a heat source, a few pieces of wood isn't much, bearing in mind what we took from them when we took over this entire country from coast to coast."

"What is a Sweat Lodge?"

The week preceding Ribbi's first service is all Salvation Army tactics. Bringing new members into the fold, Ribbi gets out there to meet the competition, including Reform Jewish services, singing services and the lox and bagel Sunday Cabala Class. The latter is my favorite. Given once a month by a Lubavitch, dressed in a heavy coat and hat no matter the time of year, and his pious wife. I've often watched those two ancient tiny Russian immigrants, nearly lost in their oversized coats, cross the wide open spaces to give service. I pull Einstein out of the pack following the Ribbi and corner him. "I finally figured out what this latest craze of yours is about."

"What craze?"

"The one you've been talking about nonstop where you're touring towns throughout the United States, I suspect with the Ribbi, spreading the gospel according to…."

"I had that idea before he even came here, Doc. Remember? Who knows what happens when the spirit is willing and the flesh is weak."

"Greed isn't a symptom, pal; it's a full-blown disease and it's contagious. You're supposed to set a good example. Why aren't you hopped-up over the Cabala classes; those little Russian Hebes are the real deal."

"Say you're going with us when we go on tour."

"Ask doncha if she can spare me."

"That's a cop out."

"No, that's reality. Do yourself a favor and go to the Cabala classes. Those people are spiritual."

Chapter Forty-Three
Camp Religious Services

Einstein's zealous attempts to persuade me to check out the Ribbi's Orthodox sundown service are going nowhere fast. "In my opinion, Professor Einstein, a short reform service is preferable to a long winded Orthodox sermon. Of course, a no sermon service is the best service of all."

Facing defeat, Einstein's bi-polar personality disorder kicks-in. "Where am I? I'm disappearing."

Now that he's impersonating an earthworm, to make sure no one carts him off or squashes him underfoot, I give in. "I'd love to go to the Ribbi's service with you. Take it easy." Untwisting him, I bring the earthworm to his feet. "What is this insane fixation you have with the Ribbi? It isn't just the money he pulls in that attracts you. Is it?"

"No matter what anyone says I love that guy. He has *higher* connections."

Yarmulke wearing, talise covered, bible bearing campers under a spell, buzz and bend and daven and sway, until I'm dizzy. Mimicking the motions, Einstein looks like a mime gone wrong. I elbow him. "Enough, screwball; take it easy with that stuff or you'll pray us right into the next world."

"I'm trying to send up a couple of good words to the Head Man. Anything I can do for you when I make the connection?"

"Hand me the phone, I prefer to speak for myself."

When the service ends, Einstein giggles. "You got into that, didn't you, Doc?"

"I'm not certain that I understood where the Ribbi was going by changing the campers into the biblical Jews. Ribbi, of course, had dual star billing as Moses and God. Stop me if I'm wrong. The G was supposed to be the Egyptians. I got that. What I didn't get was the way he expressed the degradation of his people; I found his detachment and improvisation confusing. The man's not present in his convictions and the Jews liberation never happens as he tells it."

"It will happen. For now, he's wandering. Maybe next week he'll do the plagues. You'll see, next time it will be different."

"Let me guess… God doesn't want to be overcome with the plague?"

"You'll have to go to the next service to find out, wiseacre."

On Sunday, the Ribbi and his *questionably* Holy family are in the visitors lounge. Rainbow, getting a glimpse of them, places the back of her hand on her forehead and moans. "Oy vey. Look at those hideous schmata's. No one on this planet dresses that way; only the Orthodox could have such a disgraceful lack of good taste, like the Ribbi's services. To tell the truth, my dears, I prefer the reform services, as does Doc. Being Jewish and black and gay is enough of a show for me. Besides, I don't get that Rasta/Shirley Temple thing-a-ma-jig with the banana curls dangling from the ears. If l took a good stiff brush to their hair they'd be quite lovely." Rainbow wanders off. When I mention the Ribbi's messianic complex, doncha alone listens. No one cares with the exception of Einstein, and he's not around. "My love," she indulges me, "do you think the Ribbi is delusional or manipulative?"

"I love you." I smile the words to bring her close. With lover's eyes, I look to her for reassurance. When everyone else ignores my fixations, she's there for me. "I love you, doncha." I speak words of love like a magic incantation to return us to our own world, the one we wait for all week.

Sadly, it's over too shockingly soon. Love sick, I trudge back to the dorm noting another long week will have to pass before we can again spend too little time together. Rainbow remains close and sympathetic. "You and donchie are always together. Space ain't nothin' but space. You know that, honey. It's your body that aches for her presence; your mind and heart are constant companions."

"Come in here." Gaffer pulls us into the dorm lounge. "We want you to join us next time at the Labuba's Cabala class. They serve lox and bagels. It's the fuckin' bomb."

"We did a Church thing, too. Holy Mary, Mother of God, what a kickass day for religion." Whacky's tune sombers. "Until the fuckhead Chaplain swore up and down that we're bastard Judas's and God's betrayers for money. Judas takin' thirty pieces of silver from the Jew priests to kiss Jesus ain't the same thing as us doin' what we did. We can't resemble that creep."

"I should say not." Rainbow taps her foot, indignant over the idea.

"Yep, the proverbial kiss of death." Charles lifts his head a fraction of an inch. "The Lord forgave Judas for taking the money. He did not forgive him for hanging himself afterwards."

Whacky professes, "So what if we're assholes. I begged him to absolve us. But no, that stinker would rather give us a rope to hang ourselves than give us one more drop to drink. I bet the goddamn hypocrite would like to see us all hang together...even if we're sorta lucky we didn't hang for our sins."

"Right on!" Shakey raises a fist. "Repent. The Lord will forgive us our sins."

"Yeah, repent, makes me feel better to hear that. How much we'll be forgiven? Fifty percent? Seventy-five per cent? Or alla my sins?"

"Whacky, you poor thing." Rainbow winks at me. "That was a very good question."

"Listen to this one. When the Chaplain was ready to do the sacrament thing, Charlie wheeled in the cart with the goods, chanting, "What's the word, thunderbird? What's the price? Two quarters twice." Paving the way to heaven, he handed out cups of wine. After a few rounds I pulled out the heavy artillery - larger cups." Gaffer laughs. "After the dirt bag Chaplain passed out we put him on the rectory table and lit candles around him...

"And we put a cup of quarters on his stinkin' chest to pay for the wine. Come to mass next week; it's a hella of great time. "

"Sounds like it."

"Amen." Whacky bows his head.

All together, they say "Amen."

Rainbow and I pour coffee, praying it will do them some good.

Chapter Forty-Four
The Sweat Lodge

The religious ones are a groaning moaning choir at seven a.m. "Your faces are edematous this morning."

"What the fuck is that eat 'em stuff, Doc. I don't get what you're sayin'." Whacky holds his head. "But ya don't need to be hollerin' on the top of your lungs about it."

"You're hung-over and bloated. Drink plenty of fluids, have breakfast, take two aspirins and call me if you need me. I'm going to my office."

Charles sits down gingerly in the chair across from my desk. "Doc, it's not snowing anymore. It's actually in the high forties."

"How could you tell with that stocking cap over your face?" I peak under his cap. He tries to smile. "I couldn't really. Chief told me. He said the sweat lodge would be located in the area facing the pond where there's an abundance of wild life. The Warden ordered blankets, tarps and two by fours; they're all ready to be picked up at the commissary. Chief was just telling me that."

"Good morning, Chief, I didn't see you when I came in."

Looking rather pleased, Chief lays it on thick. "The Warden asked me to pass this on…and I don't mind if I do. He said he believes the Sioux are more in touch with the spiritual message of Christ's teachings than many of his fellow Christians. Publish that in the next edition of the *Joint IQ*. Spread the word."

Charles sighs. "I guess the Warden heard about what happened in the chapel yesterday." He covers his face.

"Let's leave Charlie to suffer in peace."

"There is no peace for the wicked." Chief whispers in Charlie's ear.

We can hear poor Charles moaning all the way down the hall.

The Warden, already at the site, is not surprised to see me. "Doc, we will never witness the likes of this in the materialistic world we live in. I have been inspecting this area chosen by the Sioux for the Sweat Lodge. Whatever they need, save a few items we gave them, comes from nature."

"They never needed anything from us; we took what they had away from them."

"Sadly, that's true. The Head Chief said that after the white men drove his people from their sacred places his peopled migrated north. Then the white men killed off the buffalo. In the end, the Native Americans became dependent on the people that killed the buffalo population and destroyed their nation. He showed me a Cochina doll; a white man and a Native American attached back-to-back. Our race and his people live together without ever being able to see each other's faces. They resemble a Cochina doll."

"It's painful how men destroy what they do not understand and defeat themselves with their inhumanity."

I take a second look at the site later in the day. Walking along the perimeter of the fire pit, I try to make sense of the layout. Dark Cloud appears from the density of the woods and satisfies my curiosity for details. "The sweat lodge is structured like a tepee, covered with canvas. We place firewood inside and scent it with pinecones, needles, and other things surrounded by heated rocks. Between the altar and fire pit, the fire tenders, and no else, are allowed to cross. No one else has that privilege."

"How long does it take for the rocks to heat up?"

"About three hours. At sundown, our people invite you and the Warden to be our guests at our first spiritual sweat at FPC. Thanks to you, Doc, we have a sacred space to congregate."

Later in the day, I share some of the conversation I had with Gaffer, knowing his fascination with symbolism. "Gaffer, did you know that the reason the sweat lodge faces east is symbolic of a new beginning, new knowledge, and the possibility of enlightenment? The Sweat Lodge represents the Earth Mother, the womb."

"What else about the womb? I'd like to know all about this. I wouldn't mind going with you, now that you mention it. I was just teasing you when I asked where we should send your scalp."

✵ ✵ ✵

At sundown, a reflective glow rests on the pond. Scented smoke drifts through the lodge. Sage and pine are two immediately recognizable scents. The other scents are strange to me, and not as pleasant. The fire has been burning for the requisite three hours.

Stripped down to gym trunks, the Warden and I join the first sweat lodge ceremony of the full-blooded Lakota Sioux. In readiness for the ceremony, the Chief puffs on a pipe filled with sage and offers it to the north, south, east, and west. "To you great god of the north who brings us the wind to drive the buffalo home…" The homage, accompanied by drumbeats, are prayers that the spirits hear.

The saturated aroma affects me unlike any I have ever known. At first, I find it slightly acrid, but it doesn't take long before it soothes me. This otherworld energy, with prayers, chants, songs and laugher, is conducive to a meditative state. I embrace an inner peace, which, at first, returns me to the days when I was an Eagle Scout.

The land of the free and the home of the brave: Too bad this beautiful land didn't stay in the hands of the truly brave and truly free; I would have been a beloved medicine man among these people. My thoughts are for a peace pipe and for peace for these people and all others.

Chapter Forty-Five
Passover and Easter

I relive last night's spiritual cleansing, beginning with the part where I'm smudged with sage, followed by my admission to the Sweat Lodge on my hands and knees. The humbling posture, the simplicity of the ritual, and the richness of the rewards were as unanticipated as the clear and clean perception I have this morning. *This is what I would call miraculous. I don't know how to speak the words God, or the spirits, took my hand.*

Considering how to explain such an extraordinary experience to my roommates, Gaffer makes an explanation untenable questioning me. "You put a notch in your tomahawk, didn't you? They brought in squaws, right? You can tell me; I can keep a secret. Those guys can get anything they want on campus."

Whacker elbows Gaffer. "Let's go, nosey. We still have a lot of work to do for dinner tonight. Remember, it's Passover. You look good Doc. You must have gotten a lot of rest last night. See ya later."

doncha arrives at camp with a delivery that leaves Whacky scratching his head. "Those don't look like no fish I ever saw. Where are the fins and stuff?"

"That's how gefilte fish looks after the fish is blended together with lovely spices and herbs, eggs, matzoth meal, carrots, and I don't know what else. It's quite a production and a stinky one at that."

"They don't smell bad, they smell good." Whacky sniffs the goods again. "Kinda sweet like."

"Try one." doncha paints horseradish on a piece of gefilte fish for him.

"Mmmm. I really like Jew food." Whacky grabs another and grins. "Slap some more red stuff on it, girl. Hey Gaffer, help me unload these jellyfish. I don't want the guys getting their paws on this before dinner. Gangway! This good Jew food needs to be kept cold, even if it does come from the desert."

The Seder begins with Ribbi David, a top-notch baseball player, belting-out *Go Down Moses Let My People Go.* He can swing a bat but he can't carry a tune. His voice and the Warden's conversation unnerve the Ribbi. Suspecting the Warden is Pharaoh, Ribbi decrees, "We must immediately reorganization ourselves to cross the Red Sea and leave the sanctimonious Pharisees behind." I convince him that David is harmless and the Warden is merely curious about Jewish culture. After scrutinizing the Warden for any telltale signs of affiliation with ancient Egypt, Ribbi answers his question. "The sash around my waist separates my head from my genitals."

"A novel method to keep Orthodox Jewish men from thinking with one head only," I contribute, trying to keep it light. But the dealer passes the dice and the Ribbi returns to his role. *Before* he parts the Red Sea and leads the Hebrews out of the dining room, without any dinner to sustain them, I try to turn him around. "Listen, Ribbi, the kids are unmanageable. We need to serve dinner; eating will calm them down."

"Come here boy." Ribbi grabs a child flying past him. "Tell me why this night is different from all other nights?"

"Because I'm in the joint, that's why"

"Go look for the afikomen. I will work a miracle to free my people from this shameful imprisonment." Ribbi shoos me away. "*You*, go make your quota of straw."

"Looking for afikomen is similar to looking for Easter eggs, except the food is matzoth," I tell the puzzled Warden. "Some families are more dysfunctional than others are sane."

To prove the point, a fast working wheeler-dealer kid yells at Whacky. "You better pay up. I did so find afikomen."

"This ain't my matzoth. This matzoth has onion in it. You think you're ahead of the game don't ya, you little con job. Your type always ends up in the joint with the rest of the bums."

"Not me. I'm smart!"

"Then how come I busted you if you're so smart. Scram before I kick your ass. Bringin' in your own matzoth; what a cheater!"

"You do anything to me, *big guy,* and I'll tell about those guys making out in that room with the coats."

Following the kid, Whacky warns the little motor mouth, "Keep your trap shut and get lost!"

From behind a rack of coats Whacky hears, "Kissing on a high holiday is a mitzvah, a blessing, recognized in the Talmud." Jacob Mandelbaum, a well-known con artist, tells the truth. The sin is he's moving in on another guy's visitor.

"You Jews really know how to party. The rest of you Hebes are plannin' a dance that has somethin' to do with," Whacky looks around to make sure no one's listening, "whores." Even the Warden is goin' for it. You're gonna miss out on the action. Just tell me one thing. How can I tell which ones are the whores? The women all look pretty regular to me."

☆ ☆ ☆

On Easter Sunday, the Easter Bunny and a choir of Jewish campers sing a melody of Easter songs, beginning with *Peter Cotton Tail*. The Easter Bunny and I dance to *Easter Parade*. "Dance like Fred Astaire. You're dancing like Gene Kelley. *My* body type, as if you hadn't noticed, is more like Fred Astaire's. *You* should be the Easter Bunny, Doc, and I should lead."

"You're captivating as a bunny, Rainbow. More to the point, Fred danced with Judy, not a bunny. Besides, bunnies don't eat ham and I love ham." I tell the server, taking a twirl with us, "Save a portion of that porker for me. Hide it in my special place in the kitchen."

Lee, the PM Baker, does a passive-aggressive burn, taking the pies out of the oven. "I have watched you guys put food away for Doc long enough. He's making a pig of himself."

The culprit shows up. "Where's my ham, oink, I'm starving."

The one and only Christian not enjoying the meal is smashed out of his mind. "I want to dance, too," is how the Chaplain ends the Resurrection story, inspired, no doubt, by our dancing.

"I know where there is a case of sacramental wine. Come with me, Chaplain, Sir."

"Who the fuck do you think you are?"

"I'm the Gaffer. Gaffer means boss. Now follow me and the bunny if you want to be a nice wino."

Rainbow shakes her tail and wiggles her ears to distract the kids. "I'll help you find eggs." She drags back the precocious teenagers in pursuit of the booze trail. Not allowed wine, the little weasels corner the market on her beautifully painted Easter eggs and auction them off to the highest bidders. Just like their fathers, who are in for inside trading, probably did when they were kids. Then, they grew up and became commodity brokers.

Holiday dinners are exhausting.

Just as we're ready to hit the sack, arguing outside our door are members of Ribbi's family, with a birthright of complexes. Eba finally marches in. "Doc, I want to tell you what I never told anyone, for fear of retribution."

"We're beat, knock off." Whacky can't even lift his head.

Eba tones it down a notch. "I have to say this."

"This better be good."

"We are not the biological sons of the Ribbi."

"Like I care. Go find your real daddy." Whacky is too tired to exert himself so the Yids don't budge.

"Our ten brothers moved here to carry out the ministry and to be close to Him. Abba and Eba close their eyes and pray. "Blessed be His name." Abba opens his eyes. "Our brothers operate the Apostle Cab Company. The money, it's good, but not as good as the kibbutz scheme."

"That scheme landed your asses in jail. Did you forget that?" Whacky doesn't intimidate Abba; no one does after he's lived with Israelis.

"At our trial, and even now, we maintain that we did what we did in the name of God. Maybe we didn't make it clear enough," Abba acknowledges the Ribbi, periodically showing his face in the doorway, "that He is Him."

Whacky and the Gaffer look puzzled. My skepticism is clinical. I'm already on to the Ribbi's decided affinity with the Almighty and other celebrated powerhouses assembled in his mental construction.

"I'm trying to tell you our father is truly the Messiah."

Gaffer snorts. "You cons are out of control."

"It is written in Scripture about His coming. He will come as if a thief in the night."

"Yeah. Right. We know all about him ripping guys off with his holy rolling con salesmanship abilities."

"*We've* seen His miraculous power. *We* have witnessed *Him* heal the sick. Three years ago in Jerusalem, *we* saw *Him* raise the dead."

"Everyone recovers from the flu if you wait long enough. As for raising the dead, the deceased was probably sleeping off an alcoholic stupor when his highness woke him up." I give them that look that paves the way for "You can stay but the bullshit has got to go."

"It's about time you've drawn the line with these crazies, Doc."

"Just a minute, Gaffer; let me get this straight with these two. You're telling us that the reason the Ribbi is held hostage in a federal prison camp is, correct me if I'm wrong, the law did not deem to recognize him as God when he presented himself in federal court for questioning."

"They didn't."

"Fascinating story line and maybe we'd like to hear more, if we weren't so exhausted, and, if we hadn't heard it before. Rework the premise and we can discuss it another time." I point to the door.

Abba leaves, but he returns with the Ribbi.

"Ribbi has a brain tumor; he was diagnosed six months ago in New York. He suffers piercing headaches. We know you can help him, Doc."

"If he is who he's supposed to be, what do you need Doc for?"

Whacky agrees with Gaffer. "Why can't he fix himself?"

I take the Ribbi's sons aside. "Keep your story under wraps. You don't want the Warden to get the wrong impression. I'll see what I can do without rocking the boat."

"We knew you'd be there for us, Doc. Yahweh will reward you with many successes in your future."

I overhear Gaffer snicker. "Wonder why Doc didn't do one of those detailed exams he does with the light in the eyes and hammer on the reflexes."

"He just wanted the fruitcakes out of here. I don't think Doc wanted to touch him in case they're not makin' all this up."

"That's funny, Whacky." Gaffer lays back on the bed. "I have more nut cases on my hands than even I can deal with. I'd love to be there, Doc, when you tell Bill Warden *this* story. He'll put you on the road headed for the loony bin."

"Will you do me a favor, Gaffer?"

"Of course. What do you want me to do?"

"I want you to hold my hand when they zap me with 220 volts."

"You are nuts!"

Chapter Forty-Six
The Ribbi Sees a Brain Man

The Ribbi's interview with the Warden doesn't convince the Warden to fear God's wrath. It does however encourage the Warden to lead the Ribbi out of bondage and straight to my friend, Doctor Rich Treelman's office. The Warden (pronounced a reasonable pharaoh, in keeping with the Ribbi's principles) wants to hear what a *headman* (a neurological surgeon) has to say about Ribbi's larger than life head-trips.

My reality, too, alters. Sucked into the vortex of time, I watch Rich Treelman come around the corner walking that up beat crew cut walk of his that I remember from his years in the Navy and Annapolis.

"Books!" Rich calls me by my nickname from our Mayo Clinic days. "You look well. You're all muscle." He grabs my arm. "I can't resist the temptation to feel your bicep any more than you can resist flexing. Same ol' showboat!"

"The important thing is I'm busy. Not how it was before. Doing time, I actually have a lot more free time."

"Was it awful?'

"It wasn't good."

"You mean it was hell."

"It was hell."

"I heard you gave them what for. Our Chief at Mayo had a fit every time you stood up to him, or any of them. You were right challenging them the way you did. You will always have that fearless attitude that can't be beat." Rich holds the imaging study up to the light. "This guy is a real piece of work, Went after the nurses… tried to bless them like a regular Rasputin. He has a congenital cyst in his right frontal lobe. It causes no pressure or mass effect. He'll live a perfectly *normal* life, so to speak."

I read the films. "Operating on this one *would be* fucking with God."

We call Ribbi in for a consultation. "Ribbi, you have a cyst in your right frontal lobe…"

"There is no cyst. I dissolved it through my powers."

Rich explains the study.

Ribbi points a long wizard-like arm in the direction of the study. "Are you going to take the word of that piece of blackened evil over mine?"

Doc Frank, unable to calm Ribbi when his words are not the last or the most influential in the room, escorts his holiness to the car.

My old friend shrugs. "We call FPC, Ward 69. There have been crazy stories over the years. Don't think I'm being judgmental. I really don't know anyone that is strictly normal and interesting, too. It's all a matter of degrees. As long as no one becomes too feverish, I don't predict complications."

The Warden shakes Rich's hand. "Thanks for helping us out once again and for understanding."

I embrace my friend. "You never know where these situations may lead if put in the wrong hands. I don't think it would do the Ribbi any good to know that you seeing me diminished in this way is as humiliating for me as it is for him not to be recognized as the Almighty. When reaching for the sun it's not easy to reconcile when your dreams are associated, in *polite* society, only with the moon."

Chapter Forty-Seven
Flashman and Baseball

On the phone with her concerned grandmother, in between a blistering sneeze and a fit of coughing, doncha does little to console Katie, even though she has been trying. "It doesn't matter what people think, Bernard needs me," finalizes her decision to remain in town. In bed, conversation ended, doncha reads *Middlemarch*. George Eliot takes her mind off her fever. I don't know if literature takes her mind off freezing, to be with me two days a week.

Miles away, I'm in bed reading a swashbuckler by George MacDonald Fraser. Colonel Harry Flashman, a captivating rogue, is not too much concerned with high morality. As the Colonel is throwing the fair lady out of the dog sled being chased by villains, to make it go faster, Whacky storms in and breaks the spell I'm in. "We gotta get you to the Rec center; your presence is *mandatorious*. Get out of dat bed and get dressed."

"Have you ever heard of quiet time? And, may I remind you, that is not dat."

"Dat's right." Whacky laughs. Okay Doc, that's correct. Fuck, you weren't exactly havin' quiet time. I heard ya laughin' from a mile away. You're needed as a witness to highway robbery."

"Is Flashman in the Rec room?"

"You know Doc, he may have been doin' that flashin' stuff outside, but that pervy shit doesn't happen inside, not around here." Wringing his hands, the repulsion expressed on my friend's face worsens. "Don't put on those smelly putrid sweatpants. I'm gonna' be sick."

"Take it easy, Lady Macbeth."

"If I look like a lady to you 'cause doncha isn't here this weekend you're in bad shape. Come on, even if it isn't your woman, I've got a surprise for you. I know he's a filthy bum, but

I never heard he was a flasher or I would've burnt the thing. Doc, I promise, if it ain't…if it isn't perfect, I'll fix him."

"I don't know what you're talking about."

"I don't always know what you're sayin' but I'm smart enough to know it's smart."

"And visa versa."

"See what I mean. You're smart and I love ya." Whacky gives me a bone-crunching hug before he drags me out the door, in clean sweats.

It's difficult to travel around a federal prison camp without meeting local characters. On this fine Sunday, Action Jackson has managed to employ a crew, hard at work. The men are in good spirits, energized with the noisy machinery, the sound of their own voices, and spring fever.

Whacky whispers, "Who's in the concrete?"

"There were people who thought Jimmy Hoffa was poured into a foundation, but that's not innovative. He deserved an original sendoff, even if I didn't like him."

"So who *did* you put in this one?"

Action Jackson hands me the plans. "We're building three outdoor handball courts. The structures are…

"Ground-breaking. Come on, Doc. We have somethin' important to do." Whacky drags me away. That guy just makes-up stuff and talks to hisself all day long. He don't need nobody else to listen to him."

"Himself and he doesn't need anyone."

"What are you, some kinda parrot? I think everyone has gone screwy around here."

Montelione, approaching me in the Rec center, hasn't taken his eyes off Whacky. "Sorry, I heard you lost your coat, Doc. I found it when I was cleanin' up." Montelione's voice and hands shake.

"Thanks a lot. What happened to your eye?"

"I had an accident."

"Looks bad."

"It'll heal."

Whacky growls "You won't be alive that long. Get the fuck out of here. Everybody in this place knows you're a dirty snitch."

Montelione makes a fast exit with a crowd hissing him.

Irish collects the deck of cards the old man was playing solitaire with before we came in. "Montelione will never know peace until they bury him, and then there's no guarantee."

I thank Whacky for the return of my coat, anxious to spend the rest of the day lost in the fantasy world of Flashman. The factual world is not necessarily conducive to a healthy state of mind. That, and my calcified bones, aching from old football injuries and medication, is the reason I didn't want to stray from bed in the first place.

After spending another couple of hours in bed reading, hunger and restlessness take over. On the way back after dinner, from outside the Rec Center, I can hear Gaffer howling. By the time I get there, Shakey is summing up a heated argument. A volley of boos are a prelude to whatever is loose being tossed at Gaffer, while Shakey laughs his ass off.

Charles hums and takes notes describing bedlam. Presently, lunar cycles are affecting underbellies and exacerbating less than stellar personality disorders. Most of the time, I attempt to lead these men from their baser natures. Tonight, I don't have the will or energy.

I hear Charles, sighing right behind me; he's relieved to be out of there, too. "Doc what was that all about? Have they all gone crazy? They act like they've been struck with gamma rays."

"Full moon madness and baseball mania, Charlie, me boy; Lady Luna and sports stimulate men that way, drives them crazy."

Charles looks up at the full moon. "Do you know her well?"

"Well enough. It's better not to become too familiar with Lady Luna."

"She sounds sexy."

"Not in my experience."

Chapter Forty-Eight
Joint IQ

"Doc, I want to ask you a personal question. Don't get mad at me, but I want to know how you function being in so much pain?"

"There are ways of coping with the affective component of pain. One is medication, to reduce the noxious sensations. I prefer to subdue the main neuron - the brain. I close the gate for incoming impulses with complete involvement in whatever I do."

"You mean mind over matter."

"Stimulating another area of the brain not involved in the pain, refracts the excited pain fibers. It's called the Gate Theory of Pain."

Charles continues to look at me as if I'm the rising sun, not the waning moon. I don't need anyone exposing my lunar shadow side. I'm on it every day, Virgo analyzing, as doncha says, the darkness out of it. I often worry over my limited success. I'm relieved when the loudspeakers distract my burdened mind, announcing:

Attention campers, spring, as you may not have noticed, is here. We all know what spring brings. New York has the Yankees, Boston has the Red Sox, St. Louis has the Cardinals, and Chicago has a double whammy, the White Sox and the Cubs, but we have the Bombers. Everybody plays. It's tradition around here. Even the Mad Bomber, Fuse, DC Don, and the most unlikely of all, Rainbow...actually, she's a pom-pom girl. She won't be oiling up her baseball glove but she may offer to oil yours.

Do not miss the chance to see Gaffer and his Bombers, who are not presently a complete team, beat all pretenders. Their past record – zero for zero - has no blemishes. The captain, coach, and mascot of Gaffer's team is that large mammal himself, The Gaffer. Siegel and Nothing But Trouble will handicap the season's tryouts. Given that it will be colder than my prom date, I suggest you wear your parkas tonight. Ash can fires will keep your hands warm. The Doc and Doc Frank will be available for emergency consultations, if any of you develop frostbite. Good luck...and don't freeze your nuts off.... and don't go nuts...play ball but play nice.

After deals are made, the final teams don't resemble the original draft. Leave it to a bunch of cons; they'd rearrange God's home team if they could get Lucifer to play for them. Gaffer's Bombers are now ninety percent from our section of the honor dorm, with an occasional ringer thrown in for good speed.

"A new camper called The Rocket, famous for his speed and his agility, plays ball. I asked him to stop by."

Gaffer's scent is up. "The Rocket is now a Bomber!"

John puts a kibosh on a potential uprising. "In this case, the Gaffer's got it."

The Gaffer nearly wets himself with excitement until the Rocket shows up. "He's missing an arm." Gaffer veins are bulging. "What the fuck, you tricked me, assholes." Thinking he's slick, Gaffer trades the Rocket to another team. Not ten minutes later, watching the man with one arm in action, Gaffer moans. "He's fast with that one arm and his legs are jet propelled. I regret the day I was born."

"That's nothing, I skied in Jackson Hole, Wyoming, with a Native American who had one arm and one leg, and that guy skied the pants off all of us. Life is full of surprises."

Commenting on the way the Rocket plays ball, out of left field, the Warden pitches me a few curved balls. "I'm taking a two week holiday; I've been looking forward to going to Europe for years. Everything will continue running smoothly. The Chief of the BOP and his advisors will be here for a few days during the second week that I'm gone, but other than that everything remains status quo."

Before I say: *Chiller, the satanic asshole, will have a field day making my life hell. It's him or me. One of us is going to lose the game.* I say, "Yes, Sir." This is one of those times I hate when it's *all* about extremities.

Chapter Forty-Nine
Memorial Day

"The Warden is lucky to be out of town for this Memorial Day freeze-up."

"Who gives a rat's ass about him! I'm freezing my petunias off" is thrown back at me.

"Don't be mad at me because Gaffer and I, according to Whacky's mandate, are not allowed on the courts."

"What's the matter with him, Doc; one more gas match is all we asked for."

"Tell me something, Nothing But Trouble, is it true you sent a search party looking high and low for World War II gas masks?

"Yep, and they're not going to stop until they find them."

"In the meantime, I'm going to sink my teeth into this juicy burger. Rainbow, please pass the coleslaw over. Why aren't you having a hamburger, they're tasty."

Shivering and nibbling a brownie, Rainbow appears reflective. "There is scientific evidence that red meat is bad for you. What I want to know is, is there scientific evidence to substantiate that scrumptious food is really and truly the way to a man's heart?"

"Anatomically the areas of the brain responsible for satiety and sex are so tight they can't be discerned without microscopic magnification. May I have that slaw now?"

Picasso lies back on the space on the bench that Rainbow vacated. "Awesome food, home runs, and beatin' the tar out of cops warms the cockles of my heart."

"That expression comes from the time when the heart was thought to be shaped like a shell, a cockle shell."

"What was that about the cock? Doc, did you think it's an empty shell?"

"That's only a matter of circumstance."

In the fifth inning the score is thirty-two to zero in our favor and the cop at bat is ice cold. "Swing the bat not your ass, lady." Another camper yells, "Get your boobs out of the way and play. I'll give you *my* balls to practice with...you need it." And so on, until Mon Capitan puts his head down. "I can't stand women, even if they are cops, playing competitive sports against men when it gets so ugly. A southern gentleman never goes against the ladies." Nothing But Trouble gives him the finger. "I can't help it. That's the way I was brought up."

A sudden stillness comes over the crowd. The loud speakers screech. *Attention! Lerner, Zee, Picasso, Einstein and you too, Charles; you're all wanted dead or alive in the Chiller's office, now! And, no funny stuff, wisenheimers!"*

"Line up, mugs." Chiller points out an imaginary line. "I thought Buckaroo would have to pick you bums up."

"I had a premonition you would need us."

"I don't need you, Lerner. I never did. However, there's a call for prisoners on the northern border of North Dakota to help convert an all-girl's school to a camp." Chiller flings the paper at me.

"This is a request to do six months hard labor for six months off and it says explicitly on *any volunteer's* original sentence."

"I'm going to see to it that you volunteer." Flipping back into his chair, hard, Chiller nearly flies out of it.

"Hold your breath...you look fabulous in blue."

"In the absence of Bill, I can do as *I* see fit, which brings me to the other reason you're here. The head of the Bureau of Prisons and his worthy staff are paying *me* a visit for a few days."

Picasso applauds with the tips of his fingers. "Goody, goody, goody. Like man, are you gonna set-up those distinguished federal officers in one of the classy local hotels that have swimming pools and golf courses? It would be cool to do that even if the pools are frozen... also, playing golf with blue balls *will not* improve your game."

"I know that, and furthermore, I have made a command decision."

"I bet you want us to crease your polyester pants. No, no, that's not want you want." Picasso winks at him. "You want Juan to whip-up a pair of tight fitting corduroys that go zit zat, zit zat when you walk. That's really sexy."

"I'm not asking any of you to do anything; I'm telling you that Monday, *all of you,* will be cleaning house...*all of you*. Lerner, I'm stretching my imagination to see what I can think of to keep you on your knees."

Picasso whispers, "Cocksucker wants *us* on our knees, or is it just Doc?"

"I don't see anything funny. Shut up and listen! The code for this project is *The Eagle has landed*. What do you say to that?"

"I say it reminds me of a line from the movie *The In-Laws*. Look, Vice-Warden Chiller, you're interfering with *your* father-in-law's pet project and he's not going to like it. Remember the GED?"

"This is way more important. Furthermore, I'm the real boss around here, not you! Tell them to stop laughing."

We huddle up.

"We've discussed it and we're against your plan. I'm stating that for the record."

"I'm delighted to hear it."

While Chiller gloats, Picasso looks into his imaginary crystal ball. "I'm seeing the future. Oh no! Daddy comes home, and yes it's true, you're in for a spanking!"

"You're nuts! When he sees what I've done to impress the BOP I'll be given a raise and a promotion!"

Einstein giggles. "You're *definitely* not dealing with a full deck."

"You should know, you mental misfit. If you don't show up on Monday for your work assignments, I'll put all of you in solitary until I transfer you up north. Get out and take that zombie with you."

We each grab one of Zee's arms and legs. "Zee, wake up. Mr. Chiller wants to be alone with his psychosis."

Everyone is pissed off, with the exception of Rainbow. The magpie chirps, "Chiller told *us girls* to clean and polish and paint this that and the next thing. I nearly swooned. I said Mr. Chiller you must think we're muscle minute maids. My fingers are allergic to nasty chemicals and don't forget… *I'm a talented pianist.* When Chiller the Killer *suggested* I work with Whacky in the kitchen don't you know I was overcome with every emotion under the zodiac! I think the little corporal has a crush on me. But then why would he assign me to a butch guy like Whacky? He couldn't possibly be that stupid!"

"Rainbow, stop obsessing. If we refuse to do this we'll end up in solitary or shipped out. A little labor won't kill us… and I guarantee we will prevail."

"How's that, Doc? You want me to *kill* him?" Mon Capitan eyes are hard to look at.

"Sabotage is the answer. We will beat the little Nazi painter at his own game."

"Doc, c'mon, tell us where you're goin' with this."

"*We're* going to war."

Saying good night to my roommates, I remind them, "All wars stipulate deprivation and hardship. I hope you're up to it."

"I'm fine with it, Doc." Whacky's always a trooper.

"Speaking of war," Gaffer yawns, "brings to mind the adage all's fair in love and war. In preparation, I'm going to dream about sex."

"Good, Gaffer. Have an orgy."

"Unhappily, my morals prohibit it. And I never have more than one of my three fiancées in each dream per night…not that I haven't thought it."

"The things we worry about in life have a way of working out, with or without our permission. We just think we're in control."

Chapter Fifty
Days of Labor Begin

Instead of sweat labor, the renegade's revolt and fool around in the gym. John, worn-out from blowing his whistle, seeks comfort in another bag of Fritos. When his stomach aggravates him, too, he starts blowing his whistle and, surprisingly, he doesn't stop until everyone shuts up.

"Work assignments are posted in the hallway. If this job isn't completed on time Chiller threatened you would all finish your sentences in solitary. I think he means it…but how could he put all of you in solitary?"

"We can't see the assignments, genius. The hall is too crowded with paint, wax, strippers, pails, soap, etc., which looks like an antagonizing prelude to backbreaking slavery."

John sends the men on their way in groups of seven, but no one's whistling.

The field house is a horse of a different color. The forty-foot high walls require two crews to tackle it. With variations on *screw this bullshit* and a long and unproductive debate on the subject of how to go about painting the monster, we begin stripping the floors of old varnish. Slogging away, monotonous drudgery robs our morning; despite our efforts, only a fraction of the floor is done and it's done so poorly it needs to be done again. We break for lunch, frustrated and aggravated.

Mon Capitan finds the whole thing amusing. "Look at ya'all, covered in grunge, lookin' meaner than bob cats on fire." Head-shaking disbelief over our technique, (where was he when we needed him) he gives us instructions on the correct way to strip the floor. He takes off to a chorus of "Shit, fuck, and why doesn't someone kill Chiller; it would be a mercy killing and end our misery!"

"We have a monstrosity of a mess in the gym and we also need to keep up in the Education Department because, guess what, this isn't recess." Einstein wipes his grimy brow and finalizes his successive complaints with "How do you expect us to manage both, Doc. My aching back is already broken. I pray to God Chiller burns eternally in hell or freezes to death in Siberia….preferably both at the same time."

Talking of affirmative action whips hostile men into a feverish frenzy. Attacking the door to the gym on Friday morning, like they're storming the Bastille, moods shift. The floor looks awesome. Standing up straight, agonizing pain is forgotten. Even the weather changed for the better. Hanging around outside the gym, soaking up sunshine, we congratulate ourselves and smoke to our heart's content.

Turns out it's just another one of those unpredictable days that overwhelm us. The worst of it is the archaic heating system that won't shut down. By noon the gym is a sauna. Surly-mean and quagmire filthy we trudge back to the mess hall too hot to eat and too hungry not to.

By quitting time, stinking and stunned with fatigue, we resemble a chain gang. Mustering gratitude that our grueling sweat labor is over, bad news hits us hard. "Chiller the Killer, the Destroyer, made the field house off limits and visiting privileges are null and void." Einstein rallies the men around him. "I've worked out a plan whose time has come! Dressed like old women, we can break away from this diabolical tyranny."

"Where do we get the old ladies clothes from?"

"We can get *anything*, you already know that. We'll leave Duluth on bicycles."

"We don't have bicycles."

"Not to worry. I'll swing a deal with the Schwinn Bike factory; it may not be the best deal, but they're local and we need to make a quick bus connection and head over to the Omaha World Train Center. Once there, we hop a fast train to the coast, jump on a tramp steamer, and we're gone."

"What about money?"

"Picasso will handle that. Our very own *Great Escape* orchestrated by yours truly."

"Won't the townspeople be suspicious?"

"I guarantee the locals will cheer us on. There's nothing more reliable than a granny bike marathon to inspire people, and cover our asses. No one messes with old ladies."

"You're probably right, Einie. Who would mess with old ladies?"

Because they're taking Einie a little too seriously, I step in. "Tough it out for a few more days. All of us are in the same boat... and what you really need to take into consideration before leaving us in the lurch is who boats are named after? Right! Women. We don't want to ruin being with our women next weekend. Also, hand signals are your thing, Einie. We could never manage without you. Get us through this weekend, please, keeping women in mind. I think *that's* essential in making the right decision."

"Another news flash, Doc, we have to work this weekend!"

They look at me as if I said it.

✼ ✼ ✼

"This paint," John scratches his head, "can't be right. It's labeled *pink rose*."

Picasso opens several cans. "Pink rose is quite a long way off from gun boat gray. Tell your leader there's a hurdle to overcome with the hue."

"What's a hue? And, who's my leader?"

"Like the color, man. Go tell the asshole that the color is wrong."

John doesn't look happy on his return. "Mr. Chiller was sort of sleeping...but he said for me to tell the morons, I mean you guys, to get to work and paint the goddamn gym or he'll throw your asses in solitary. Sorry."

I grab a bucket of paint and a spray gun. Watching me paint, the men realize the possibilities. Placing extension ladders against the walls, they climb aboard. Pink rose goes on nicely in a spray gun or on a roller. "Use brushes for the tight spots, guys."

"It feels good painting a color that is so feminine."
There's something soothing in the work, like women are in the color.

Mon Capitan stops by after his usual rounds, which means he's not bowling or brewing. He laughs his ass off. "It's lookin' more like a bordello than a joint field house in here. Well, at least ya'all are happy....that in itself is a blissful change."

Rainbow twirls, dancing. "Pink is exactly what this *testosteronic* place needed. I bet no other field house in the country has the quality this one has."

The wall mural Picasso designed for the weight room gives everyone pause. Deciphering the glyphs, I laugh. "I grasp what you mean, Daddy-O. Those two are traditional male symbols." I point to the two three foot high circles with arrows pointing in the direction of one o'clock. "The plus sign in between them signifies male plus male."

Picasso stands back to admire his work. "You know man, this is the first time I've done a mural... it catches the eye, makes you think, and breaks up the monotony. You're diggin it?"

"The male plus male symbols are behind bars - the white vertical lines. I get that. Then there's the equal sign with a question mark to follow...and another male symbol and the female symbol together....I get it. Men plus men behind bars can be or are potentially bisexual. That's my take. What do you think the BOP people are going to say?"

"They won't get it; they're not cognitive after the eighth grade. I want them to think we're all gay so they'll get the hell out of here and take Chiller with them."

Whacky, joining us in the gym, sniggers. "Freud says everyone is *potentially* bi-sexual…is that what your saying, Picasso?"

"That is good news, indeed."

Whacky, to show he's sophisticated doesn't punch, Rainbow.

Chapter Fifty-One
The Eagle Has Landed

At noon, twenty-five numb dumb spit shined hacks slouch around the intake center waiting for final orders. Commandant Chiller has his bullhorn with him. He nearly skips, singing out "In preparation for the arrival of the esteemed Chairman of the Bureau of Prisons, Herman Hoodstrong and his most excellent committee of twelve from Washington, D.C., we will now synchronize our watches on the count of three. Get ready. And, a one. And, a two. And, a three. Great, great! Now test your two-way radios to see if we're all on the same frequency."

"I didn't realize there were so many resident hacks."

Mon Capitan, an old pro on the ways and means of life in the joint, informs me, "Hacks keep a low profile. Sleeping during shifts here allows them to be slick for their night jobs, bagging groceries and pumping gas. Those boys are ambitious."

"I just heard them say The Eagle has landed. I guess the bigshot assholes are here."

Chiller is radiant with an entourage of Blues Brothers suited G-man behind him. Rushing through the gates flanked by fifty full-blooded Sioux with garden tools in hand, Hoodstrong, the head man dressed in a orange jumpsuit, whispers "They look *mad*." Chiller replies, "We're all *glad* you're here." Chiller didn't notice that our Native American brothers white washed stones spelling out *Home of the Indians - Home of the Brave*. The *Welcome BOP* banner is not on display.

No matter how ridiculously the man in the orange jumpsuit is dressed, the hacks hit themselves in the head saluting him, until the man in orange suggests lunch.

"You're not obliged to do this," Gaffer entices the servers serving the Celebs roast beef, oven-browned potatoes and grilled vegetables, "but, if you want to do something cool and I know you do, piss in this cherry bug juice. We must refresh our less fortunate guests, fresh from the source of real men."

Cooperation knows no bounds.

Hoodstrong takes a whiff. "Unusual aroma. What do you call this flavor?"

Chiller volunteers, "It's the camp specialty. We serve it to all our honored guests. I knew you would like it. I do, too."

"I would be indebted to you for the recipe, if you can part with it."

Gaffer is tap dancing in the kitchen. "Whacker, bring out that special chocolate cake....the one I baked."

"I put it outside. It's got a stinkin' bad smell."

"Hey, if they like pink piss they'll really like my cake. One man's poison is another man's golden shower punch, no apples. I personally endorse my special treats as a way to end an exhausting day."

"Or life. Don't do it." I warn him. "They'll have it analyzed if one of them croaks."

Hoodstrong, to give him credit, isn't impressed with any of the house beautiful improvements he's seen so far. He just wants to bowl. On the tour, Juan of San Juan, found napping in his haberdashery, rubs his eyes and addresses the vision before him. "Senor, I haven't seen that style in years. A man of your dignity should not wear… that color." Juan shudders.

Not in the habit of criticizing without alternatives, Juan outfits Hoodstrong in officer's khakis, a smart dark blue blazer, and a powder blue shirt.

"Now you look like the Senor in charge!"

"My wife will love this." So does he, he hasn't stop looking in the mirror. You may drop me off at the bowling alley, Mr. Chiller. I wouldn't want to keep you from whatever it is that you do."

Wiping grease from his hands, Mon Capitan slips out from the crawlspace behind alley eight. He concludes his introduction with "These automatic pin spotters are antiques. First generation Brunswick have a zillion parts and are as enormous as an old oak tree, like the original computers use to be."

Examining a disassembled pin spotter, Hoodstrong gets to the point. "You don't by chance have any two-holers around, do you?"

"No, Sir. You must throw a mean hook. Solid oak cut planks are much better than concrete. Care to give it a whirl? We have real kangaroo leather shoes. Saddle soap goes a long way."

Hoodstrong nods. "And I noticed something else…there isn't any fresh paint around here. I'm glad someone used what God put between their ears. How did you end up in residence, if you don't mind my asking?"

"I'm a high octane man equipped with diverse multiplicities. I'm also a self-made and a self-taught master mechanic. In the good ol' days, I dissected airplanes, trucks, autos, boats, any machinery I could lay my hands on. I was principally fascinated with the charms of armored cars. Those money carryin' vehicles haunted my dreams…made me morose with desire. Because of the improbability of gratifyin' my yearnin' anytime soon, I redirected my energies elsewhere and did a bit of importin'. When I took up a more or less permanent address, I took up bowlin'."

Mon Capitan rolls the strike that sets in motion the first of many games with the head of the BOP.

The smell of fresh paint and wax in the field house does not bowl Hoodstrong over, although it nearly asphyxiates him. Chiller turns several shades brighter than the walls. "I would like to show you a mural of Sioux tribal symbols."

We wonder how Chiller manages to believe so much misinformation.

Everyone, excluding Chiller, doubles over laughing. When Rainbow pirouettes, Gaffer informs Hoodstrong, "She. Rainbow. I mean, he is being symbolic, like Picasso's mural."

Before telling Chiller to take a hike, Hoodstrong gives him some sanity orders. "Have a memorandum sent to the dorms and work places telling campers to return to their usual occupations immediately."

When Hoodstrong tells us "Resume your lives, men," he wins favor.

Chapter Fifty-Two
Functioning under Pressure

*The trouble with summer, warm and sensual with gentle breezes, is
that it passes quickly, coming so suddenly to an end it could break your
heart. The NorthWoods are magnificent turning to autumn. I listen to
the rambling streams and smell the blossoms bursting full and fragrant.
Temperate faultless nature graces us with her loveliness. Like a tale of
Courtly Love, admiration is from a distance.*

The spell I'm in is interrupted.

"Where in the fuck is Einstein?" Picasso bangs the table. "Am
I supposed to take notes for him? This place is going to pot."

It's not the usual Monday morning briefing before classes
because it's already Thursday, more than a week later and the men
are already miserable, not having had any visiting privileges over
the weekend. Reading doncha's letter helped, but it's not the same
as having our women with us. I suck it up and say, "You guys aren't
worth anything if you can't function under pressure."

Einstein, giggling like a maniac, finally shows up. He waves a
paper in my face. "Could any of your high pressured neurosurgical
shenanigans replace this copy of an old GED test?"

"I'm impressed. Shall we discuss this maneuver over lunch,
gentlemen? We can prep the guys more efficiently....the tests are
never the same, so it's kosher."

John is breathless. It's strenuous for him to haul his three
hundred pounds across campus in a hurry. "I've come to report.
Hoodstrong told Chiller that he prefers to have lunch in the mess
hall with you people. Mr. Chiller's face turned bright red when
he heard that. Mr. Hoodstrong also said that instead of being
warehoused here, all of you should be working in community
service. And the Warden's back." John scurries away.

"Mind if we join you?" The Warden asks as he and Hoodstrong sit down. "Doc, Herman and I were just talking about fishing. Chiller is no longer allowed on campus, so that won't be a problem...and I must apologize for the aggravation he caused when I was away."

"You might want to check out the Boise Brule River. It has some of the best trout fishing in the country."

Action Jackson and Nothing But Trouble come up behind me. "The Warden's back and he isn't happy. I just snuck out from the bushes in front Chiller's home. I know everything was going along smoothly so I don't know if I should tell you this. Should I? Asshole Chiller crawled out from under his rock a few minutes ago and brought his subterranean self with him. Mrs. C won't let honey hangout at home....so the Warden is permitting him to return to campus on the condition that he remains *exclusively* in his office. Do you think he will? Personally, I don't. What do you think Nothing But Trouble? What are the odds the Chiller will stay in his office and not harass anyone?"

"C'mon, that's a sucker's bet."

Tormenting sadism is the stagnant soil Chiller plots in. Threatening, "I'll single handedly up-root a huge conspiracy going on right under the Warden's nose," thought flares his nostrils. A well-developed olfactory system defines him, with his huge limbic lobe. Sniffing for evidence, snooping around, the snake's head rattles when he hears me say, "You will get an idea of where you stand. It will also reduce anxiety because you'll know what you really need to study and what you're up against..."

"Bingo. I've caught you red handed in an illegal con swindle." Chiller nearly wets himself. His mania is satisfied as easily as any other boorish bureaucrat's. I push him out the door. "The Warden is on his way over here. I'd get lost if I were you."

I tell the men, "Chiller's return is annoying but it's not going to be an obstacle. He's lost. The man's mind is gone. Stay on track determined to be triumphant. Don't let him frustrate you. Don't act impulsively. You'll learn that doing the right thing for the right reason becomes second nature."

"When will that happen, coach?"

"It's already happening."

"Yes, sir, coach."

"You weren't born playing ball and you play like a pro. Now all you need is pro behavior to stay in this game. Same thing. Put in the time and play it straight through. There is no end to becoming better."

The men work well under the premise that they are adult students living on campus. The reality is their minds are ravenous; something they were unaware of up until now. Nourished from the tree of knowledge these men gain confidence.

Hungry for trouble, hanging out in the shadows, Chiller advances. Picasso seizes the opportunity to fan flames fueled with animosity. Picasso goes classic with Milton, reciting, *"The mind is its own place, and in itself can make a Heaven of Hell, a Hell of Heaven,"* remember that Chiller the next time you order everything to be painted purgatory pink. "

"You can't fool me with decoys. I heard Lerner brushing you up on your criminal skills the way I brush up…"

"Spit it out."

"The way I brush up staying on top of you outlaws. I'll see to it that you schemers get what you deserve."

"Thanks a lot. It comforts us to know you have theories to keep you busy when you're not decorating."

"I happen to know you put in the fix."

"You're right. Can't fool you." Picasso pretends to inject himself *with his pen*.

Chiller's lip curls. "You're sick!"

"And you're tripping."

"I'll catch you in the act if it's the last thing I do around here."

"We're always in action. There's nothing we've got that you can catch; it's a personality type. Don't take it too hard, but you haven't go what it takes. Nothing personal."

"I do take it personally. I'm going over the Warden's head to my own people in the BOP. I have clout." Chiller's off and running, a legend in his own mind. We're always glad if we have to see him, to see the backside of him on his way out.

"Sorry that the GED and the Drug Education classes provoke Chiller," I tell the Warden, knowing Chiller flustered him. "But they are what you asked for. The *high* the men are on is authentic and natural, and it has nothing to do with drugs. No one is crashing from a heroin overdose. Learning is all we're doing; there's nothing suspicious in that."

"We need to hold classes in the baseball field bleachers or the fire department will be on us for code violations. The number of campers in attendance *is* staggering."

"Wasn't that the point?"

Picasso takes this opportunity to impress the Warden further. "Now that I'm involved, the men call the Drug Education classes the Trinity. Doc, being scientific and all, is the Father figure. Gaffer is the son. He is the type of son who improves bad boys with relevant personal stories. When it's about self-growth and social responsibility within the community, I am the representative Holy Ghost, focused on the spiritual aspects of inner healing. Eastern mysticism meets western physics is not Doc's line but he listens, he always listens."

The Warden glances at Picasso's bible. "*The Tao of Physics*: Do the students read that?"

"They're groovin' on particles and waves being one and the same. Particles traveling backwards in time naturally brought up the subject of reincarnation. Does that ring any bells for you, Warden?"

"Can't say I know anything about it."

"Check out the lecture schedule, it's posted. A rather precocious student holds the opinion that since matter is vibrating energy, he's assimilating enough brainy energy in the environment to become brilliant." Picasso strokes his goatee. "Changing your head to change your life is not jive talk. Thoughts can change your molecular structure and come right back and change your head, where it all began in the first place. Right, Doc?"

"All we have to do is tap into our resources with awareness. We're wired for it."

Just when I think it might be appropriate to suggest cocktails, the new recruits pile in and the Warden takes off. Presumably, he's gratified. Unquestionably, we stimulated *his* little grey cells.

Rocky shuffles in. "Give me a cigarette and someone to tutor, before I go crazy. I'm having a pukeavating day."

Gaffer assumes his let me shrink you demeanor. "A quick head fix would do wonders for your ego and prevent you from going crazy, Rocky. I'm willing to give you a special no fee consultation, with an installment plan. Just so you know... I'm totally Jungian."

"Listen, Gaffer, you could end up doing extra time for impersonating a shrink."

"Really?! You've heard I'm that good?!"

Chapter Fifty-Three
Burning Off Bad Karma

doncha is in a huddle. I stand on the periphery and listen to her say, "Your age is an asset, not a liability. It enables you to be fully conscious for this rather remarkable journey that you've undertaken."

When the men lose confidence and distrust themselves, doncha reinforces their goals. She hugs me and kisses me on the cheek before she returns her attention to one of the babies whining about his past. "You're right, you didn't make good decisions and you screwed up. What's in the past is never undone until you change the present. What you're doing *now* is fabulous. You're smart and you're a crazy cat with a good grip on reality. An outstanding combination to shape your future."

"Sexy, too?" He drools. He needs a bib.

"You must be. Your wife adores you."

Irish adds, "I think you should take into account that we will have the burden of earning money once we're out of here."

doncha bristles. "How many material possessions do you estimate you will need later? Objects aren't satisfying on a meaningful level or people wouldn't always be looking for the next new thing. Character is the impressive possession. You're an organized person, Irish. File your mistakes away or better yet get rid of them. It's time. We'll do a ceremonial farewell." doncha writes *Irish's past life mistakes* on a piece of paper. "Go on say your good-byes and burn it. It's magic. Go for it!"

Irish lights a match. "I don't know what to say."

"Repeat after me. Goodbye worries. I've had enough of you. I'm on my way to a fabulous future. One that is without superficial needs, wants or desires." Irish repeats the words with doncha.

When she hands him the matches he lights the paper on fire without hesitating.

"You just burnt off a lot of bad karma, Irish. I could tell you meant what you were saying."

"That felt good. I feel relieved."

I, too, feel relieved. Finally, the wench is all mine - no more sharing today. We all have insecurities and everyone, to include me, needs reassurance.

Chapter Fifty-Four
Doc's Eligible for Parole

The Warden hands me a cup of coffee and offers me a chair. "You happen to be eligible for parole under a new law that was just passed. I took the liberty of ordering a copy of your PSI, anticipating you would review it before meeting with the parole board at the end of September."

"I'm sorry, I don't what you're talking about. What is a PSI?"

"It's your Presentencing Investigation report. To be honest, Doc, paroles are unusual."

I'm relieved when the Warden's phone rings and he gets tied up.

My thoughts are consumed with coincidences about what doncha told me so long ago I almost forgot. *Iris Saltzman, the psychic, told doncha that someone she knows in prison was going to receive important papers. Is it likely there was a mistake made in my paperwork? That's what she said. A mistake was made in the important papers of someone doncha knows in prison. I know they made a mistake. Iris Saltzman is no phony, but she can't always be right. And yet, maybe she is right and maybe I'll be released early. No, she didn't mean me...but.... doncha doesn't know anyone else in the joint.*

I stop rationalizing and obsessing when Whacky shows up. "What did the Warden want, Doc? You look upset. Can I help? *Vant* to come into our office....the space we share."

I have to laugh every time Whacky plays Freud.

"It would be a dark day, Whacky, if you and the Gaffer were to part ways like Gustav and Siggy. Their friendship broke up over irreconcilable differences in opinion. Freud didn't like his young colleague, Jung, going his own way with his own ideas."

"Sooner or later everyone goes their own way. It makes me sad but I'll be fine because I'll still have the good memories. It's just one of those things that's part of livin'."

"It's bittersweet."

Whacky sighs. "I know."

✣ ✣ ✣

We spend a lazy late Friday afternoon in September soaking up what may be the last Indian summer day. Sitting on pilfered lounge chairs in the area known as the beach, we pass around a couple of brews and discuss the upcoming parole board. Rainbow shows-up in a two-piece bathing suit with the news. "PSIs are ready at the administration building. You sun worshippers signed up for the parole board, didn't you?" When no one stirs, her hands go to her hips. "Cat got your tongues. Are your legs broken?"

Shakey, about to get up, leans back in his chair. "I'll pick mine up tomorrow. You know the old saying. You've got nothing comin', so take it to the wall, Paul."

"Did you come to suntan?" Whacky does not want to make an issue of Rainbow's attire.

"I came out here to improve my honey color."

"Is that possible?" He looks at her over his sunglasses.

"It is. You guys don't have to keep me company, the girls are coming."

"Let's go get our PSI's...c'mon, don't be pussies." We follow Whacker's lead.

Chiller, delighted to have fresh victims, doesn't waste a minute. "Poor little misfits...bunch of losers want their PSIs."

The Whacker steps up. "If you want to give me a shot, Chiller, I'll give you a fuckin' good reason to do it. Excuse my profanity, Gentleman." Whacky winks at us. Einstein giggles. "Ha, ha, we're all here to pick up our PSIs and it doesn't say we should be harassed in the process. We know our rights."

Chiller grabs my PSI from John. "This thing says you're convicted of a drug crime. A brain surgeon with all his de-brained buddies; the only thing you'll ever operate again, if you're lucky, is a car."

"That's enough, Mr. Chiller. No more hazing."

"Thanks John, but I can handle this." I swipe my PSI from Chiller's hands. "Your suppressed anxiety over not beating or getting beatings from your wife recently has resulted in hostility and unrepressed anger. Are my findings accurate, Doctor Jung?"

Chiller gasps. "You heard that, John. That asshole can't speak to me like that. That's insubordination!"

Dr. Jung, expressing his opinion through his arsehole, farts. "Freud, you approve of my meaning, too?"

Freud gives Jung a thumbs-up.

Chiller's mouth is wide open. "Write them up! Write them up before I throw them in solitary!"

John shakes his head. "I can't; I didn't understand what they said but it had something to do with your wife."

Chiller slams the clipboard down on the desk. It appears he can't write the report, either; mentioning beating his wife would be an act of insanity.

We collectively install ourselves in the library.

"I thought you guys like it here." Rocky greets us with his customary salutation. "It's a shame to attempt early release when you're all so content. Check me out; I'm in high spirits. With all your PSIs to work on, I'll have smokes enough for a month."

We are genuinely attentive as he turns lawyerly.

"On the very day you were convicted, or made a deal with the G, a stupid social worker called a probation officer cornered you in their cubicle workspace to torment you like a cat torments a mouse. When the bully begins questioning you, it's in the most condescending way possible. Your story could be a completely different story from what you were convicted of, which only makes it better for them as they rub-in how you're going to be punished. Fucking sadists don't believe in rehabilitation. Doc's probation officer had some doozies. KISS - keep it simple stupid and one day at a time and crime doesn't pay. Dumb stuff like that. Meanwhile, you're fucking amazed that your life can go off over some bizarre nothing, and boom, it's all over..."

"Rocky, some of us actually committed crimes."

"Okay, back to you guys. Several days before *your* sentencing hearing, your brainless probation officer goes over your PSI for *maybe* two minutes. They bullshit because they never read the documents; that would take time; it's easier for them to declare you fucked for life."

"Can we get unfucked?"

"When I go over your presentence investigations with you I'll concentrate on the federal statues, the backbone of your sentences. I'll show you why once you're fucked almost nothing will help undo the screw. Welcome to the Hotel California and remember the lyrics. *She said we are all just prisoners here, of our own device.* Just the same, I'd be glad to help check you out, if it's possible, in this *best of all possible worlds.*"

Chapter Fifty-Five
Rocky Gives Doc the News

"Mind if I bum a smoke?" Rocky puts his hand out the minute I show up for my PSI review.

"I brought you a pack; I heard you haven't *bought* one since you got here."

"That's right, and I'm better off for it. Give it a try, Doc."

"Come on, Rocky, what's the buzz? I can tell the news is bad just looking at you."

"Of all the gross incompetence I've ever witnessed, your PSI, cooked-up by Fass the ass, your probation office, is the most nauseating piece of work I've ever come across in all my years practicing law. Not only did Fass fuck up royally, the bastard judge, the indifferent prosecutor, and your incompetent criminal attorney fucked up as well. The idiot post conviction attorney didn't read the material or even check it for accuracy. They are all either butt fuck dumb or did it on purpose. Who knows....maybe money changed hands, but I doubt it. My position is that they're dangerously stupid and criminally lazy. You even paid good money to get fucked."

"They made a huge mistake didn't they?"

"That's what I'm telling you. They all did because not one of them read your PSI. If they read it they would have caught the misplaced decimal point that turned you into a felon. Instead of medicating yourself with prescription medication, they charged you like you were dealing. Whichever way you look at it, the cock-up is deplorable." Rocky places a hefty tome titled *Federal Statutes on the Subject of Drug Crimes* in front of me. "I know you can read, so read these two paragraphs aloud."

"I'll read it silently."

"Fine. I already read it hundreds of times."

I look up from the page. "In drug-related crimes the mass of the drug determines the sentencing guidelines from probation up to life depending on the drug mass."

"Correct. Converting to gram equivalents of heroin ensures the accuracy and uniformity of all drug crimes relating to opiates."

"I think I'm about to be told for the first time how they got me inside."

"The drug you were taking was prescription dilaudid. Still, they calculate two grams of dilaudid as one gram of heroin. That's just the way it works. It's two for one with that drug. In your case, convicted of sixty prescriptions, some were for methadone when you tried to get off the dilaudid. It's amazing they charged you for that medication. The scripts written to your patients were for reasonable treatment and they charged you with those, too. Let's forget the Ludes and coke; who didn't do Ludes and coke back then. Now it's Ecstasy – XTC. Anyhow, using isn't a federal offense, only dealing is."

"What are you getting at?."

"Bear with me. Sixty scripts, two counts each. One count was for subterfuge, which is for writing scripts to someone else and taking back the medication. The rest of the counts are for taking back the medication illegally. None of this is anything more than legal mumbo jumbo. In other words, if you had another doc write the scripts for your medication there wouldn't have been a case. Fuck, there was never a case in the first place. The whole thing reeks."

"Tell me something I don't know."

"The long and the short of it - Fass, the idiot probation officer, misplaced a decimal point. The killer is, in so doing he turned you into a felon convicted of possession of 360-gram equivalents of heroin instead of 36 grams, or one hundred times the actual amount of dilaudid you took for pain. There was no dealing. Where they got that from beats me. The error they made is ridiculously sizable, in anybody's book. I cannot believe this happened to you.

A talented guy like you and those careless pigs ruined you. Sorry, Doc. I know this is brutal."

"So why am I in prison?"

"Take into account drug mass threads the sentencing guidelines of a drug crime. If you look at the guidelines, 36-gram equivalents of heroin, if you were *selling*, which you weren't, would buy you a sentence of probation to six months. That's if you were selling. They never had a case against you because there never was a case. Let's face it, Doc, instead of taking the medication for pain, which is what the real deal was, you were tried and sentenced as a regular neurosurgical drug kingpin. The kicker is there wasn't any supportive evidence for a criminal case. What's up with this? How is it that *everyone* missed the mistake? And what's worse, how did they get away with this preposterous shit?"

A searing pain inside me is the consequence of silent desperation. *It's so unfair. I feel sick.*

"I understand they're all idiots. Above all the rest your post conviction attorney Steinbutt… Steinbeck, what the fuck is the difference, should be ashamed to show his face in public. He's supposed to know better. In fact, had he done his job he would have found the mistake and the whole mess, that never should have happened in the first place, could have been straightened out. I don't really understand why it wasn't. But I can tell you it ain't kosher. No way, or we're in sad shape when this many people aren't doing their jobs. What are the odds of that. Are you okay? You're in shock, aren't you? This knocked the shit out of you.

"I find all of this hard to grasp." I'm suspended in animation inside a horrible recurring nightmare. Where does that leave me? Nowhere. I'm nowhere. They've ruined my life.

"Write the asshole Judge a letter. The creep will write back to you: You're case came to mind this morning at breakfast and it was my judgment and discretion that even if it was one milligram, being a Doctor and such, forty-two months is what I deemed and still deem you deserve.

In other words, Doc, you can't win outside the parole board. I still think you should rub Assbern's face in his fuckups. He doesn't belong on the bench. Maybe you'll join me with the ice picks when we check out of this hotel. Schmuck attorneys robbed you. Now, you have to jump through hoops to reinstate your license, and, if you can, start over. One hundred times more than you deserve is what you got and you didn't deserve any of it. You know, Doc, ice picks and ball-peen hammers are a cheap way to get revenge. If all those lazy shits did their jobs correctly you wouldn't be here. They should wear something like the mark of Cain to identify them, so they can't damage anyone else."

I stand up, unstable on my legs, and I can't hear my voice say "What I thought all along is true. I shouldn't be here." Everything has gone hollow.

Picasso taps me on the shoulder. "I bumped into Bill Warden. He's all hepped-up. What's going on? Did I miss something? Okay, don't answer me. The Warden wants you to come to his office on the fly. Maybe you won the Nobel Peace Prize or somethin'. What happened? You're not lookin' too cool."

"I feel worse than I look."

Chapter Fifty-Six
The Warden Commiserates

I end up, although I'm not sure how, sitting in the Warden's office. "The mistake made on your PSI is a horrendous miscarriage of justice and one more reason I dislike working as part of the penal system; and it's a rather significant reason. The truth is, Doc, you shouldn't be here. What is this about?"

"What can I say. It wasn't my decision."

"I faxed a copy of your PSI to Hoodstrong in Washington. The Judge's sentencing statement insinuating, no it was more than that, that you were actually dealing drugs....even with the enormity of the error, I don't know how he came to that conclusion. There wasn't a shred of supportive evidence. The parole board will have to release you. I can't imagine any other alternative."

"We'll see. In the meantime, I have a lot of work to do. I need to return to my office."

He puts his arm around my shoulder and walks with me. "I'm terribly sorry, Doc. I speak from my heart when I say you're a great man and you have some spectacularly unusual qualities."

"That's the reason I'm in the joint."

The Warden pauses and looks at me. I don't know if he really gets it. "This shouldn't have happened. I don't know what else to say." I know the Warden, he's deep like the guys, he'll think about this.

Word travels at the speed of light in the joint. A funereal atmosphere prevails. All week long men come to offer me sympathy. The Jews sit Shiva with me, mourning my lost life. The Irish praise me. The Native Americas bring silence and a peace pipe. Several druggies swear atonement in my honor and the hippies draw close in loving kindness. Showing respect and paying tribute, every one of these men let me know they are here for me. And most of them don't belong in the joint, either. It's a sad state of affairs in this country when we turn our social issues into criminal issues.

I unburden myself to my friends, but not by much; they have worries of their own. "It's comforting to know I have support. I could have used it when I got into this mess. But there's work to be done and, if nothing else, I'm a professional. My priorities are a successful outcome for the GED students and finishing the softball season. After that's accomplished I'll think about this."

My dejection, lessened with a little wisdom, allows for a philosophical tone. Asked about the parole board I answer, "I don't expect anything. I'm no longer the man I was who expected everything and got it. The G, no doubt, will rationalize a way to keep me inside. Shock therapy is an affront on the human psyche that doesn't last forever."

On my way over to call doncha the realization hits me, I can't ask her *exactly* what it was Iris Saltzman, the psychic, said about my legal papers because I was so damn dismissive when she originally mentioned it. Iris Saltzman said an error made would be found in my legal papers. That's all I know. No matter how much I want to tell doncha that Iris is correct, I can't; not on the phone.

Chapter Fifty-Seven
Facing doncha with the News

Waiting to go into the visiting room, I answer my friend's questions. "I can only say understanding the value of doing what is correct has been a hard lesson. It's crucial to do the right thing without the distraction of wanting anything in return, even if it's just praise. Not being sidetracked by temptations that are not good for us, my friends, is imperative for avoiding all kinds of aggravation."

"I never know what's not good for me if I like it." A statement followed with nods of affirmation from fellow campers of like mind.

"Was any of it worth the loss of your freedom?"

"No."

"Then the singular value of what you did and what happened to you as a consequence is that it gives you the opportunity to be better. Not bullshit better. Really better. Which one of us wouldn't be happier without the stress that went into our debut at Club Fed? Own it, gentlemen, at one time some of us thought we were masters of the universe." Swallowing an immensity of self-consciousness, I choke on my ego. "I never told you guys this. The sentencing Judge compared me to the protagonist, Sherman McCoy, in Tom Wolfe's novel *Bonfire of the Vanities*. It's easy to be dismissive with people you don't respect. Now I can see the similarities between that character and myself that I didn't see at my trial. Flawed human being; what does that mean...above the rules... no boundaries? My imperfections were clear the day they slapped handcuffs on me. Before that I defined myself by the *usefulness* of my hands. From the time I was a kid I was devoted to the idea of practicing medicine. When I was able to operate, I loved it. But it stands for nothing when it was sacrificed, along with my vainglorious ego. Every thoughtless thing we do comes back to haunt us."

Picasso pats me on the back. "I would like to mold your PSI into a word problem for the math class. It's the best way I can think of to teach the practical value in learning fractions." When he grabs me and hugs me I know we're all in this together; none of us are so different from the other that we can't recognize pain.

"Go for it. Everyone already knows I'm an asshole and they still like me."

"Was there ever a more serious person than you, Doc? Even when you first came to FPC, you accepted as true that the best part of yourself was lost when they took that knife out of your hands. I'm here to testify that you had plenty more to give. You gave the other best part of yourself to us. You saved many lives around here. Your bein' here has symbolic meaning. It provided a truly moral lesson for all of us to learn by. Trust me; if after this happened to you and you still had it in you to share with us, we owe some major paybacks. You think we would have recognized our depravity without you as a guide? You're a gentleman and a scholar."

"Thanks Gaffer. I feel better now."

"You should, you Quack, quack."

Rainbow, painting her nails, is among the group waiting to enter the visiting room. She has been unusually quiet. "Please, I don't want to hear the Q word ever again, even if you are kidding."

"What's wrong with you today, Rainbow?"

"I'm on the rag, Whacky, if you must know. For your information, I happen to understand how intolerably useless Doc felt without his surgical instruments. He did the only thing a man of his caliber could do; he developed new ways to serve; he came to our rescue, and I will be forever grateful to him. He sat with me through many dark and lonely nights. And he managed to get me medicine I needed when I had that terrible infection."

"Thank you for all for being such good friends and most of all for your loyalty and support. It's a terrific compensation for all the betrayals. They called my name… I have to tell doncha. I couldn't tell her over the phone. As much as I want to see her, I'm dreading opening old wounds."

doncha is appalled. She sees malignant design in the magnitude of the *error*. Sickened, she judges life crueler than she ever imagined possible. Never having forgotten what Irish Saltzman told her about my legal papers, the mistake in its magnitude and its actuality turns her raw emotionally. Desperate to confront every one of the criminally negligent personally with their evil deceit, she falls silent. Her lips press together. I can tell she is holding back an existential shriek - one that may never stop coming if she surrendered to her anguish and cried out.

Holding her shoulders, I penetrate her eyes, green and gold. I see the cat has claws and I want to crush her with love. "Listen to me doncha, I'm forgetting this for now and I want you to do the same. We'll be fine."

"I want to melt into that safe place inside you. Hold me, tight," she pleads. Bringing her close, consoling her, she breathes her way into equanimity. Every breath is a retreat from heart-breaking grief.

"I'm determined that the day I'm released legal complications are over for me. Let's talk about something else. I started reading *Perfume*."

Whacky and Gaffer join us. The timing is perfect. Gaffer scratches his head. "*Perfume*? I think I read it.

I keep a straight face. "It begins with a child born with no scent to his body. His body has no odor, no smell at all...."

"Shit!" Whacky nudges Gaffer. "That's somethin' you shouldn't read. It'll make you self-conscious."

So it goes; an initially traumatic but loving weekend passes with tears and laughter, but mostly laughter. The truth in the scheme of things is: this is just a day in a life... if we're lucky we know how to make it bright.

Chapter Fifty-Eight
The Art of Memory

"Listening at the back of several classes, the tension in the air is the reason I called for this assembly. I want to offer you scholars advice that worked for me. In medical school, when I had to take a test I stuck to the principle that what I couldn't absorb I memorized. I went back later and learned thoroughly what I needed or wanted to know. We aren't going for a show of knowledge. Most of the work you're doing is for test taking. Knowledge doesn't come all at once. It's a lifelong pursuit. Trust me, many of you have gone further than high school level studies; you're doing university work. The rest of you aren't too far behind."

Chiller rolls his eyes in his head and leaves the auditorium getting in the way of Montana, loaded down with books. "Why are you breaking your neck for this bunk junk? Memorize. You know Lerner is a pushy son-of-a-bitch. C'mon, guy, you're better than that. I heard you took a shot at him."

"Doc and I straightened that out a long time ago. Not only did he apologize to me, he helped me overcome a lot of issues. Like Doc says, once you taste pay dirt there isn't any going back."

"I won't put up with this radical infiltration in my department. I know what's up around here. No one's fooling me."

Losing his power to victimize Montana, Chiller hangs around to annoy anyone willing to listen to him, which leaves me for target practice. He's confident that he hit the bull's eye, but he's never on target. "I get it. I finally get why you put in so much over-time. You're paid an immense secret salary under the table. I've got your number, bigshot ex-doctor."

"Cute, Chiller; the next letter after x, in case you've forgotten, is y and then z. It's good that you finally completed something. You must be ready to retire."

"Enough of your dumb jokes. I know what's important to you, Jew boy."

"When you die, if you're fortunate enough to come back as a superior being, kicking into your historical roots, opposed to your hysterical roots, you'll return as a monkey. Perhaps then you might understand what is of value to me....but I doubt it."

"Leave Darwin out of this. I suppose you think the error made in *your* sentencing report makes *you* special."

"You see *these* hands. They fly." My technically trained fingers form knots, one-handed-ties, repetitively, on fishing line procured to keep my fingers nimble. Walking away, I pray, *Please let me do this again with suture material. Please let me operate again* is the energetic communication I put out to the universe with every strand of my DNA. If stretched out that would be five-hundred-million miles of prayer.

Chapter Fifty-Nine
Gaffer's Troubles with the Wrong Word

Burning the midnight oil, our well-disciplined team is preoccupied with success every minute of the day. In the mess hall, in the shower, watching games or taking a dump, the men fire questions at each other and someone always has the answer.

"As I predicted, you created monsters, Daddy-O. At times they're groovin' on being smarter than we are."

"At any rate, they're doing precisely what I want them to do."

"What, exactly, is that, Doc?"

"I want them to use the frontal lobe. I want them to think. This part of the brain," I press on the bone over Picasso's frontal lobe, "is called the key hole. It separates the frontal lobe from the temporal lobe. Drill a hole and it is approachable from both sides. Anyway I can I'll get across that they are intelligent, not just street smart. The frontal lobe is intellectuality and the temporal lobe is memory. Connecting the two will support them through this and any other difficulties they encounter in life. That's the point of all of this, isn't it?"

"And all they have to do is exercise their lobes. Is that right, Doc? Mentally fit and physically fit, what more could they ask for?

"Moral perfection. Factor that in and we'll be surrounded by men that make God proud."

"I think you're fab, Doc. You're one in a million. You're…"

"Are you trying to butter me up?"

Mon Capitan shows up and brushes Picasso aside. "Excuse me, but those boys are turnin' into gators. I'm sorry if this offends you, Doctor, but you and those boys need a break… and Nothin' But Trouble is so bored he's been takin' bet on future test results. What do you say? Give 'em a break."

I do give them a break or Whacky wouldn't be next up with two outs. He hits a line drive. The shortstop catches it and the Whacker returns to the dugout, bummed out. The Gaffer exchanges the wrong word with him and the next thing I know Whacky is chasing fat ass Gaffer, going after him with a bat. Tired out, Whacky returns to the dugout. Cooler heads prevail at the bottom of the seventh, until Gaffer shifts positions, from left field to pitcher.

With two outs, if Shorty, on first, scores the winning run the game is over. Gaffer has one strike on the Monarch batter. He tries a pick-off play. Shorty has a lead off. Gaffer runs to first to cover it, in case there's a play between second and first, piggy in the middle. His strategy doesn't work; Shorty returns back to the bag in time. No one hears what transpired between Shorty and Gaffer before Shorty wrestled Gaffer to the ground, screaming, "No one calls me that!"

"You're out. The game's over." Gaffer kicks up a storm. "Get off me."

Shorty stays in Gaffer's face. "You called me the N word. I hate that more than ever coming from a white bread boy like you."

Gaffer jumps up. "I never said it. I never would. All I did was compliment you for not getting tagged out."

"You're a fucking liar, Gaffer. That's a direct attack on my honor."

Before they put on the gloves, John the Hack steps in. "As Commissioner of FPC Softball League, I say the game is over. For the first time in the history of FPC softball there's a tie for the World Series."

When opposing sides complain to me, I advise them to calm down. "Don't judge an entire group on one man's faults. This is a gentleman's joint." I hope that the words will trigger a truce, if Gaffer shuts up and behaves himself. I confide in Whacky, as we go over the events, that John saved us a lot of grief ending the game with a tie.

"Yeah, the Gaffer has got to cheat and use his garbage mouth. We're all tired but he's got to start up."

Of course, Gaffer thinks he's a legend.

"If I was you, I'd formally apologize to Shorty and everyone else, or stay in the dorm for the duration."

"Don't get carried away. I have lots of black friends. Shorty knows that I'm super-competitive when I play competitive sports. C'mon on Doc, you know that. I always have a sting operation to fall back on."

I put my hand up for him to stop.

"You mean you had a lot of friends, dummy." Whacky smacks him with a rolling pin.

"That wasn't nice. That makes me feel BAD!"

"No shit!"

Gaffer doesn't lose time begging Shorty to forgive him. When Shorty doesn't budge, Gaffer jumps up on the mess table; although the gesture is grandiose, he humbles himself. "I beseech you, Shorty, and all of you, to forgive me. I honestly don't remember what I said in that heated moment, which goes to show what a competitive prick will do to win. Because Shorty says I said what he says I said, I'm really scum for having said it. I'm humiliated for being such a jerk. Please believe me when I say I am repentant. I love my soul brothers. I hope you find it in your hearts to love an asshole like me again."

They will forgive him in time, even if presently the encouragement is minimal. "Blow the rest of your crap out of your ass somewhere else, Gasser," teaches our friend that his compromised integrity isolates him and puts him into a solitary confinement of sorts. Hopefully he'll improve his strategies and learn that success or the lack of it has so many layers, peeling even one of them away can make you cry. What's the good of a sting, when there's no flavor worth savoring.

Chapter Sixty
All Knowledge is Precious

"I'm always happy when I have excellent news to report. This morning, I found out what all of you are dying to know. Nearly killing each other and ourselves, at times, in the effort to achieve this event, I am pleased to announce that everyone passed the GED with flying colors... and more than half of you are above the ninetieth percentile in the country. No one is below the eightieth percentile. Had it not been for word problems the scores would have been off the wall. Nothing to be ashamed of as they stand... I'm damn proud!"

"Doc, you told me I would pass. I'm like a diamond in the rough. I'm a venereal genius."

Whacky cracks me up. "You mean a veritable genius."

Charles comes back from searching for Greco. "Mr. Chiller is holding Greco hostage in his office."

"Cheat!," reverberates down the hallway. "Confess right now. You'll end up in a penitentiary anyways, you senile old fart....and I'll make sure they're harder on you if you lie to me."

Sister Mary protests. "I was in the room while Mr. Greco took his GED test. He's worked very hard to succeed."

"He took the test last year and he wasn't even in the fortieth percentile. How do you explain that, you conniving geezer? I'll make you own that you and Lerner are nothing but con artists.... this whole thing was a scam! Go on prove me wrong! I dare you!"

Greco turns to us. We encourage him to continue. "Okay, it was like this....I won't say I had an inferior teacher then and better teachers now."

"Watch it, Mister!" Chiller turns to the troops at the door. "You're all history, now. He's going to spill the beans."

Greco points his finger toward his meaning. "It came to me from above. You know. Heaven."

Chiller pushes Greco out the door. "Go to hell. If I'd been around, all of you would have been stopped in your tracks."

"I wouldn't brag about that if I were you. I must have a word with your father-in-law about your pathologic behavior."

"You're nothing but a snitch. Watch your ass if you report me. Do you hear me, Lerner?"

Walking out the door I hear someone from somewhere in the building shout "Shut the fuck up, Chiller, we're trying to think in here…try it sometime, asshole."

Watching the sun set in ribboned flames makes me want doncha, badly. For her not to be present on this occasion after she contributed so much, coaching me, inspiring me, helping me on days when I was so overwhelmed that only she could charge my batteries, saddens me. She saw me through this. I listen to the men congratulate each other, warmed with Mon Capitan's reserves and a bonfire. "Good thing the BOP sent spies. No one can say anyone cheated. Everyone aced the GED exam." I'm relieved when Whacky picks up the ball. I don't want anyone to sense the melancholy mixed-in with my gratification.

"We showed 'em we're nobody's fools. The world looks beautiful from where I'm standing. Didn't I tell you I was a genius?" Whacky crows with the right to be heard. "I feel like I made my Bar Mitzvah." Whacky raises his cup to Greco, the other scholar most elated with his excellent test results. Greco, seeing everything through rose-colored glasses, sobs, "My friends, I like it here because of you. Best of all, I'm happy that I don't have to go to the Big House. I never thought anything like this could happen to me." Greco kisses Irish, his proud tutor, the way he kisses his eldest son when he leaves the visiting room. Even though Irish is not accustomed to Italian emotion, he lets himself be kissed. "Thank you, Irish and all of you, from the very bottom of my ol' turkey buzzard heart. Life is beautiful. L'Chaim."

"Doc, what's the matter with you? I think the booze paralyzed his facial muscles. You'll recover, Doc. But Doc, listen to me… don't you agree that the Gaffer and I would make sensational shrinks if we do our Internship with you?" Whacky crosses his arms over his chest and cocks his head waiting for the right answer. After several attempts to speak, I finally get out, "And, pray tell, what do you think you've been doing?"

Chapter Sixty-One
Graduation

The next thing I know, I'm on a ship and Montana is shaking me. "Doc, get up. doncha will be here soon. You made me promise to wake you at seven o'clock. It's seven and that's not an answer to a multiple choice question."

"How did I get on this ship?"

"You're not on a ship; it's just a hangover."

doncha does her best to revive me. With the last of first kisses, she confronts me. "Why didn't you call me last night?"

"You're jealous, doncha!" Rainbow takes her head back and around. "I didn't think of *you* as the jealous type."

That makes me laugh. "This woman, in a fit of jealously when she *thought* I was with another woman, burnt all of my clothes. Armani. Gucci. Prada. Suits, ties, shoes, everything."

"Were you innocent, Doc?" Rainbow scrutinizes my face.

"You never know what this redhead will do."

"I do the same thing everyone else does when you're perfect, I sing your praises. You're everyone's hero and you'd better remain mine, if you know what's good for you." She displays an impress bicep.

Lucy Greco's face flushes. "Excuse me for interrupting. I wanted to do more to thank you, Doctor Lerner, but I made you a German chocolate cake. I heard it's your favorite…"

"I only showed Greco the way to get started. He and Irish did the rest. Greco is a remarkably intelligent man."

"Yes he is and I'll always be grateful that you encouraged Irish to help him."

Graduation is one of those remarkable days when appreciation and dedication have their rewards. On this exceptional day, visitors mingling on the lawn drink lemonade and exchange pleasantries.

"The weather is perfectly mild."

"My boyfriend knows all about brain chemistry."

"Mine reads literature. He used to read comic books."

"The sun came out in the nick of time."

"It certainly did. I know that I'm going to have a good life, at last."

The setting may be different, but in this community it's comparable to a graduation tea served on a college lawn. The elderly sit in the shade, children play, and adults visit. The ushers open the doors and announce the main event is about to begin.

This is where things get *really* unusual. Rainbow, playing the piano, is outfitted in a black graduation gown emblazoned with a constellation of rhinestones; she's a cross between Tinkerbelle and Liberace. As light refracts from her star-sparkled robe, she and the stellar voice of the Barber singing *Stouthearted Men* accompany the graduates marching in to take their seats. They're singing:

> *Give me some men who are stouthearted men,*
> *who will fight for the right they adore.*
> *Start me with ten who are stouthearted men*
> *and I'll soon give you ten thousand more...*

Bill Warden looks like Father Christmas standing at the microphone. "Ladies and Gentleman, I give you the first GED graduation ever to brighten the reputation of this house. When the booming applause subsides he invites the Chaplain to the microphone. "The Chaplain will now give the benediction." The Warden joins Sister Mary, fast at her rosary, praying that the Chaplain, wobbling at the microphone, will not fall head first from the stage.

Gaffer restored the Chaplain to a somewhat suitable state, re-buttoning and dusting dusty clothes. Re-straightening the man's clerical collar, Gaffer places the unholy relic on stage. Remaining close behind to manage any missteps, when the Chaplain doesn't move a muscle, Gaffer pokes him. "Say something, stupid."

Startled, the Chaplain blurts out, "Dearly beloved, we have gathered here today…"

Gaffer cues him. The third time the Chaplain gets it wrong, Gaffer, positioned behind him, like a ventriloquist, speaks for him. "May God bless and keep this fine class and send them on their way to be of good use in society. Amen."

"What the fuck do you think this is the graduating class of Notre Dame?" Gaffer escorts the Chaplain, pissing himself, off stage, making room for the Warden at the microphone.

"My name is Bill Warden or Warden Warden. Even with my name and my profession being the same, it's strange to say that I happen to be Warden of this institution. If any of the graduates have been offered the position it wouldn't surprise me….but I doubt they would find satisfaction in a system that values punishment and calls it rehabilitation, any more than I do. Rehabilitation is a word I dislike nearly as much as I detest the institutional concept of punishment. My preference has always been for a system that strives to attain a transformative ideal. Blessed with an intelligent and dedicated group of well-educated men who devoted their time and energy to provide a stimulating academic environment, we have been triumphant putting an idea into action.

The recipients of this enterprise were our graduates. Realizing their best selves, they worked toward a secondary school diploma and in the process surpassed all expectations. I am proud of the academic achievements and the team spirit of these men. When asked why they worked so hard, they replied with their motto - *Once you taste success, it's difficult to accept anything less.* I'd like to introduce the instigator of this motto and the headman of the

Department of Education. Doctor Bernard Robert Lerner. Please come forward, Doc."

Given a standing ovation that stuns me, it takes me a minute or so before I regain my composure.

"You men certainly know how to say thank you. I really appreciate that. Now that I can speak, I'll tell you that this has been a gratifying, and obviously successful operation. I can say unreservedly that the process included healing ourselves as we healed each other. Coming from a damaged society, as damaged men, we overcame our spoiled vision of what life should be and concentrated, instead, on how to best live on this planet with respect for what we were given. Tikkun olam means healing or repairing one person or one thing at a time with the intention of healing this truly disfigured world. We figured out, not without pain, how to do this as we went along. After all, we weren't born with all the essential knowledge required, and we aren't finished products. We have, however, shared an illuminating and worthwhile path. I'm proud to have traveled this road with these men, celebrated today. Be proud of yourselves for doing something truly worthy of your efforts. Love you, guys. Professor Picasso, we call on you."

The audience is exuberant once again.

"When Doc arrived I was teaching art. You guys never became great artists but you developed first rate minds. Before I knew what hit me, Doc talked me into tutoring art history, history, English, math, and anything else that came up short. No second bests around here. Everyone had to be first in the class. From the start, I was my usual pessimistic self. But, after a while, if Doc asked me to swim the English Channel, which I once remarked might be the next project he and Warden would dream up to keep us in tip-top shape, I would. I'd have to ask Juan of San Juan, our fabulous tailor, to fashion a pair of water wings for me because I can't swim and I would never say no to them. Good going, Graduates, you deserve our respect. No kidding, you men worked all-out and you've gone a great distance in a short time. You made us proud. Next up is our very own Einstein."

Einstein giggles before he begins, the way he always does.

"Honoring these men today is a pleasure." He wipes away a tear. "And it is a far cry from my old selfish behavior, wiggling on the ground like an angle-worm to have my own way. If these men copped-out like I did, I'd still be an earthworm. From now on I'm straight-up. Doc made sure our heads were screwed-on the right way, enabling us to create a utopia. Utopia is defined as nowhere. I know there's no where like this on the planet, but it's not in my head alone, it's in my heart, too. I know these men and I know they are a phenomenon that can be repeated with the outstanding leaders among you. Lead by example is your beautiful and elegant motto. Also, about Einstein's theory of relativity….because I'm not particularly fond of my relatives, I hang-out with people I admire. Friends of mine, you are the greatest. You changed my life. Thanks! I will never forget any of this. Zee, take it away."

"I loved teaching and reading literature with the graduates. Their mature insights made an enormous difference in what they brought to the table. You see, living among *real* character is inspiring. I'm proud of the Graduates phenomenal success. Congratulations to this awe inspiring group. We're bigheaded with pride because of you. Charles, the Co-Chief of Education, will address this fine gathering."

Charles blushes. "Thanks for being friendly; you helped me find confidence and a purpose. I wish you all success in all your future endeavors. Your achievements are outstanding." The men cheer and applaud Charles who made it his business to go out of his way for them on every occasion.

Bill Warden takes over at the podium.

"Two students graduating today have been chosen for outstanding accomplishments in academics. Whacky has additional honors in humanitarian affairs. Whacky and Greco are true representatives of this class. They are the class valedictorians. Whacky, please come up and say a few words."

Whacky stares at the microphone. "I never gave a speech before. This is tougher than I thought. Well, here goes." He crumbles the paper with the speech he prepared. "You heard the Barber and Rainbow and all us graduates sing *give me some men who are stouthearted men*. Well, here we are. The song says *hearts can inspire other hearts with their fire for the strong… obey when a strong man shows the way*. That man, I am proud to say, is the Doc, my roommate and one of the best friends I ever had in my life, and he's my teacher and he tutored me." Whacky pauses to compose himself. "He taught me to do somethin' not too many people would have thought was possible for me. But I did it. I became successful in what is worthwhile and I am conscious about how I live *almost* all the time. I speak for everyone I know here at FPC when I say we love you Doc. Now that I'm done, if anybody disagrees with me I'll see them outside. Come up here, Greco, you genius." Whacky gives Greco an affectionate hug and leaves the stage.

Greco takes a cavernous breath. "I am a dinosaur of sorts. In this house filled with big-hearted men, Doc and his gang helped me. Doc got Irish to tutor me, calling in a favor. You didn't think I knew that did you, Doc? That was my lucky day. I'm like the Scarecrow in the Wizard of Oz. Not only did I get a brain, I got instructions on how to use it. When I leave here, Harvard is the place for me….even if it's just to sweep the Quadrangle. I don't mind as long as I can use their library. Thank you, Doc, and Warden, and Irish, and all of you great men that made this day possible. God bless."

The Warden and I call on the graduates to receive their official diplomas. With diplomas in hand, throwing graduation caps into the air, they march out of the auditorium singing *Stout Hearted Men* to a standing ovation.

I'm happier today than I was when I graduated second in my medical school class because today it's a first for everyone…and I love these men; they're family.

Arm in arm walking to the mess hall, Rainbow, teary-eyed, sighs. "That was a beautiful sight. I'll never forget it."

"Rainbow, why didn't you fling your cap like all of us did? That's tradition."

"Whacky, I'm surprised at you… it's a designer's piece and my souvenir forever."

"Why didn't I think of that? Now it's too late."

doncha, knowing Whacky is too finicky to keep just any hat, consoles him. "Whacky you will always have the memory of the high honors you received today. The memory of this day will last you a lifetime…not to mention what you have become in the process."

"As the Doc says, when you're right, you're right." Whacky hugs doncha. When he hugs Rainbow, she blushes.

"I'll never forget *that* for the rest of my life. Thank you, Whacky. Thank you from the bottom of my heart."

"You're welcome."

Rainbow is speechless all the way over to the mess hall.

Leading the crew of campers serving dinner, waltzing from table to table, Gaffer has that mischievous shit-eating grin that makes Whacky nervous. After a magnificent dinner, Whacky gives Gaffer one of his genuinely generous hugs. "You did a fabulous job. I'm proud of you. I thought for a minute that you were going to, but you didn't pull any of your usual shtick."

The Gaffer, a fiend for praise, looks like a good little puppy receiving a delicious bone. Whacky's behavior modification program, influenced by reading about Pavlov and his dog, produced verifiable results. Obviously, in Whacky's version, he's Pavlov and the Gaffer is Pavlov's dog, no matter what Gaffer says to the contrary.

This perfect day ends with the men singing *Stout Hearted Men*, toasting each other in the dorm. Psycho, secretly AWOL for an undetermined period, returned with the goods. After partying so hard, we pass out like students who overindulged at a *smashing* graduation party.

Chapter Sixty-Two
Junk Food Junkie

It's a crisp autumn morning. The air is sweet, scented with burning leaves. Rainbow takes a devouring breath and tip toes over to admire us sleeping beauties snug in bed. "Oh you handsome specimens of male physiognomy, it's time to get up and out. It's the maid's day in." Her tune goes flat. "What is that awful smell?" One hand over her mouth, she shoves John out of our room with the other. "What's that mess you're stuffing in your fat face?"

"Nothing."

"Don't speak with your mouth full. God you're gross."

"Get the fuck out of here, man." Whacker covers his face with his pillow. "I thought a rat crawled up *someone's* asshole and died."

"Wait, wait, I'm finished." John crams the remains in his mouth. "I came to tell you," gulp, "that football season is…" Death's spitting image embraces John. Clutching his chest, John falls to the floor.

Scooping masticated taco out of John's mouth is no way to begin the day. "This is the garbage that you're so crazy about, Gaffer." To return blood to John's head, Whacky helps me position him flat on his back. Because he's seen me do this before, Whacky elevates John's legs thirty degrees. "Rainbow, tell Doc Frank that John is in cardiac arrest. Fly, girl!"

I extend John's fleshy face into position. "Gaffer, John needs mouth-to-mouth resuscitation. Make sure he doesn't swallow his tongue." I demonstrate, repeating the directions, to bring Gaffer into the rhythm. "Whacky, using the heel of your palms, one on top of the other, compress John's chest exactly like I'm doing. Make it approximately 40-60 compressions per minute."

"Take it easy, Doc; you'll hurt him."

"I'm trying to cause electrical activity to ignite his engine. Now you do it... and make sure you pump hard!"

"Is this hard enough?"

"You pump like a pro. Keep going. His arteries are coming to life. You've got it... that's right. Keep it up. Now hold it a second so I can to listen to his heart. Damn. No activity yet. Continue."

"I felt somethin' crack. I think I broke his rib."

"If you don't break a rib you aren't doing it hard enough. Look at him. He's a thirty-seven year old beached whale. I warned him off junk food. He wouldn't listen."

The crowded hallway parts like the Red Sea to make way for Doc Frank pushing the medical crash cart. An arterial line and several large I.V.'s are employed immediately to intubate John.

"Gaffer, you're as green as peas."

"My head is floating a mile from its circumference. I need to throw up."

I indicate the trashcan. "The electrical monitoring device reads poor activity." I grab the stethoscope and listen to John's chest. "Good air exchange. We're in the right place with the endotracheal tube." I cut and thread an I.V. catheter into John's jugular. Doc Frank does the same with a second catheter in John's elbow-joint.

"He's almost there. Don't look do terrified; I wouldn't let anything happen to John anymore than I'd let anything happen to any of you." I hand Gaffer a sponge. "Wipe the blood off John's neck and arm and tape the I.V. lines down." Gaffer barfs like a trooper, again, and gets right back on the job.

The monitor signals distress. Three jolts of current do the trick. "I want all of you bystanders to pray for the ambulance. Go on! Do your part. I know you've all gathered here to lend moral support. Put your all into it!"

✳ ✳ ✳

Doctor Hernandez, on his post op rounds, attempts to set John straight. "Culo gordo, I'm warning you that you have to lose a hundred pounds."

"I'm hungry."

"May I suggest you wire his mouth shut, Doctor Hernandez."

"How's the patient?" the Warden asks when I return from the hospital.

"Fat."

"Knowing you that means John is fine."

"He's fine for a placoderm."

"What is a placoderm?"

"In this case, it's a mortal that eats more crap than is reasonable and becomes extinct in the process, if he doesn't quit stuffing himself."

Chapter Sixty-Three
Passing Up a Weekend Pass

If anything goes wrong after a surgery, it's bound to happen within the first six to twenty-four hours. A note from the Warden first thing this morning worries me that John has had a surgical complication. To make it worse the Warden's explicit look says this is going to be up close and personal.

"I just wanted to tell you that The Eagle and I have discussed the parole board hearing, which is a mere ten days away. We are both of the opinion that you're going to have your sentence reduced, or better."

"Any news about John this morning?"

"John is fine. Herman and I want you to call your post conviction attorney and fire him. You'll do better on your own, with the help of the Governor. I don't have to tell you that Dan Walker is not only intelligent and spiritual, he also knows his way around the law. It's safer to travel this road with someone trustworthy, which brings me to the second item on my agenda. Put together a lesson plan for next year's classes. I can't have the department falling apart when you leave."

"Good idea." I walk around the Warden's office. "You should be proud of these." An eloquent silence follows. I remember the distain and contempt I felt for the Warden and his photos when I first arrived. After a wrong turn and a misplaced decimal point rubbed my nose in my circumstances, I learned how to share abundant human resources, no matter where they might be found.

Across from the Warden at his desk, I light a cigarette. "Some say there are no mistakes and that there's no such thing as an accident. Others say watch out for what you wish because it may come true. Strange, when I desired to work in an environment that is *perfectly,* if there is such a thing, productive. I never thought I'd have to go this far to have that experience....but I did."

"I'm glad that we met...although I wish it never happened... not here."

"You're a terrific guy Warden but I could have lived without knowing you, too....but I can't say I'm unhappy."

"I'm giving you a weekend pass. That should make you happy. It's the least I can do after you saved John's life and everything else you've done around here."

"No matter how tempting, and thank you for the offer, but I can't accept. The real heroes of the day are Whacky and the Gaffer. I've been trained for medical emergencies; they haven't."

"Are you sure? You don't want to take this weekend for yourself?"

"I wouldn't do it."

"Can they be trusted?"

"It appears they can be. They're not at risk to escape. They like it here."

"We laugh but it's true."

Noticing the Eagle standing in the doorway the Warden calls him in. "Hoodstrong, what do you think about the two Irishmen out on the town for a weekend?"

"I'd like to be a fly on the wall hanging out to see what happens with those two playboys on a spree."

Whacky and the Gaffer are in seventh heaven, floating on cloud nine, chattering about their up-coming weekend.

"Gaffer will be applying his famous half-nelson on some sweet thing before the soon to be historic date night is over. I've seen him in action on weekends. He's a handful."

"How's that, Doc?" Whacky asks looking up from his plate.

Mon Capitan suggests, "You guys might want to do the deed slower than you eat."

"That's what I'm talking about. His speedy hands are everywhere. They don't call him The Octopus for nothing."

"Slow down, boys. You *must* take time to delight in nibbling a juicy piece here, sucking sweetness out of a piece there. Savor the succulence." Mon Capitan winks at them. "Get my drift?"

Gaffer howls.

In the dorm on this moonlit evening, the laughter is male and lusty.

"Thanks, Doc. You're responsible for the carousing we're gonna do, until we drop, and we know it." Gaffer and Whacky make slobbering kissing noises kissing me on both cheeks. "Stop it. Save your smooching for the women. Return on time and no wheelbarrow stuff."

"Who us? You must be kidding. I don't know about you Whacker, but I'm going to start my weekend tonight."

"Bullshit." Whacker turns out the lights.

"Gather me bags, I must dream me dreams about it."

"We've got to give Gaffer credit. He knows how to make the most of anything."

"Then I'm goin' to gather me bags, too. Hey, Gaffer, wait for me."

"Have a good time, gentlemen. I'm just going to sleep."

Chapter Sixty-Four
Sit up Straight

Familiarity breeds contempt is the dominant mood as we sift through last year's work to organize it for next year's students. Einstein has that *I'm bored and about to turn reptilian gaze*. "Our standard is much higher than the basics. This is for kindergartners..."

"I know you'd like to start with quantum mechanics but the thing is, the job ain't that easy. We start at the bottom and work up proportionately, meeting the needs of the incoming wounded. This has nothing to do with your thirst for excitement."

"Listen to me, Doc, quantum..."

Sometime during this grueling debate, Chief came in. Picasso places the envelope Chief delivered to his forehead. "My vibration is this is from the Warden and the Oscar goes to...." He rips open the envelope. "Wait! This is hilarious. The Gov expects Doc in his office at noon. His office, working for the anti-Christ Chaplain, is the broom closet in the chapel. You better jump into your suit and tie, super-guy; you don't want to spoil any delusions."

"As hard as I try, I haven't disturbed yours."

✧ ✧ ✧

"Governor, I'm grateful that you offered to help me out with the parole board."

"My pleasure, but it's my impression that any time you get off has already been settled before the board meets with you. Since our time is limited, let's work on demeanor."

I light a cigarette, look down at myself and shrug. Treated to the Governor's hospitality, I'm told how to look, speak, act, and think from a man who is sincere, instead of phonies.

"I hope you don't mind if I advise you that I agree with the Warden about firing your post conviction attorney."

"When?"

"When you leave here."

✿ ✿ ✿

The Warden offers me his chair. "Use my phone to call the one who thinks *he's* your Higher Power."

Disliking confrontation, I do it because it needs doing, and Steinbutt must be curious because he takes my call.

"Lerner, have you bolted?"

"I'm calling from the Warden's office. You don't accept reverse charge calls and it's the only way we can make calls from here."

"If I spoke to every one of my clients in prison I would be on the phone all day."

You don't mind accepting money all day long for doing absolutely nothing. "I made a decision..."

"I'm glad you called."

"Really?" *Bullshit.*

"I just this minute finished a letter to you. I represent a high profile politician of importance and a body shop..."

"I don't know the politician that well and I don't know your other client the chop shop guy at all. I didn't call to discuss them."

"Look, I can't really in good faith deal with all three of you on the same day and you've only been in for a short time....how long is it? Anyways, the point is, I made a decision to postpone my appearance for you until the next parole board hearing... in nine months from, yes, from today. That way, I'll have more time to concentrate on your case."

"That won't be necessary. You are officially relieved from your professional relationship with me."

He sputters. "Who will represent you?"

"Someone who knows my case."

"You will *not* have a positive resolution without *my* help. But hey, have it your way." He hangs up.

I sense the Warden hovering behind me.

"Good, Doc, you did fine. I believe I'm correct in saying that he hasn't read your PSI or the motions you filed. No one, including those who prosecuted you, will want to take responsibility for their negligence. Spend another hour with the Governor in preparation for the hearing...you only have a week to prepare but you're going to win."

"Thanks for your support, Warden. Steinbutt is a loser anyways. He got knocked-out in fifteen seconds in the first round of a Golden Gloves boxing match. A young Puerto Rican kid did the honors. Rocky told me all about it. Doing what he has no aptitude for he's a failure, more than ever because he doesn't put out any effort."

I find the Whacker waiting for me outside the Warden's office.

"I had to tell you, Doc, that I had a premonition about you being a short timer. For the Gaffer and me the parole board hearing will be another day down with the polyester people. We're here for the duration. But not you. What are you going to do when they let you go?"

"You mean what will I do if I have to leave my friends and fantabulous life? You know I really haven't thought that far ahead. I can tell you that anything, including Disney World, would be anticlimactic after living with you guys."

"I'll miss you, Doc."

"I'll miss you too...but I'm only going to be with the Governor for an hour."

Chapter Sixty-Five
The Parole Board

The day of the Parole Board hearing, Whacky is first in. Coming out, he's slamming the door, hard, behind him. "From the way the assholes were hammerin' at me, I thought more time was gonna be slapped on me. Asshole Buckaroo and chump change Chiller dished me out two shots each. Wait 'til they don't see what goes in the food I personally serve them, *after they've eaten it.* I told those phonies in there that I never took a fuckin' drug in my life, other than alcohol, and that's legal. I would never turn down a good drink. Since the parole pricks know so much about me, I asked if any of 'em knew when I'm gettin' another weekend pass."

I laugh. "I like that."

Whacky puts his arm around my shoulder. "I'm gonna miss you. I mean it. Life won't be the same without you around. Here comes Blossom. He went in fired up for action.... three stinky portions of huevos rancheros would do anyone but him in."

The parole board's commissioners, choking for air, race out of the conference room behind Gaffer, and we know why. Nonchalant as the day is long, Gaffer struts over to us. "They didn't see my defense weapon against liars coming at them from behind." Gaffer is rewarded with thumbs up from the guys hanging around lending moral support.

On the other side of the room, Steinbutt and his equally ineffectual partner are promising their enraged client, snarling obscenities at them, "We'll win on the appeal."

"The fuck you will. You're fired." Another client bites the dust. The chop shop operator, who put used parts in cars and charged the insurance companies and paying customers for new parts, is treated to a dose of *I don't give a shit*, lack of professionalism.

Amazing how infuriated some people can get, never expecting to have some of their own back.

I hear the epic drum roll. My time to face the Inquisition, skillful turners of the screw, is upon me. Savvy at not betraying their humanity, they sit across from me – five against one. I visualize them tossing a coin in the air and both sides are heads, mine, just as they called it.

Sitting tall, looking slightly downward, chest expanded, expressing firm confidence, my composure is an act expressed only in my well-rehearsed demeanor. Slowly enunciating "Good afternoon, Gentlemen, thank you for this opportunity," I sound like a male version of Liza Doolittle.

The monkey in the middle fidgets. "This is an unusual situation." He fumbles through a stack of papers. "I can't recall ever examining a neurological surgeon in front of the parole board." He passes the stack of papers to the quint next to him on the right. "We have received one hundred and fifty letters from fellow inmates on their personal development in your drug education classes. Their knowledge of the effects of drugs has surpassed *my* comprehension."

"I was not aware of those letters. Are they nice? I mean, that's nice." *This is painful.*

They get a kick out of that.

"I was informed that you were responsible for educating your fellow inmates to pass the GED, and you were successful with flying colors. This," he pats a letter, "is a note from the Warden and another from Mr. Hoodstrong. I won't beat around the bush. We've seen your PSI and we've read the motions you wrote to the court. No one is willing to take responsibility for the error made in your case - not the courts, the attorneys, or the probation department. Therefore, because of the error made when your drug mass was calculated, and for giving the impression that you were distributing drugs for profit, this board is granting your petition for relief and releasing you to the custody of a halfway house."

Released released released reverberates in my head.

"The process will take approximately three months. Your probation and parole will be fulfilled and there will be no further requirements to your sentence." The five members of the Parole Board reach for their water glasses simultaneously, glancing sideways at each other. Returning their glasses to the table in unison, Mr. Maypole, the man in the middle, clears his throat. "Do you have any questions?"

Even though I don't trust a word they say and I'm so unnaturally stiff I can barely breathe, I manage, "Is it possible for me to remain in residence here until my papers are cleared? If it's all the same to you, I'd like to finish my work here before I leave."

"An unusual request but I'm willing to grant it." He makes a few changes on the paper work. "Incidentally, it works out that your release date is Christmas Day and this meeting is concluded."

Wiping the sweat from my brow, I'm concerned about how my friends will receive the news I can't conceive to be true. By the time I compose myself enough to show my face, Steinbutt has polished off another dejected client. Hearing congratulations going around he's curious. Surprised that it's me who won the day, he stammers, "I guess you had a smattering of good luck."

"I should report you to the Attorney Registration and Disciplinary Committee. And I would if it would do any good."

The Warden shoos the brief boogeyman away.

"Congratulations, Doc." The Warden shakes my hand vigorously. "Amazing how the government takes three months undoing what they messed up in the first place. I'm rendered speechless that you chose to remain in residence. May I know why?"

"First of all I would miss you and my friends. Also, I need time to adjust to the idea of separation. Second thing is Mon Cher told me the halfway house is in a terrible neighborhood with loads of restrictions. Besides, the food being bad, he said the place is a dilapidated dump. The third reason is I have to be here to finish the job I started, so nothing goes wrong when I leave. That's probably more than three reasons."

He takes me aside. "Call doncha from my office."

Relieved that my friends have taken my good news, and their bad news so well, I follow fast on his heels.

Through tears of relief, she tells me "Your Yom Kippur prayers *once again* have been answered; you can be optimistic about your sins being forgiven. I love you. You are so strong."

I close my eyes. "And I love you, doncha, you're so incredibly extraordinary."

"Yes, I know." She laughs. "But nothing can compare with you."

Chapter Sixty-Six
Something to Cry About

I can't fathom why the Warden would say, "Carry on as usual. Don't disconcert yourself about a thing."

Edgy about what Chiller will do next, while the Warden is in Washington attending the post parole board hearing, I go through a list of possibilities too numerous to imagine. I head over to the library to join Charles, knee deep in literature sent to us with best wishes from a Good Samaritan. .

While delving into our loot, Chiller, the spoiler, stalks in. Swarthy hues shroud his discounted neo-Nazi sneer. He thumbs his boxed moustache and narrows his beady eyes to match his microcephalic head. Less man, he's more archetypical villain.

"I heard *your* sidekick, lame-brained Charles, is going to take over your responsibilities, *if* you're ever released."

"Get lost, Chiller." It's easy to dismiss little men with nothing creditable to say; nothing you'd want to hear unless you're sub-humanly ignorant.

"Charles Dickens," I put the Chiller incident in historical perspective, "knew a thing or two about life as an insider. He had his fill of supremacists running Victorian prisons with impunity. When you live as a prisoner and write about emotions, the pain is deep within the page."

Walking over to the dorm, Charles conjectures about the page in my life that's about to turn. "Doc, I'd like to ask you how you're going to get along without us looking after you."

"I'll be fine, but it won't be easy."

"You don't live on the planet like the rest of us. I'm nervous about you. You need someone to look after you. I know how involved you become in your work. Whacky knows how forgetful

you can be. *What will the absent minded professor do without me lookin'
after him?"* Charles does his Whacky imitation. *"Doc's gonna cook me
to death while I'm sleepin', smokin' all them butts and then he has the
nerve to try and talk me into lettin' him come into my kitchen. I love Doc
but he can't mess around in my kitchen."*

"I wouldn't mess around."

"Addicts are never entirely present in their body. That's how
you can ignore your pain…and other stuff. I started taking care
of myself because of how much you care about me. I noticed that
you don't even listen to doncha when she talks to you about your
health. Smoking like a fiend and God knows what else you'll do
when you're released."

I blow a smoke ring.

"I'm nervous about you."

"I could blow off *almost* anyone, but not you, Charles."

He hums a tune and he doesn't stop until we're back at the
ranch, so I join him on my imaginary sax.

Playing cards, puffed up like his best pastry, Whacky assures
the audience. "Guys, I'm not going to say no if they ask me to be
the first guest speaker of Doc's Memorial Chair and…"

"What are you talking about?"

"Don't you know anything, Gaffer? The Chair's like the big
cheese."

"And you're the big rat?"

"Listen to me. I'm goin' in and I'm gonna fire-up those bad
boys to learn. Isn't that right, Doc and Charles? You guys know."
Whacker solicits support when he sees us standing in the doorway.

"Charles and I are counting on you."

Gaffer high fives Whacky. "Am I taking over the kitchen or will
I be directing the Psych/Sociology Department?"

"I said guest speaker."

After fulfilling his social obligations, Gaffer comes in for the evening with his mail. Dancing around the room, Casanova shows off his scented letters, exhausting himself with the effort. Flopping down on the bed, he tears open a pink envelope. After reading a few words, he tears open the yellow envelope before he covers his head with a pillow to muffle his horror.

I glance at the first few lines of each and hand them to Whacky.

"Hey man, you really fucked up. You sent each of your fiancées the other one's lovey dove letter. How stupid is that. You'll never be a valedictorian. Now that you have only one fiancée left, you need to take the other two pictures off the wall. Schmuck."

"We never liked the idea of you thrice-timing women, but being found out is unpardonable."

"I can't do it. I loved them sooo much." Gaffer wails.

On that note, we go to bed and leave lover boy to figure out his dilemma on his own.

Chapter Sixty-Seven
Somethin's Cookin'

I wake up to find Rocky smoking my cigarettes. "I thought you loved it here, Doc. The parole board was of the same opinion. That's why they're sending you away."

"Let's not talk about it. I don't want to jinx anything."

"Superstitious is a strange thing for a neuroscientist to be."

"I'm a strange guy."

"I came to tell you that you have a new job assignment in the kitchen. Bizarre, huh."

Gaffer and Whacky, now wide-awake, yelp, "What are you talking about?"

"I'm a bit soured on the optimism I've been cultivating lately, too."

"Yeah, yeah, yeah, what were you sayin' about Doc working in the kitchen?" Whacky, praying for the best, holds his breath.

"Chiller's a troll. He's a draconian dirt bag. What do you think, Doc?" Rocky takes a long drag from his cigarette.

"No way is Doc working in the kitchen. Not even over my dead body." Whacky jumps into his clothes.

I shrug. "I guess I'll have to work in the kitchen. Chiller may want a shooting match before the Warden returns on Saturday but I'm not game. Nothing is going to interfere with me leaving on Christmas."

Whacky heads for the door.

"Please don't fall into his trap, Whacker. Let's have breakfast. I don't want to do intelligence on an empty stomach. Gaffer, are you joining us?"

"Of course. I'm not going to standby and let Chiller fuck you around."

With all my co-conspirators present, I discuss what I hope to be my final shot at Chiller. Whacky, demoralized and convinced that his kitchen will be reduced to ruble in no time, prays his sacrifice helps the cause. He wants me to win the war against Chiller quickly and end my stay in the kitchen. With that in mind, I am welcomed into his domain.

"Now that you're on KP, Doc, I'm giving you the important job title of PM Baker."

"All I have to do is be in the kitchen from one to four in the afternoon. That's my work day? What do I do the rest of the time? I like a full work day."

"Work out, sleep, read, plan menus, whatever."

"Planning menus...now that's good."

"It's not an easy job. Shakey and Little Lee will be back there to help ya out. Incidentally, doncha told me you fuck up soup out of a can and that you start fires makin' toast."

"Did the snitch tell you about my coffee?"

"She said you make the most perfect coffee she's ever tasted. You grind the beans forever. She told me all about your secret method. Putting butter on the bread before toasting it isn't your best idea. Take it easy. Your good buddies will cover for you. You don't have to do much besides show up."

"I can't wait to get my hands in the batter."

His eyes roll up in his head; he prays to Saint Basil the Great, patron saint of kitchens. "Please help me survive Doc in the kitchen without losin' it, or losin' your good protection, Saint Basil. After you get a load of Doc in the kitchen maybe you won't forsake me."

"I think I'm going to surprise you."

My staff, flying without their pilot in the Education Department, continues their work on the curriculum for next semester. Chiller shows his twelve o'clock shadow at eleven o'clock, three hours late.

"Everyone get in my office for the morning meeting right now!"

The guys come running.

"That's more like it. Now that you're cooperating, confess that Lerner got his sticky fingers on the answers to the GED. Tell me the truth right now and I'll spare you, or else you all go down."

Einstein licks his imaginary wounds. "No one cheated, no one had to. I resent the implication."

"Cut the baloney, liar. From now on you won't speak unless addressed by a superior...."

"When you say superior I suppose you mean anyone in gray polyester sporting a bunch of rusty keys. What's up with that anyways? You sound like you need oiling, most exalted ex-Chief of Education. And, if it pleases you..."

"Don't use that pseudo-sophisticated college professor flowery bullshit with me, Picasso. What a stupid name. You're all executed...excused. Get out!"

Einstein checks to make sure Chiller isn't behind them. "I know what mental illness is and that guy is unbelievably fucked up. He's a delusional, hallucinating, dyslexic, megalomaniacal douche bag. And those, my friends, are his good qualities." Having said that, the entire Education Department staff make themselves scarce.

Meanwhile, in the kitchen, Little Lee hasn't stopped nagging me. Now it's "Why did you put that much flour in the Hobart?" Lee dives into the huge stainless steel mixing bowl removing the ingredients I put in. "What made you do it? The directions are clear. Whatever possessed you?"

Exasperated, I try to put it into plain words once again. "Because we're baking... "

Stop arguing with me. I told you we pre-measure everything in smaller quantities... stop eating my candy."

"Common sense man, multiply and shorten work time." I explain to Lee for the tenth time why he should do it my way.

"This is not math. There are variables in baking. What are you doing in the kitchen anyway? You don't know a sifter from a whisk. You don't know measuring cups from coffee mugs. I asked you for measuring spoons and you brought me ladles."

"I do know that you need a very hot oven to bake, for starters." Pleased with myself, I pop another piece of candy into my mouth.

"I distinctly told you not to eat any more of my Jolly Ranchers."

Forgetting myself, I toss another one in the air. It lands on target.

Lee hurls a bowl of flour at me, grabs what's left of his candy, and runs. Faster than he'll ever be, I grab the shrimp and put him headfirst into the industrial sized mixing machine. I'm tempted, but I don't turn the machine on. Only in my imagination does little boy Lee disappear into the cake batter as the machine spins on the whip cycle.

I hear Whacky behind me. "Calm down, Doc." He takes Lee out of the machine. "Anyone can make a mistake."

Whacky, once again, knows what to say.

"That's true." I admit being the bigger man.

Shakey sums it up. "Doc is gung-ho with no where to go."

They're all trying not to laugh at Lee dredged in flour; he looks like a chicken. I'm a sight, too. Whacky, about to put his arm around me, thinks better of it.

"Look, Doc, not everyone is born to be a chef. From now on, knowing your appreciation for perfect tomatoes, you can check out all the produce to guarantee it's on the money. And, if you wanna be really busy, you can serve on the cafeteria line. What do you say?"

"I won't disappoint you, buddy. I mean to make my mark in the kitchen."

After I leave the scene of the crime, Whacky confides in Gaffer. "Fuckin' Chiller wants *me* to kill Doc. Thank God the Warden will be back on Saturday."

"Yeah, that's it, breathe, Whacky, breathe. doncha taught you that?"

"No. Yeah. I saw her do it when she was upset. I asked her what she was doin'. I thought she was goin' into a trance. Then she was relaxed from breathin' deep like that."

Gaffer takes a few deep ones himself. "I never knew Doc could be such a menace."

Dressed up in my white chef's hat and short white coat, busy hawking beans, singing out, "Get your beans here, baked to please both you and your regularity. *Beans, beans, the musical fruit, the more you eat the more you toot, the more you toot the better you feel so eat your beans with every meal.* After finishing that number, I do others from my anthology to include Frank Sinatra, Josh White, Woody Guthrie and Muddy Waters.

After dinner, Whacky trails me to the phone room. When he hears me ask doncha about various recipes, he thinks he's ahead of the game, but I've got ideas of my own. He grabs the phone. "doncha, I've got to tell you somethin'," and then he tells her everything.

"Before you snitched me out, she thought I was Chef Gourmetvous."

"Even you couldn't convince her of that."

337

Chapter Sixty-Eight
Solitary Confinement

Chiller heaves a stack of yellowed papers at Charles. "This plan is perfect, use it or I'll put you and those mongrels in solitary until you're a bunch of flea bitten…" In the middle of Chiller's harangue, Charles does an about face. "We've had enough of your denigrating tirades. Let's hit the road, men."

Eight hundred men have been alerted that something is not kosher. Ordinarily, Doc in not on KP and his name is not included when Chiller's hysterical voice comes over the loud speakers. "Picasso, Charles, Zee, and Einstein, report to the entrance of your dorm. I mean now! No one messes with me and gets away with it."

The sidewalks line with campers cheering the plucky spirit of Doc's players. Buckaroo shocks everyone when he handcuffs the troupe and shoves them into the back of the van, a makeshift paddy wagon.

A cavity exploration is Buckaroo's next big mistake. Picasso shits on the idiot's hand. Everything in order, the defiant ones are bullied into a huge bright airy room with seven beds and a private bathroom.

Zee chooses the bed in the far corner. "It's good that Snow White's in the kitchen; our portions will be extra large. I'm going to rest before dinner. Peace at last." He's asleep quicker than you can say once upon a time.

Herr Chiller, arch tormenter, marches in. Making a white glove inspection, he sniffs around. "I told you it wouldn't be pretty if you didn't obey me. Any comment, punks?"

Einstein sobs. "The bars, the rack, the filth, I feel like the Prisoner of Zenda. See to it that I have my meds, will ya, sweetie."

"That, and meals, and not one thing more is all you'll get."

Picasso examines his fingernails. "How about demerits? Can I count on demerits?"

"Not if you come back to work and tell the truth about Lerner. He put you up to this defection, didn't he? Cheating on the GED test was his scam, too, wasn't it?"

"Huh?" "Duh?" "Say what?"

"Stay here until you rot. Fools! I don't give two hoots about any of you. I'm not like that silly penguin, Sister Mary, sitting in front of the building praying for you; as if prayers could save your souls. What a crock. You'll all rot in hell."

"I think it's *your* soul that needs to be saved, dude." Picasso bites off a hangnail and spits it out. "Let me get this straight. You don't believe in heaven but you believe in hell."

"I'm finished listening to you. You can't save Lerner, now. He's already doing hard labor." On his way out Chiller nearly knocks over the camper bringing in food. Poking around, Chiller uncovers a nail file and a note under the cake. *We'll spring you guys Saturday at noon. Signed, good friends.*

Vice Warden Chiller, with napkin in hand, picks up the nail file. "I'm sending this to the lab for finger prints. Planning a jail break is a serious violation of prison protocol."

"Get real." Picasso snickers. "There aren't any bars here. That file wouldn't file my nails. Take the needle out of *your* arm."

"My case against you is sealed with this instrument."

"That's good, man." Picasso pushes Chiller out of the door. "We're going to eat now so leave us alone and rush right over to the forensic lab. We wouldn't want to keep you from doing your job."

Zee groans. "Everything was perfect until the asshole showed up. Being conscious for about two hours a day is plenty with him in the neighborhood. Let's dine and entertain poor Charlie. He doesn't have any books."

Charles finds the soliloquies an acceptable substitute for the books that are not available, until Einstein gives Hamlet a definitive *not to be* with a harrowing suicide scene that leaves his friends doubting that Einie is taking his medication regularly.

"I think Hamlet would have, or should have, done the deed like that, instead of talking about doing it. It's important to take action. And now, pals of my heart, I'm going to draw up practical plans for our departure. Picasso, will you help me, please."

To pass the time, Picasso indulges Einstein, telling the guys, "I'm worried that Einstein might have a psychotic episode, if he isn't having one already. Einie's, 'I've been put behind bars for life' routine, coming sporadically out of the blue as it does questions the boundaries of the stage....or he might be rehearsing. It's best not to overtax him asking too many questions."

Balance is maintained primarily with a yoga practice attempting postures called happy baby, warrior, downward dog and cobra, to name a few. Picasso is the single member of his class that can stand on his head or maintain a seated meditation for any length of time; although Zee says he's meditating, not sleeping. Good intentions bring the group safely to Saturday.

The Warden, just back from Washington, heads over to the bowling alley to find out what's *really* going on. Mon Capitan comes out from behind the lanes. Because he is busy, he is succinct. "Could be Chiller's had a nervous breakdown."

"Where's Doc?

"Doc's on line in the cafeteria serving lunch."

The Warden's hand is heavy writing a note. "Bring this to the administrative building and give it to the person in charge of solitary."

The Warden cuts in line and gets in my face. "What are you doing? Have you gone crazy?" He doesn't wait for an answer. "Come with me to my office, right now! This place has gone to pot."

"But Warden," I protest, "I'm needed here. Who else can sing and serve the way I do?" Crooning into the serving spoon, *Down in the west Texas town of El Paso, I fell in love with Mexican beans. Night time would find me in Whacker's Cantina, the music would play and the beans would whirl, tooting and ...* Before I can amaze him further with my talent, he puts his hand up. "Enough. Come with me."

I take a seat, hoping the Warden has finished interrogating me, to explain that Chiller is a mammoth piece of pre-historic protoplasm walking this planet in too tight wingtips. After raking me over the coals once more for good measure, the Warden finally relinquishes. "You did the right thing, Doc. Go back to work" does not end the matter.

"In the kitchen?"

"In the Department of Education."

"May I ask you a question after you've given me the third degree?"

"What is it?"

"I just want to know if you're going to leave that destructive sadistic deviant in charge again. And, may I go back to work serving on the line?

"No. I will never leave him in charge again. Spooning beans makes you happy?"

"Yes, it does. I like to sing and I like to serve, if it's a good cause."

"Of course, I should have known. Go back and finish the day, but let that be the end of your kitchen duty. You're needed elsewhere. Unfortunately, there's only one of you. I must say you have a nice voice. I like when you sing Josh White."

I walk out singing, *Delia's gone, one more round, Delia's gone. The first time I shot her she staggered out the door. The second time I shot that bitch she fell dead on the floor. Hallelujah! Delia's gone.* I'm singing Delia and thinking Chiller.

Chiller and Buckaroo contest their new work assignment. The Warden attached the dynamic duo to a detachment of criminals doing backbreaking labor in the frozen tundra.

The Warden gasps. "I'm stunned at your resistance, Vice-Warden! This is a perfect opportunity for you to put into practice your crime and punishment theories. Traveling on a bus with one hundred and fifty hard-core criminals in chains, reeking from every deprivation they are forced to endure, will break you or make you a better person."

"What about my poor wife?" Chiller wails.

"She, like you, favors rehabilitation through punishment."

John the Hack, just back from the hospital, missed all the action. He's brought up to date as he makes "thank you for saving my life" rounds. Nothing But Trouble follows behind him taking book on how many pounds everyone thinks John has lost, how many pounds John is going to lose, and how many pounds he will gain back after he has lost them.

Running to shake my hand puts him out of breath. "You saved my fat butt, Doc."

I pat him on the back. "It's all right. I was glad to do it. Don't cry, John."

Whacky drops his ladle and grabs the puppy dog hack. "What did you loose, fifty pounds? Swear you'll never touch food that isn't cooked or approved by me. Go on, swear it."

"I swear it." John wipes away tears of gratitude.

Now that Whacky's in charge, Nothing But Trouble makes John's weight loss a favorite.

"Thanks, Gaffer, for not letting me die because of my taco breath. I hope your weekend pass will make up for all the trouble I've caused."

Gaffer pinches John's cheek. "So you heard that Whacky and I are double dating. We've made *super duper naughty* plans. Maybe you want to have a stroke when we come back."

"You're kidding, right?"

"Not unless you can fake it."

You can hardly shut Gaffer up, although John is glad to listen, primarily because Whacky is feeding him, albeit with portions reined-in.

"Our plan is to not go far from here. We want to spend every second with our dates. We have at least ten already, but we expect to have more."

"Gee, that's amazing! I bet you're not too mad at me then?"

"Naw, cover our asses when we return. And think about faking that stroke."

☆ ☆ ☆

Sunday night, the devils return from their weekend in an ostentatious stretch limo. Men with radar for the opposite sex are lined up at the gate. Everyone stops cheering and begins to drool. At least twenty women in the limo are kissing and hugging those two drunken Irishmen. Because the camp is hauntingly quiet we can hear the women talking.

"Sweethearts, we had fun."

"You're adorable."

"We loved spending time with you."

"See you next year, if not sooner."

"Can't wait, honeybunch." The smooth operators answer all kissy faced. "We'll have to go into business saving lives." Whacky climbs out of the car and hands the driver a fistful of dollars. "Take my harem home." Disoriented and drunk, he trips over Gaffer and passes out next to him.

Eight men load the lover boys into the van and unload them in the shower. Their faces, covered in various shades of lipstick, look like tutti-frutti ice cream cones as the colors melt under the hot water.

Gaffer gurgles, "When I told you guys that living here forever wouldn't be half bad if Saturday nights were date nights....well, I changed my mind. There's nothing like freedom with lots of women to share it with and there will never be enough days in a week to do that. Beautiful soft women have curves and wear perfume and... tits. I love tits and silk lingerie. You guys don't wear beautiful silk underwear."

"I beg your pardon. I wear exquisitely beautiful undies."

"You're not my type, Rainbow. Such stuff as what was in that limo – that's the stuff my dreams are made of. Women are so different from guys."

Chapter Sixty-Nine
It's Never Over

Thanksgiving dinner, served up with all the traditional trimmings, would have made the Native Americans and the Pilgrims proud. Chanukah, too, with crispy potato latkes as treats that we trudged through snow that glowed to eat, also passed Gaffer and Whacky by without notice. Unvarying North Pole, day before Christmas, cold doesn't mean a thing to the Gaffer and Whacky. Still hot over their weekend of debauchery, they don't seem anywhere near cooling off. Not that anyone wants them to.

Hornier than jackrabbits, Whacky and Gaffer pulled off a lustful two-night three-day randy weekend, managing more philandering in that short time than most men of similar inclination can get a shot at with all their years on Viagra, hankering after heftier hard-ons. Getting longer, taller, and more enhanced, the stories the machos tell have them consorting with concubines enough to entertain themselves and the guys well into the next decade.

"Beautiful sexy dames were swarming around us like bees around honey. I'm telling you, men, they couldn't get enough of my sweet meat right up to the last minute. They were grabbing me as I crawled from the car, begging me not to go."

"Whacky is that really true? Is it Gaffer?" Newcomers are mesmerized with every word.

"Sugar plum lips...that's what I'm talkin' about. The limo scene will stand forever in camp history as testimony to our mind-blowing studly prowess long after you guys are gone. Whacker, tell the naysayers the story about the blonde with the leopard skin high heels."

"She was somethin' else."

"And what about the brunette with no tan lines on her gorgeous bod because she's going to be a nude Santa, and that hot to trot redhead…."

"Stop boasting, Gaffer."

"We satisfied all of them."

Another slogan as popular as *Fucking with the boys* is *Don't hock with the Doc.* Unexpectedly this one came from the Warden. Apparently, *Don't hock with the Doc* translates into a victory over stupidity for him, specifically Chiller's defeat. *Fucking with the boys* stands for a supreme act of unselfishness, in the Warden's estimation, because I passed up the famous weekend in favor of Whacker and Gaffer, never dreaming of the aftermath it would cause. At the core of these two slogans is an emblem of honor and community that is uniquely, but not exclusively, ours.

In all the many camp conversations that aren't about the wild weekend, no one mentions my imminent departure. My ambiguity over not finding the idea of leaving camp altogether gratifying worries me. Mustering the strength to do battle on the outside, where the fight for my right to practice medicine awaits me, is not the setback. What keeps me down is the fact that I will never again be valued or supported in the same way that I am now. It's ironical that the saying *no good deed goes unpunished* is unfounded inside the joint but not on the outside…not in my experience. Perhaps that's why I cling to my tenure here.

doncha senses my apprehension about leaving when we speak on the phone. "What happens next is a mystery, my love. Don't torture yourself about the future, it will spoil your last evening with your friends."

"It feels like the Last Supper."

"You carry too much of a burden, Bobby. I agonize over you, but I'm deliriously happy because starting tomorrow I'll have you forever."

"I don't want the guys to see me leave." I tell her, not for the first time.

"I know. You want to take off at the crack of dawn when all through the house not a creature is stirring. Arrangements have been made."

"It will be strange not having my friends in my life everyday... but I have to...I mean I *want* to go home. It would be ideal if they were released too, or soon. With their support anything is possible."

"A bittersweet dilemma, my darling."

For the first time, in too long a time, I can say, "Goodnight doncha, I love you sweetheart," without spasms in my gut...can't say the same about my loins.

Crazy combo pizza is placed in my hands and a cup of joy juice hooch is poured down my throat the minute I return to the dorm. My mouth is full. My heart is full. My spirit soars. "A farewell bash for me. You guys are the best. Hey, John, you look like you're in a partying mood."

"I'm in charge of the honor dorm tonight. Fire escape lookouts aren't necessary" puts everyone in the right frame of mind and earns John an extra swig.

A mass of campers present themselves like candles. To lighten my way, they shake my hand and drink to my health. I don't need to slam another one down. I smack my lips. "Good, but not as good as this. Nothing is better than this."

"We know you'll forget all about us when doncha gets her hands on you. She'll be better to you than we could ever be. They don't call me Einstein for nothing."

The talk this night before Christmas turns to the *man* Christ, who drank and ate and loved and cared. "More than the words and sentiments, which are all heart-felt and often humorous, I have a sense of the admiration Christ must have felt at the Wedding at Cana. I'm spiritually elated surrounded by an effusion of love that fills me with such a sense of awe I have to ask myself *where am I?*"

"That's good Daddy-O." Picasso slaps me on the back. "Be a prince and leave us with the secret of how to turn H_2O into vino. We don't want to run out when you disappear from this Siberian shack."

"Did I ever tell you guys about the time I was on an oil rigger off the coast of Mauritius when they dragged up a bottle that was dated from the time of Christ? Inside the bottle was a note."

Mon Capitan rubs his whiskers. "I seem to recollect hearing about that. Remind me, what did the note say?"

"It said congratulations on your wedding Morris and Esther Lefkowitz...must have been from the Wedding at Cana."

"I hope you kept it as a memento. You'll need bucks...unless Picasso handled that."

"Doc taught us how to be good. And I'm never gonna be a Judas and forget. So if Doc says it's true, it *almost* always is cause he wants to make everyone happy." Whacky burps.

"A profound insight from a man with a heart of gold and a soul to match his giant body. If any of you ever betray yourselves, Whacky will know what to do."

"Thanks Doc." Whacky wipes a tear away. "No one but you will ever understand me so good...I mean so well."

✵ ✵ ✵

"I'd like to read my will, now that we of the inner circle are alone. It's time to pass on my worldly possessions to those nearest and dearest to me. First, I want to drink to your health and your well-being. Because we supported each other, we became better in the ways men should be better. For that and many other things I am grateful to all of you."

"Doesn't Rainbow always say that... be better in the ways men should be better."

"I knew I heard that somewhere. So to you, Charles, given that you're always using them, I'm bequeathing you my glasses. Be sure to point out any lapses in the men, like you did for me."

"I wouldn't be of much use without these. I feel like they make me stronger; like they have magic in them. Thanks, Doc."

"Gaffer, you're inheriting my collection of books for your soon to be famous library. Sorry, there's no pornography but you have that covered on your own."

"If I read through this lot, I'll be offered an honorary degree at a university the minute I'm out of here."

"Grab the first offer you get. And, Whacky, because you've admired my watch, it's yours."

"This watch will always remind me of doin' time our way... thanks for giving it to me and everything else. I can't say anything else....or I'll cry."

"You're welcome, Whacky. Thank you from the bottom my heart for giving so much of yourself to me and the guys with your friendship, loyalty, and your amazing culinary skills. You turned this place into a hotel with a four star restaurant. As for you, Mon Capitan, you are now the proud owner of my custom trench coat. I will remember you, your friendship, your adventures, and your brew for the rest of my life."

"I will cherish it, my friend. Our memories will have a long and glorious history because I vow to keep them alive."

"And, Einstein, my friend, step into my new gym shoes with the unstoppable ambition to remain healthy, mentally and physically."

"I will, hoping my physique and psyche match yours some day."

"That's the nicest thing you ever said to me."

"I have a lifetime of good thoughts to remember you by, Doc."

"Thank you."

Picasso presents me his painting *The Pope behind Bars Praying.* "This was a vision I had of you, before you arrived."

"I thought I noticed the resemblance the first time we met. Why, if you don't mind me asking, did you paint it in watercolors?"

"That's the point Daddy-O, we all knew havin' you on board would make our lives more temperate and more colorful than it was in our black and white days. You gave us a hell of an easier ride, easy rider. We never thought about how you would react to us, or that it would turn out like this."

"I want you to keep this painting here for everyone to remember me by and because I know how attached you are to your work, except if it's minted."

"Always the one thinking of the other guys needs. Thanks. It *was* hard to part with but not as hard as parting with you."

Words of friendship so genuine they may not sound natural for straight guys choke our voices. A stronger bond is rare. You never know where or when you'll come across others that have an almost unbelievable ability to share.

Mon Capitan raises his glass. "This is the beginnin' of a new society. All of us will be out of here in three to four years. On the Christmas Eve I'm out, I would like ya'all to join me in a celebration on *The Bonnes Riches*, stashed in Florida."

Cheering, we sign a buccaneer's pact.

John comes in to say goodnight. "I want to tell you Doc that you will forever remain in my prayers. You are the one man I ever knew who should never have been a prisoner and you saved my life. Makes me wonder."

Telling me they are grateful to have known me, the men hug me and say goodnight. The goodbye part is too tough to articulate. We turn in for the evening knowing it will be the last one we share, for a very long time, maybe forever.

Unable to sleep, I light one cigarette after another, try on my clothes, and make several rather futile attempts to read. I pace and I wait for morning to come in its own time. Dressed in my re-tailored suit, I find a note in the pocket from Juan speaking of his admiration. *This is tough.* I brace myself and slip on the coat I arrived in over a year ago. I look in the mirror and expect to see the man that I was then. He's gone. In his place is a saner man, a quieter version of the original.

Life has its own rhythms. The idea of leaving quietly, well so much for that; on my way out every man on my end of the dorm wishes me a Merry Christmas. They wish me a good life with such intensity I can barely breathe in their farewell crunches.

Rainbow trips out of her room on her mules. "Doc, I almost didn't come out to say goodbye. I look terrible. I've been crying all night. I'm going to miss you and donchie sooo much."

"Here, sweetheart, this is for you."

Wiping away her tears, she gasps, "Oh! This scarf is lovely and French. Ooo la la. doncha has impeccable taste in all things. May I kiss you…on the cheek, of course?" I put up my hand. "Do away with the lipstick first. I don't want to start off with donch on the wrong foot. You witnessed how possessive she is. Remember?"

"Oh honey, she's not jealous of me. We're good friends."

I leave the dorm with the indelible embrace of the men I care about more than I can presently perceive…and that's saying a great deal.

I take my first steps outside as a free man.

The dorm fire escapes fill with campers. Windows wide open are full of faces. Guys have collected in the freezing cold in front of the dorms. They clap and chant, "Doc, Doc, Doc," and they don't stop. They run over to hug and wish me well. I can't keep the tears back. I walk backwards waving to them, saying goodbye and God bless you. It's strange and beautiful.

The Warden hands me a box of tissues and takes a fistful to mop his own face. "We'll miss your stellar presence. I have to admit, I've never known anyone like you and from the appearance of things, neither have they. Before you go, Doc, say a word or two for us to record to remember you by."

I clear my throat and wipe my face again before I turn back to face the men. "In this twilight moment, suspended in the moving picture called life, I'm the proud owner of this outstanding display of affection. I'm framing it in my mind to conjure it at will. It will remain ageless, undisturbable and indestructible and it will always bring a smile to my face and fill my heart with gratitude.

I learned a valuable lesson that has branded me forever. Because I once thought the egotistical diversions I got off on were the prize, I missed a lot. With your help, I found that the most meaningful rewards are abundant in daily interactions. It is the simplicity of a well-balanced existence, not without obstacles, that cemented our hearts and souls. Everything we shared made life magnificent. Happy Holiday, Gentleman. Live worthy lives. That's what we're on this planet to do. So go forth and be brilliant. You're the best and the brightest."

The Warden turns off the tape recorder. "No matter how much we benefited from your presence, I am glad to let you go. Godspeed, Doctor Bernard Robert Lerner. I'll never forget you, Doc."

"Keep up the good work, Warden."

Before I get into the limo, I look back again. I'm not dreaming. This is better than any dream I've ever dreamt where I'm the hero. Flooded with emotion, wowed with the most spectacular show of humanity imaginable on my behalf, I wave a last goodbye.

I enter doncha's encircling embrace. I'm held like I'm never going to be released. "I want to crawl inside you." She means it. doncha can't come close enough and I pray she never stops loving me because there's nothing quite like a hero's welcome.

When we come up for air I lean back and light a cigarette. "I can't believe it's over, sweetheart."

She smiles at me, indulgently. "My love, it's never over for people like us."

With cheering echoing in the background and the north wind blowing at our backs, we're driven away. Our future is waiting and we intend to make the most of it.

"Bobby, what are you whistling?"

"I don't know. I must be whistling a new tune."